The Gebusi

Lives Transformed in a Rainforest World

FOURTH EDITION

BRUCE KNAUFT

Emory University

WAVELAND
PRESS, INC.
Long Grove, Illinois

For information about this book, contact:
Waveland Press, Inc.
4180 IL Route 83, Suite 101
Long Grove, IL 60047-9580
(847) 634-0081
info@waveland.com
www.waveland.com

Photo Credits

Latham Wood: Front and back covers, p. 219, and color inserts 14, 17, 18.
Eileen Knauft: pp. 4, 11, 22, 35, 50, 56, 66, 72, 88, 97, 103, 106, 128 (left), and color inserts 1, 3, 5.
All other photos by the author.

To the Gebusi

Past, Present, Future

About the Author

Bruce Knauft is Samuel C. Dobbs Professor at Emory University in Atlanta. He has published numerous journal articles and two substantial monographs about the Gebusi of Papua New Guinea: *Good Company and Violence* (U California Press, 1985) and *Exchanging the Past* (U Chicago Press, 2002). Dr. Knauft is a widely known scholar of Melanesia, including his books *From Primitive to Post-colonial in Melanesia and Anthropology* (U Michigan Press, 1998) and *South Coast New Guinea Cultures* (Cambridge U Press, 1993). He has also written extensively about contemporary directions in cultural anthropology, including his books *Genealogies for the Present in Cultural Anthropology* (Routledge, 1996), and *Critically Modern* (edited, Indiana U Press, 2002).

During the past decade, Professor Knauft has directed projects that relate to applied and engaged anthropology in West Africa, East Africa, Inner Asia, South Asia, and the Himalayas. He has mentored students who have conducted fieldwork in diverse world areas and who have become established professionals in their own right. He enjoys teaching undergraduates and regularly teaches Introduction to Cultural Anthropology. The present book was written especially with undergraduates and a larger general audience in mind. Professor Knauft has remained keenly interested in the Gebusi people of Papua New Guinea since his first fieldwork among them in the 1980s, and he anticipates returning to work with them yet again.

Professor Knauft's CV, selected papers, photos, online teaching modules, videos of him with Gebusi, and music links are available on his website at *www.bruceknauft.com*.

Contents

Preface

BACKGROUND

Anthropology is little without powerful portrayals of diverse peoples and their cultures; for beginning students as well as advanced professionals, learning about different ways of life can be both thrilling and provocative. We are challenged to push our envelope of understanding—and to reconsider our own beliefs and practices. Over the years, a number of short books have exposed students to the richness of cultural diversity as lived experience. These typically take the form of short ethnographies—book-length descriptions of the people and culture considered. The present book follows this pattern but attempts to be distinctive in two connected ways. First, I have written this book without the formality and jargon of technical scholarship. This is not to dismiss scholarly writing. But having published some 1,500 pages of academic description and theoretical analysis concerning the Gebusi and related peoples in Melanesia (see "About the Author"), I can take the liberty here to write more concisely, personally, and lyrically for a larger and more general audience. While *The Gebusi* is based on what I think is detailed and rigorous scholarship, it tries to portray Gebusi and my experience with them in evocative and engaging ways.

Second, as a teacher of undergraduates, I have enjoyed writing this book to dovetail with topics and issues covered in cultural anthropology courses and textbooks. This aspect of *The Gebusi* was important to me from the start but has evolved further in the book's present edition.

FOR INSTRUCTORS AND STUDENTS

This Fourth Edition of *The Gebusi* has been completely revised and re-designed in a highly readable format. No major details from previous editions have been omitted, but tightening and further clarifying the book's contents have made way for significantly updated material based on new fieldwork with Gebusi in 2013.

Update sections now follow chapters 2–10 in Parts One and Two, bringing the chapter stories fully up to date. Major new material from fieldwork in 2013 as well as 2008 is brought together and discussed in Part Three. The Update sections allow the book to be read as a story of cultural change topic by topic and chapter by chapter, while the book retains its overall structure of sequential change portrayed over three different periods of time.

Revised and updated "Broader Connections" bullet points at the end of each chapter link the chapter content to anthropological concepts, which appear in boldface. All of these sections include updated material based on fieldwork in 2013. For ease of reference, each chapter's Broader Connections themes are listed under the chapter title in the book's Table of Contents. And an alphabetized index of the highlighted Broader Connections terms, with their page references, is included on my website, per below.

A striking 8-page insert of color photos of Gebusi, in addition to black and white photos in every chapter, showcase people and topics. Together with the book's cover, a rich array of 61 photos link directly to portrayals of Gebusi in the text.

A List of Persons, which indicates what has happened over time to many individuals mentioned in the book, is included prior to the index.

Online Features

- Eight video modules that were made in large part during on-site fieldwork with Gebusi in 2013 illustrate updated topics and link them to larger issues in anthropology. These segments are available for the following topics at *www.bruceknauft.com → Gebusi → Gebusi video modules online:*

    — Entering the field
    — Studying Culture
    — Language
    — Subsistence Livelihood
    — Social Organization and Kinship
    — Gender

— Sexuality

— Development and Underdevelopment

Additional Gebusi online modules may become available in due course; check the above website for updates.

- A narrated photo presentation summarizes Gebusi and their changes through 2008 [68 minutes]. This can be used in one longer class or divided into two or three segments (corresponding to the parts of the book) for use in shorter class periods. See *www.bruceknauft.com* → *Gebusi* → *Gebusi narrated flash presentation.*

- A large photo gallery of fieldwork with Gebusi has been organized and categorized by chapter of the book. These photos and captions with additional information are available at *www.bruceknauft.com* → *Gebusi* → *Photo gallery of Gebusi, chapter-by-chapter.*

- Gebusi music clips—including traditional singing and contemporary string band music—are available at *www.bruceknauft.com* → *Gebusi* → *Gebusi popular music, church music, and preaching (2008).*

- Probing more deeply, chapter-by-chapter Thought questions are available at *www.bruceknauft.com* → *Gebusi* → *Thought questions.*

- Updated Notes and References are available at *www.bruceknauft.com* → *Gebusi* → *Notes for* The Gebusi *4/E* and *References for* The Gebusi *4/E.*

- A list of the bolded anthropological terms that appear in the "Broader Connections" sections of the book's text is indexed with each entry's book page referenced at *www.bruceknauft.com* → *Gebusi* → *Broader Connections highlighted terms Index for* The Gebusi *4/E.*

- Instructor's resource materials are obtainable online via a password from Waveland Press. They include thirty objective quiz questions concerning *The Gebusi* 4/E, and objective ten-question quizzes for each of the author's eight Gebusi video teaching modules.

In all, this Fourth Edition of *The Gebusi* is a significantly revised, enhanced, reformatted, and updated book, and is enriched by a host of exciting new teaching aids and online resources for instructors and students.

THE GEBUSI

Who are the Gebusi? When I first lived among them, they were a small ethnic group or "tribe" of some 450 forager-horticulturalists living in longhouses in the deep interior rainforest of Papua New Guinea, which is located just north of Australia in the South Pacific. At that time, Gebusi life was rife with dramatic practices of ritual and body art, sorcery and divination, feasting and camaraderie, violence, and alternative sex practices. When I studied with the Gebusi again in the late 1990s, they had largely transformed. They were then a Christian people of about 615 who frequented the local market, attended government development meetings, played in the regional sports league, attended the local church, and whose children attended the local government school. In the mix, they had become engaged with other ethnic groups in a regional process of nation-building, and they had given up many of their previous beliefs and practices. In 2008 and yet more recently in 2013, Gebusi, now approximately 1,000 people, have weathered a collapse of the local cash economy. Government and its services have been withdrawn, and the airstrip has been closed. In the bargain, Gebusi have rediscovered and rejuvenated much of their previous culture. Now, however, ExxonMobil, the world's largest energy company, is contemplating building a multibillion-dollar pipeline for liquefied natural gas that may cross part of Gebusi territory.

In all, our knowledge of the Gebusi spans a great arc of social and cultural transformation—from remote isolation to active engagement with national and global lifestyles, to resurgence of many previous cultural practices in a new key, and now to the possibility that one of the most expensive energy projects in the world will intrude on their lives. In the process, Gebusi vividly illustrate important features of social change, marginalization, globalization, and inequity—as well as topical issues of subsistence, kinship and marriage, politics, religion, gender and sexuality, ethnicity and nationalism, expressive and public culture, and applied or engaged anthropology. Amid and across these issues and topics run indigenous Gebusi orientations and their cultural elaboration over time.

Most importantly, I think, Gebusi are amazing people—funny, funky, high spirited, and at turns both relaxed and intense. I hope you will agree that they are as wonderful as they are different from a Western perspective. I am privileged to be able to work with Gebusi, many of whom have become deep friends for many years. And I feel fortunate to have the opportunity to convey vital aspects of their lives as well as parts of my own when working among them.

Personal names used in the text are in most cases actual names, used with permission, and in a few cases pseudonyms, including when a depiction is potentially unflattering or embarrassing in a modern context and the person is still alive. Quotations taken from my Gebusi fieldnotes have been lightly edited from the original to make them clearer or more compact.

ACKNOWLEDGMENTS

It is hard to express the personal and professional debt that I feel toward my Gebusi friends and acquaintances. Deepest thanks go to Sayu, Didiga, Mus, Halawa, Keda, Mosomiay, Kilasui, Yamdaw, Uwok, and Abi. I gratefully acknowledge help from officials and staff formerly at Nomad, officials at Kiunga, and clergy of the Roman Catholic Diocese of Papua New Guinea's Western Province. Especially in remote regions, field research is difficult if not impossible without financial assistance from funding agencies. I gratefully acknowledge support for my work among Gebusi from the US National Science Foundation, the US National Institutes of Mental Health, the US Department of Education, the Rackham Graduate School at the University of Michigan, the Wenner-Gren Foundation, the Carnegie Corporation of New York, the Harry Frank Guggenheim Foundation, and Emory University.

Thanks go to numerous persons who have read and commented on various drafts and editions of this book, especially, at present, wonderful editors Tom Curtin and Jeni Ogilvie at Waveland. I am grateful to Elena Lesley for help with proofreading and to Kate Bennett for conceptualizing the photo layouts with me, as well as detailed editing of the book's previous edition. Stuart Kirsch, Laurence Goldman, and a range of other colleagues have alternatively given me general insights and specific clarifications that have informed my work, though they bear no responsibility for the book's shortcomings.

Photo credits are listed on the book's copyright page. I give heartfelt thanks to Eileen Knauft for permission to print a range of her photos of Gebusi from 1980–82, at which time taking quality photographs and maintaining film were difficult and challenging in a tropical rainforest environment. To Latham Wood goes credit and thanks for the cover photo that graces this book as well as several other of its photos. I was most fortunate that Latham was able to take time from his other obligations to go with me to the field in 2013, during which time he was a wonderful presence and much appreciated by Gebusi.

I owe a special debt to my students at Emory University. They have given me the courage not simply to teach anthropology from the heart but to go back to the field—and learn it all over again!

This book is dedicated to the spirit embodied by my friend Yuway (c. 1961–2009), to Sayu Silap and Didiga Imba, and to the past, present, and future of all the Gebusi.

Entry

It looks so grand from a thousand feet up, glowing green and vast. The broccoli tops of the trees stretch out as a broad carpet, an emerald skin shielding worlds of life within. You look down to see two blue-brown ribbons of water etching through the forest canopy. You follow them through the window of your tiny plane as they snake toward each other and merge in gentle delight. Below, in the crook of these two rivers, you look closer, to where the green shifts from dark to bright, from old forest to new growth that gets cut but always sprouts anew. Inside this lime-green patch you see a score of white squares arranged in two neat rows, standing firmly as if at attention. Ten line up evenly on one side while their partners face them across the lawn, their metal roofs glinting in the hot sun. You recall how these structures were built long ago by the first Australian officers, so colonial and rugged, trekking in across muddy rivers and swamps. Alongside these structures, a long rectangle lays out flat, its grass cut short and trim. Your plane will swoop down on it now, the gilded spine of that book you have come so far to read. But its substance is not what you thought it would be, not a text at all. As you descend, its meaning becomes the faces that line the airstrip, bright and eager as their skin is dark. They watch expectantly as you land. You open the door to a searing blast of heat and humanity. Welcome to Nomad Station.

Introduction
In Search of Surprise

Like most anthropologists, I was unprepared for what I would find. Eileen and I had been married just a few months when we flew in 1980 from Michigan across the Pacific. We were going to live for two years in a remote area of the rainforest north of Australia, in the small nation of Papua New Guinea. I was 26 years old and had never been west of Oregon. I had no idea what changes lay in store either for me or for the people we were going to live with.

Well into the 20th century, the large and rugged tropical island of New Guinea harbored people who had had little contact with outsiders. In the area where we were going, first contact with Westerners had not occurred until the 1960s. The 450 people whom we encountered had a name and a language that were not yet known to anthropologists. As individuals, the Gebusi (geh-BOO-see) were amazing—at turns regal, funny, infuriating, entrancing, romantic, violent, and immersed in a world of towering trees, heat and rain, and mosquitoes and illness. Their lives were as different from ours as they could be. Practices and beliefs that were practically lore in anthropology were alive and well: ritual dancers in eye-popping costumes, entranced spirit mediums, all-night songfests and divinations, rigid separation between men and women, and striking sexual practices. A mere shadow to us at first, the dark side of Gebusi lives also became real: death inquests, sorcery accusations, village fights, and wife beating. In the past,

3

The author in 1980 with Soliabo, a senior man who is attempting to understand what writing is.

cannibalism had been common (we later discovered that a woman from our village had been eaten a year and a half prior to our arrival). As I eventually realized, the killing of sorcery suspects had produced one of the highest rates of homicide documented in human history.

Living and working with the Gebusi turned our own lives into something of an extreme sport. But in the crucible of experience, Gebusi became not only real to us but also, despite their violence, quite wonderful. With wit and passion, they lived rich and festive lives. Vibrant and friendly, they turned life's cruelest ironies into their best jokes, its biggest tensions into their most elaborate fantasies. Humor, spirituality, deep togetherness, and raw pragmatism made Gebusi for the most part great fun to be with. I have never felt more included in a social world. And what personalities! To lump them together as simply "Gebusi" would be as bland as to describe Beyoncé, Barack Obama, and Bart Simpson as simply "American." The Gebusi were not simply "a society" or "a culture"; they were an amazing mix of unique individuals.

Anthropology is little if not the discovery of the human unexpected. I initially went to the Gebusi's part of the rainforest to study decision making, to see how all-night séances produced concrete results—the collective decision to mount a hunting expedition, conduct a ritual, fight an enemy, or accuse a sorcerer. But spirit séances were more like off-color YouTube clips than a political council. The spirit medium sang of spirit women who flew about seductively and teased men in the audience. The male listeners joked back while bantering lewdly with one another. In the bargain, their own social relations were intensified, patched up, and cemented. That meaningful community resolutions could actually emerge during such raucous all-night festivity seemed impossible. And yet, they did, including some that were really important. Sorcerers could be scapegoated and threatened with death; people could be accused or found innocent of infractions. Politics and conviction combined with sidesplitting humor, sexual teasing, and spirituality in ways that made my head spin.

You might imagine the first time I tried to translate a Gebusi spirit séance from one of my recordings. I sat with Gebusi men in all seriousness as the track played. They were astonished at first to hear their own voices—but they quickly then shifted from amazement to hilarity. At my prompting, they attempted, word by laborious word, to explain the humor I had recorded. It was tough, as I had no real interpreters and was learning Gebusi language "monolingually." As it turned out, their spiritual poetry had as little relation to their normal speech as the sentences of an anthropology textbook have to hip-hop. Gleefully, the men responded to my confusion by repeating yet again the bawdy jokes I had recorded. Unable to turn nighttime humor into daytime clarity, I realized at first that the best thing to do was to laugh along with them and enjoy their camaraderie. Seeing our strange interaction, the women said many of the songs were "no good" or "rotten."

Mostly, Gebusi were not just jovial but considerate and quick to apologize. I came to like most of them a lot, and over time, I grew to appreciate their culture—including their rituals, beliefs, and customs. But I remained keenly aware of my own ethics and values. What was I supposed to do with my morality when it collided with theirs, including in areas of sex and violence?

So, too, cultural anthropology is driven by a dilemma of competing desires. We want to appreciate the cultures we study. But we also confront others' difficulties and injustices. In Western traditions, appreciation of cultural differences extends from Herodotus among the ancient Greeks to thinkers such as Giambatista Vico and Johannes Herder in the 18th and 19th centuries. Broadly speaking, they argued that cultures should be appreciated in the context of their own time and place. This same basic principle was emphasized by American anthropology's "founding father," Franz Boas. Similarly in recent decades, cultural anthropologists have been passionate to understand other peoples through the lens of their own customs and beliefs. Why should Western ways of life be thought superior?

But anthropologists are also mindful of problems and inequities in the societies they study. Some of these injustices are caused or fueled by outsiders. During centuries of colonialism, Westerners have exploited or enslaved people across the world, including in North and South America, the Pacific, Africa, and significant parts of Asia. Many indigenous peoples have been subordinated, stigmatized, or simply decimated on grounds of cultural, racial, or religious difference.

But such injustices do not always link to external forces. Among Gebusi, the oppression of women and violence against suspected sorcerers grated roughly against the splendors of Gebusi ritual performance and festivity. Such paradoxes cannot be explained away by the impact of outside intrusion.

These opposing trends underscore the challenge anthropologists face as we investigate problems and suffering: how do we reconcile the wonder of cultural diversity with difficulties caused by subjugation or violence in the heart of the social lives we study? During fieldwork, ethnographers frequently experience social life through the crosshairs of ethnocentrism, sexism, racism, religious intolerance, ageism, or other forms of discrimination. In the mix, we become more aware of the ethical standards we ourselves hold—as well as the risk of projecting these too easily onto others. This is a real dilemma I have felt when working with Gebusi.

Ultimately, Gebusi surprised me beyond the delightful "good company" of their social life and also the unfortunate violence of their sorcery beliefs and gender practices. The biggest surprises have come each time I have returned to live and work with them again. Not knowing what lies in store, I brace myself, quell expectations, and take new conditions on their own terms. Over time, momentous changes have rocked Gebusi. Modern development has come and then largely gone, including government and market intrusion, Christianity, and hopes for business based on money. In this mix, some traditional Gebusi customs seem to have died out for good, but many others have continued or been revived, or rejuvenated in new guises. This checkered and remarkable pattern persists—and will continue yet further.

By 1998, my old community had picked up and moved its settlement—lock, stock, and barrel—from deep in the rainforest to the outskirts of the government airstrip at Nomad. Previously isolated, they were now part of a large multiethnic community of persons speaking five different languages. They became Christian and went to church. Their children went to school. Their women went to market. Sweet potatoes were now a starch staple, and new crops such as manioc, peanuts, squash, and pineapple were grown for sale as well as for consumption. Gebusi considered themselves citizens of the nation of Papua New Guinea.

In the mix, Gebusi spirit séances were replaced by soulful modern songs accompanied by guitar and ukulele. "Parties," "videos," and "discos" were the rage. Children in school drew pictures of their future selves as pilots, policemen, soldiers, heavy-machine operators, nurses, teachers, rock singers, and Christians in heaven. Traditional dances were a thing of the past. And without spirit mediums, Gebusi couldn't reliably communicate with their traditional spirits. As such, sorcery inquests were replaced by Christian funerals—and violence against sorcery suspects happily plummeted. Gebusi said their old spirits had been exchanged for new ones, and for new ways of life. But in the process, they also became far more subordinate to outsiders than they had been before.

Since the mid 2000s, Gebusi have again been changing radically. Due to inefficiency and graft, the Nomad airstrip has effectively been closed. Government officials have gone, the health clinic is shut, the market is desultory, church attendance is down, and schooling is compromised and sometimes nonexistent. In the vacuum of this decline, however, Gebusi have rejuvenated many of their traditional customs—and they have become much more in charge of their own lives and society. If Gebusi seemed uncommonly "traditional" during the 1980s, and if they became surprisingly "modern" by the late 1990s, since then they have creatively combined strands from both these legacies. In the mix, crucially, they have kept control of their own land, maintained a thriving rainforest livelihood, and increased their population without pushing on the limits of their territory.

My good fortune is to know a remote rainforest people who now find meaning by combining earlier customs with new modes of experience. Gebusi don't and can't reflect the lives of people elsewhere. But they do illustrate how society and culture change over time. Like Gebusi, people around the world become modern by both retaining and reshaping their unique identity, drawing on the past while creatively launching it into the future. As an anthropologist, I see culture as the diverse colors that refract through a prism of ongoing experience. By considering these refractions, we understand how people across the globe share a modern world while retaining and expanding their distinctiveness. Some people resist outside influence; others adopt new customs and cast old ones aside. Some agitate for autonomy; others accept or embrace the political or commercial authority of outsiders. Amid these alternatives, though, most people weave a rich tapestry of hybrid cultural developments.

Exemplars in this regard, Gebusi provide an excellent framework for considering topics covered in anthropology courses. These include distinctive features of livelihood or subsistence; how kinship and marriage organize people into groups; dynamics of economic exchange, distribution, and consumption; the politics of leadership, conflict, and violence; religious beliefs and spiritual practices; issues of sexual and gendered diversity; the construction of ethnicity and race; the impact of colonialism and nationalism; the role of the anthropologist; and, through it all, the dynamics of sociocultural change. Rather than describing Gebusi in general terms, I present them as individuals whose lives have unfolded across decades along with my own. My goal is for Gebusi to come alive for you, for you to get a sense of their past and their present, and to connect this striking story with current trends in cultural anthropology.

Note: See www.bruceknauft.com → Gebusi → Gebusi video modules → "Preface" and "Anthro & Studying Culture" to watch Bruce's surprise and uncertainty when reentering the field in 2013.

BROADER CONNECTIONS
Cultural Anthropology

- Through **fieldwork** and the writing of **ethnography,** cultural anthropologists such as Bruce become highly engaged with and attuned to **cultural diversity.**

- Cultural diversity leads anthropologists to appreciate **cultural relativity,** the value of each culture on its own terms.

- Anthropologists are also attuned to **social inequality,** including how differences of sex, gender, age, ethnic identity, religion, and other factors lead some people to dominate and subordinate others.

- Some aspects of social inequality derive from external constraint or coercion, including **colonialism, imperialism,** or **nationalism.**

- Other aspects of social inequality may derive from **internal social discrimination or stigma,** which may be informed by long-standing beliefs and practices.

- In current practice, most cultural anthropologists appreciate cultural relativity *and* critique social and cultural inequity.

- Collectively, changes among Gebusi illustrate the relationship between **traditionalism, globalization,** and how people become **modern.**
- Because people such as Gebusi draw upon larger influences in their own unique way, they become **locally modern** or **alternatively modern** in their own way.
- A key concern for modern livelihoods is their economic and **environmental sustainability.** Gebusi are fortunate to have land, subsistence, and customs that provide for a thriving and sustainable livelihood.
- The fact that **cultural change** is not easily predictable also makes it is especially interesting, surprising, and exciting—and crucial to helping us understand our human world.
- Like peoples throughout most developing countries, Gebusi have recent histories that reflect both strong traditions based on indigenous customs and the desire to participate in and benefit from modern activities and institutions.

A Gebusi boy, Gwabi, in traditional dress, 1981. →

Part One

1980–1982

Chapter 1

Friends in the Forest

The bananas were piled up, hot and grimy. Steam floated up from them—as if the air around us could have gotten any hotter! Some were stout as well as long, but most were slender, and a few were quite tiny. But their variety in dozens was a mystery to us then. Though all of them had been carefully scraped, long strands of soot and globs of charcoal remained from their time in the fire.

What to do with this mound of starchy bananas, presented to us so formally in that first village? Kukudobi villagers had probably not seen a white person since five years before our arrival, when the country had become nominally independent and all the Australian patrol officers had left. During the seven years or so before that, after first contact, a patrol officer would try to tramp to major Gebusi settlements once a year and count as many inhabitants as he could find. That was about it. Against this backdrop, our own arrival caused quite a hubbub, a tempest in the forest. Women and children fled while men gasped with curious excitement. Emerging from the forest, the four local men who were carrying our supplies took the lead and we followed them ("When in Rome . . .") to the central longhouse. As we sat down cross-legged, a flood of villagers did likewise all around us.

They must have done the cooking quickly or already known about our arrival, since it wasn't long before the smoldering mound of starch was brought in on a palm leaf platter and laid with gusto directly in front of us.

Suddenly I was the focus of great public scrutiny. Short men with bamboo tubes through their noses looked on from all around. I was too embarrassed to check with our carriers or even with Eileen about what to do. Everything was heat and stickiness. I took one of the sooty bananas and began to munch on it, trying to show appreciation. The bananas were dry (technically they were "plantains"), but I forced myself to chew through one and pick up another. The people around us started to grin as I swallowed their food. Progress was slow, however, and, judging from the size of the platter, ultimately hopeless. Using my hands, I signaled that the pile of food was large, my stomach was small, and many people could certainly be fed. What a relief when they broke into pleasant conversation and stretched out their arms, sharing the bananas throughout the longhouse. We had apparently passed our first test.

Anthropologists often talk about "The Gift," especially in Melanesia. How people produce things through hard work and sweat, infuse them with hope and good intention, and then just give them away speaks volumes about human connection. Gifts are at once a social economy and a materialized emotion. As Marcel Mauss suggested, gifts reflect and reinforce social bonds between givers and recipients. In American society, gifts at Christmastime are heavy with meanings that reflect who we are most connected to, the strength and character of the relationship, and sometimes, as well, what we project or anticipate we will get in return.

As in many societies, Gebusi believe gifts should be given to visitors who are peaceful. Their most basic gift was the fruit of their most regular work as well as their primary source of nutrition: starchy cooked bananas. Well beyond food, however, material exchange creates social connection. Gebusi define their relationships by the things they give or don't give to others. In short order, I established a "gift exchange name" with each man in the village—derived from something that was given or shared between us. Gusiayn was my "bird egg"; Iwayb was my "Tahitian chestnut." Based on gifts I myself gave, Yuway became my "fishing line" and Halowa my "salt." Whenever we saw each other, we called each other by these terms, and our relationship was referred to similarly by others: "Here comes your 'bird egg'; there goes your 'salt.'" To have a social identity and to have shared something that was memorable were one and the same.

In that first village of Kukudobi, we were fortunate to have accepted those starchy bananas, to have eaten a few and shared the rest. It was a simple act, but symbolic in ways we barely appreciated. The patrol officers before us had also come to forest villages. But they had brought along servants or "houseboys" to cook tins of meat and bags of rice they hauled around. In our case, word had already spread that we were looking for a rainforest village to live in and that we ate local food. So we received a hopeful reception of cooked bananas. The other features of local welcoming etiquette were not yet known to us—the calling out of gift and kin names, the hearty snapping of fingers, the dramatic sharing of smoke-filled tobacco pipes, the drinking of water from nine-foot-long bamboo tubes, and the palaver that lasted until the hosts arrived with great whoops to present more food. But even in that first village, the invitation of social life, the giving of food, had been extended, and we had accepted. It was a good start.

As we quickly found out, all the villages we visited wanted us to live with them. Though bossy, the Australians had provided a trickle of outside goods, and when they left, the trickle had dried up. Local people craved the trade items they now associated with white-skinned outsiders: cloth, salt, beads, fishing hooks, soap, and, especially, metal tools. Compared to an adze made of stone, a steel ax goes through rainforest trees like a knife through butter. Metal axes made it easy for people to clear bigger garden plots, grow more food, and build stronger houses. Metal knives and machetes found many additional uses, from skinning animals to clearing weeds.

Besides stoking a passion for trade goods, the Australians left a political legacy that the Gebusi also appreciated: they pacified the Bedamini. More numerous and aggressive than Gebusi, Bedamini formed war parties that burrowed deep into Gebusi territory. Using brutally efficient tactics, they would surround a Gebusi longhouse at dawn, set it ablaze, and slaughter the residents as they fled. The Gebusi had been repeatedly victimized by these raids, and whole settlements had sometimes been wiped out. Typically, the victors cut up the bodies of slain Gebusi and carried them home for feasting. Though it's important to distinguish rumors of cannibalism from the real thing, the eating of Gebusi has been well documented and admitted among Bedamini—and by Gebusi themselves following the killing of their own sorcery suspects.

With just 450 people against the Bedamini's 3,000, and with smaller settlements, the Gebusi were no match for Bedamini war parties. If Australian patrol officers had not forcibly stopped Bedamini raiding, the Gebusi would have become only a remnant people. By 1980, Gebusi were still visibly scared of the Bedamini, but they were seldom killed and no longer massacred by them. And despite outside intervention, Gebusi themselves hardly felt the boot of colonial domination; the benefits of Australian presence far outweighed the costs of their brief annual visits. The officers' main objectives were to update the local census and lecture villagers, via interpreters, to keep their settlements clean and not fight one another. Seen as victims rather than aggressors, Gebusi were portrayed in patrol reports as "quiet, tractable people" and were left largely alone. Hence the irony that even as Bedamini were pacified by armed colonial patrols, Gebusi were left to continue their own sorcery inquests, executions, and even cannibalism within their communities. Living deep and scattered in the rainforest, they hid their actions from Australian awareness.

Though Gebusi appeared at first to be a pristine people, what we took to be traditional customs had actually flourished during the colonial period—along with the use of steel tools to clear larger gardens and build bigger houses. Because Gebusi associate growth with spiritual support, these changes affirmed their religious values as well as their social life. Like streams converging in the forest, material production and spiritual vitality came increasingly together in major Gebusi rituals, especially the initiation of young people into adulthood (as described in Chapter 6.) Ironically, colonial intrusion nearby gave Gebusi freedom to intensify their own customs, allowing them to become even more "Gebusi-like" than they had been before. Although they seemed unacculturated, Gebusi traditions underscored the importance of change all around them. A tribal powerhouse had been laid low while the lowly Gebusi had been left on their own to recoup. Over time, Gebusi resented Bedamini not so much for their former raids as for being recipients of government development projects that Gebusi wanted for themselves.

That Gebusi had both exuberant traditions and desire for contact with outsiders made them perfect for us. Little wonder that we were enamored of them or that they wanted us for themselves. At first, however, we weren't interested.

My journey had begun with a blank spot on a map. That was where, back at the University of Michigan, my graduate advisor and I had thought that I would find the most fascinating people. The largest scale maps then available were produced by the US Army—in case even the remotest parts of the globe needed American involvement. The map of Papua New Guinea's Western Province showed an unknown space that stretched across a swampy rainforest north of the Tomu River. We could roughly triangulate the culture of the unknown people who lived there from what was known about groups not too far away. Lacking a name for Tomu River people, I talked by phone to a missionary who had completed an aerial survey nearby. He said these people were probably the "Kramo." Armed with this information, I obtained funding from the US National Science Foundation and the US National Institutes of Health to study political consensus formation led by spirit mediums among people called the Kramo in the remote rainforest of Papua New Guinea's Western Province.

But there was a good reason for the blank spot on the map: no one lived there! We finally accepted this after leaving Kukudobi and trudging for what seemed like forever to the far distant village of Honabi. The inhabitants there told us consistently, and in as many ways as our inadequate language would allow, that there was nothing farther ahead of us but swamp and mosquitoes, both of which we had already endured to our limit. They informed us that the few people called the Kabasi who had previously lived in this area had deserted it to live near a crocodile skin trading post to the east. Even if we had wanted to continue trekking ahead into uninhabited territory, our carriers would not go with us. In professional terms, we had traveled across the world to Papua New Guinea on doctoral research grants to study people whom we couldn't find or who didn't exist.

Sensing our uncertainty and perhaps our fear, the people of Honabi brightly insisted that we stay and live with them. Though they claimed to have a tradition of spirit séances, their assertions were hedged with ambivalence. When we probed about their living conditions, they admitted they typically abandoned their settlements during the dry season, split into tiny groups, and foraged for food even deeper in the rainforest. As the evening

grew longer and the mosquitoes bit harder, the prospect of adapting to
their lifestyle for two years seemed more dreadful than admitting failure.

Not knowing what else to do, we trudged back to Nomad Station via
the village that our carriers lived in, which was not altogether out of the
way. The more we found out about this impending stop, the more interested we became. By this time, our carriers had become real people to us.
Yuway was a wonderfully decent young man—tall, sensitive, and strong
for a Gebusi. He had a spontaneous sense of concern, interest, and
patience even though we couldn't yet speak with him. He would wait to
help us over slippery log bridges and often volunteered to shoulder the
heaviest load. Gono never said much, but he was as sinewy and depend-
able as a stout tree, and always alert. Hawi was our nominal interpreter,
and though his translations ultimately proved more troublesome than
helpful, he was socially and physically agile. Finally was Swamin, older

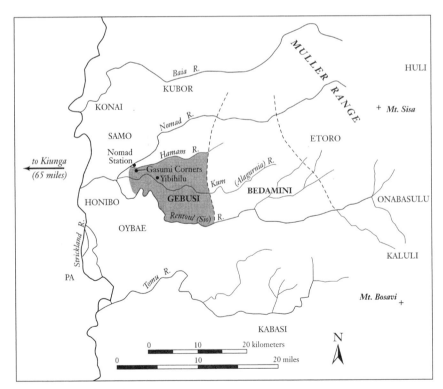

The Gebusi and nearby groups.

than his unmarried companions but more muscled than they. He would flash a captivating smile under his impish hooked nose and pepper his remarks with articulate bursts that, given the reactions he got from the other three, convinced us that he was both very funny and very smart. As Hawi informed us, Swamin was also a spirit medium who regularly held communal séances.

When we finally reached their village of Yibihilu, the "place of the deep waters," we thought we had reached nirvana. Having stumbled for days through a sea of leaves, mud, and vines under a closed rainforest canopy, we felt like the miniature children in *Honey, I Shrunk the Kids!*, navigating enormous obstacles in a galactic backyard of foliage. I yearned to look up and out, to see more than the next hidden root that could send me sprawling. By contrast, the "place of the deep waters" was perched on a 40-foot bluff overlooking a serpentine bend in the Kum River. The porch of the longhouse extended out over a canyon through which the river rushed before pooling in a serene basin some hundred yards wide and across which we could see a crocodile lazing in the sun. Farther downstream, the watercourse was calm enough to be traveled by canoe—which was far preferable to tromping through the muddy forest. At dusk, the sky above the river became a breathtaking sunset. The villagers stopped and stared. *Bubia maysum*—"The crimson is being laid down."

If the village seemed majestic, the people were yet better. Having learned more about us from our carriers in five minutes than the other villages had in five days, their kin and friends gave us the kind of warm welcome, especially in such a remote place, that made us feel on top of the world rather than at its end. As the traumas and troubles of our journey were discussed to the tiniest detail, the villagers laughed good-naturedly. That we were already trying to speak their language—however haltingly—was widely and enthusiastically noted. That we ate local food and that I had somehow carried my own backpack, which the men enjoyed trying on, were also taken as positive signs. Eileen's presence was also a bonus. White women had rarely been seen by the Gebusi, and probably never in Yibihilu. Eileen shared food and laughter with the women and played with the children. They were enthusiastic and responded in kind. If the men "had" me, the women took Eileen into their own world.

In remarkably short stead, our physical presence, possessions, and desire to speak the vernacular painted us as paragons of beneficence, a gold mine of goods, and a three-ringed circus of entertainment. Our hands were shaken, fingers snapped, and bellies gorged with countless gifts of food. Everyone seemed quite genuinely to want our friendship. If our reception was anything less than overwhelming, we were too euphoric to notice. As if we needed further encouragement, Swamin held an all-night spirit séance. Word of our presence had drawn villagers from surrounding hamlets, and given the convergence of many people in high spirits, a songfest was almost inevitable. The stars shone as they only do when there is no competing light for hundreds of miles. The songs of the men swelled as the moon rose from its silhouette in the forest canopy. Beneath its glow, their deep-throated harmony echoed as if in a wild cathedral. The music was nothing like, and more amazing than, anything I had heard before. I knew that Gebusi believed in a world of unseen spirits and in places that come alive through the spirit medium's songs. But as the sound washed over me, I knew almost nothing of its meaning. In the moment, however, this only added to the mystery and splendor of their cosmos—a world of wonder I had come to explore.

There was so much we didn't know about the Gebusi at first—including their name. Our ethnographic maps and the missionary who had told us about the "Kramo" had placed a group called the "Bibo" at our present location. But the people of Yibihilu found this terribly funny. They brought us a large starchy banana and indicated that this was the only "bibo" in their territory—one of their three-dozen varieties of plantains. There were no people called "Bibo," they said in no uncertain terms. Their own identity, and also their language, was "Gebusi."

The discoveries of fieldwork had already brought us full circle. We had gone halfway around the world to study a Kramo people who didn't exist. We had projected their presence based on our incomplete maps and our imaginations. But the people we did find—and came to like so deeply— were, in name, an undiscovered group. As green and insecure as we were at the time, this was a comfort. In retrospect, though, our nominal "discovery" of the Gebusi exposed as much about us as it did about our tribal friends—namely, the Western desire to label other peoples and to project onto them our own sense of discovery. Like many anthropologists, we confronted our own projections at the same time, and in many respects for the very reason, that we were trying to reach out and understand the lives of others.

Beyond the Gebusi's name, we also quickly encountered one of their central concepts—one that took much longer to understand. With predictable difficulty, we had been trying to explain why we had come to the rainforest. To Gebusi, we obviously didn't fit the mold of other Whites they had previously seen or heard about—patrol officers, who ordered people around and then disappeared for another year, and Christian missionaries, who read from a big book and told villagers to give up their customs and believe in a new spirit. We tried to convey that we wanted to learn their language, to understand their songs, to watch their dances, to join in their feasts—in short, to be with them as they lived and to learn what they were like. In a flash, they seemed to grasp our meaning: we wanted to learn their *kogwayay*. They appeared so certain of this that we had no choice or desire but to agree with them. But we had no idea what *kogwayay* actually meant! In truth, however, they were entirely correct.

Kogwayay is—or at least was, during that early period—the single word that best describes the heart of Gebusi culture. In a way, the term represents their concept of culture itself—the beliefs, practices, and styles of living that are special and unique to Gebusi as a people. At one level, *kogwayay* refers to customs that make their culture different from others. As Gebusi themselves used the term, it refers especially to their distinctive traditions of dancing, singing, and body decoration. But what is the term's deeper meaning? The Gebusi were not much help here. For them, *kogwayay* was a catchall marker of cultural distinction rather than a tool for dissecting it.

When you think about it, it's not surprising that people have a hard time explaining concepts that are central to their culture. Such meanings are often "beyond words." How easy would it be for the average American to define and explain what "love" is to someone who had never heard of this term? In the case of *kogwayay*, we were fortunate that the word breaks down into three distinct units of meaning, what linguists call morphemes: *kog-*, *-wa-*, and *-yay*. *Kog* conveys "togetherness," "friendship," and "similarity." These meanings reflect the collective and communal nature of Gebusi life. Gebusi prefer to do things with as many other people as possible. They hate being alone; they are the opposite of loners. The *wa* component of the word is the Gebusi root of *wa-la*, "to talk." It refers to pleasant

Two unrelated
young men of
Yibihilu indicate
their friendship by
dressing in a similar
costume, 1981.

casual conversations that are roundly shared. This is what the men did in the longhouse at night—they "*wa-la*'d" by sharing news and gossip, joking, fantasizing, and telling stories around the small glow of the resin lantern. Hour after hour and evening after evening, I came to realize how rare it was for Gebusi to get angry with one another in these gabfests. Disagreements were tempered by friendly smiles, embarrassments covered over by jokes and shifts of conversation.

Yay supplied the exuberant conclusion to *kog-wa-yay*, its exclamation point. Particularly for men, to *yay* or to *kay* is to cheer, yell, joke, and cry out as loudly and happily as possible—and preferably in union with others. These yells have bodily meaning as well. When a Gebusi calls out in concert with those around him, his "breath-heart" (*solof*) rushes out and mingles with that of others. To *yay* or *kay* is to send forth and unite human spiritual energy; it is a vital assertion of collective life.

Taken together, what do *kog-*, *-wa-*, and *-yay* mean? And why should we care? No single English word captures their essence—and this fact is important. As anthropologists, we are charged with learning and conveying concepts that are important to other people even and especially as these exceed our initial understanding. *Kogwayay* was clearly important to Gebusi. The word was frequently used and talked about, it evoked strong feelings, and it was highly elaborated in central rituals and ceremonies. In Gebusi culture, *kogwayay* was what anthropologist Sherry Ortner has more generally called a "key symbol." Collectively, the three meanings of the word—togetherness, talk, and cheering—conveyed core Gebusi values of happy social unity, of living in good company with one another. And *kogwayay* permeated Gebusi social life. This was evident on a daily basis and was epitomized at important events such as feasts, dances, spirit séances, and the initiation of teenagers into adulthood.

Although *kogwayay* was a powerful and deeply held concept, it did not stand alone. It highlighted the positive side of Gebusi culture, the bright side of their moon. Most peoples try to depict themselves in a good and favorable light, and the Gebusi were no exception. If you were asked to name central values in American and other Western societies, you might use words such as "freedom," "economic success," "love," "self-expression," "family values," or "tolerance." Of course, these are sometimes ideals more than realities. Many marriages end in divorce; people can be shackled by poverty; and discrimination based on race, ethnicity, sex, or age can be as deeply ingrained as it is illegal. A critic from another culture might argue that American society is cutthroat, egotistical, hedonistic, imperialistic, and much less equal or free than we like to believe. If culture is an assertion of ideals and values, these can sometimes hide problems or difficulties. In this sense, culture is a double-edged sword of beliefs and representations. On the one hand, it emphasizes values and ideals that are often, if not typically, good and healthy. On the other hand, extolling these values can cover up less pleasant realities. Certainly it would be shortsighted to dismiss the importance of cultural values. Where would we be without them? So, too, it is good to appreciate the values of other peoples, including Gebusi. But it is also important to recognize the underside of culture—realities that are neglected by cultural ideals. Both sides of this coin are important.

Where do we draw the line between an appreciative view of culture and a critical view of its inequalities? Do we emphasize the fight to free the slaves during the American Civil War? Or the history of slavery that made that war necessary? Do we emphasize the human benefit of toppling a dictator like Saddam Hussein? Or the tens of thousands of lives lost as a result? Such questions have few simple answers. But asking them makes us more aware of both the positive power of culture and the problems it can hide.

Gebusi culture can be viewed from this same perspective. The good company of *kogwayay* was a strong practice as well as a wonderful ideal. But *kogwayay* was also controlled and dominated by men. It was men rather than women who collectively cheered and publicly yelled. Men were the ones who gathered for public talk each evening on the large porch that overlooked the river. During this time, women were largely confined to whispered conversations in a cramped female sleeping room along one wall of the longhouse, away from the men and older boys. In terms of decision making, it was typically men who determined which settlement their families would live in—who would have togetherness, and with whom. Men took charge of the events most strongly associated with *kogwayay*—ritual feasts, dances, spirit séances, and initiations. At feasts, men from the host village would proudly present visitors with piles of cooked sago starch—though this food was produced by women's labor. In the evenings, it was men who dressed up in stunning costumes to dance. At initiations, young men were the main focus and were decorated most elaborately. As if to deny the notion of motherhood, boys were nurtured to manhood not by females but, as described in Chapter 5, by the men themselves—through the transmission of male life force from one generation to the next.

Male control was especially pronounced at spirit séances. Late in the evening, men would gather in the dark longhouse and arrange themselves around the spirit medium while he sat, smoked tobacco, and went into a controlled trance. The medium's own spirit would leave his body and be replaced by a soul from the spirit world. After a while, the new spirit's voice would start chanting through the spirit medium, whispering at first and then singing in soft falsetto tones. As the words of the spirit became clearer, the men clustered around the medium and formed a chorus to echo him. Their singing encouraged the medium's spirit to sing louder and with greater confidence. Gradually, the spirit's chants became full songs, each line being repeated and chorused in full-throated harmony by the male chorus.

Gebusi women, however, were excluded from the séance (though they could hear it while sitting or dozing in their own quarters). The men, meanwhile, shouted, joked, and laughed in an all-night songfest of masculine bravado. Perhaps most strikingly, the primary spirits who sang through the male spirit medium were young women. And not just any women, but gorgeous young spirit women who longed to have sex and joke with Gebusi men. In effect, the men's séance singing voiced, projected, and received back their sexual fantasies of women—at the same time real Gebusi women could be beaten by husbands or brothers for being flirtatious. By contrast, spirit women were literally embodied by the men themselves, first in the voice of the male spirit medium and then in the men's collective chorus. Spirit séances were, at least to some degree, a male fantasy that celebrated men's sexual desires at the same time that real Gebusi women were excluded, controlled, and sometimes disparaged.

Given this male bias, what were we to make of Gebusi "good company"? Was *kogwayay* merely a cultural value that disguised male dominance over women? This question brings us to the crux of anthropology's appreciation of cultural diversity, on the one hand, and its critique of inequity on the other. For the most part, Gebusi women accepted and appreciated the culture they lived in. At spirit séances, they sometimes took offense at male joking, but more often they indulged and genuinely enjoyed it. Women were excited and galvanized by ritual feasts and initiations, and they actively played their own roles at these events. On these and other occasions, they enjoyed interacting with women who visited from other settlements. It was true that Gebusi women often lived in the cultural shadow of Gebusi men. Sometimes they resisted their second-class status. But for the most part they accepted and embraced it. Women swelled with pride at their own and the men's accomplishments, even when men presented the fruits of women's work as their own. So, too, women tended to accept men's collective prerogative to take violent action against sorcery suspects, and usually as well the right of a man to beat his wife.

In many if not most regions of the world, the activities and experiences of men and women differ. Among the peoples and cultures of New Guinea, the division between male and female realms is often especially marked. Women had their own world, their own lore, and their own female-centered interactions. I found the social life of Gebusi men, for the most part, to be a lot of fun. I enjoyed their banter and horseplay, smoked their tobacco in big bamboo tubes, joked with them, and participated in community feasts.

To both men and women, and for Eileen and me as well, Gebusi children were a great source of pleasure and happiness. We took a particular liking to an impish little boy named Sayu. He was four or five years old and simply the most charismatic child either of us had ever known. His mother, Boyl, was an attractive woman with a broad smile and, we thought, the strongest intellect in the village. Her husband, Silap, was one of the more important men in the village, one of the principal founders of the main longhouse, and a feisty character with a quick smile.

In the beginning, we didn't know what would happen next. We knew the people of Yibihilu were vibrant and welcoming and their culture was alive with song and celebration. We had naiveté, energy, and trust in our purpose. These were indispensable for fieldwork that was both deeply difficult and ultimately limitless. After several weeks of visiting, it was time for us and for the people of Yibihilu to decide if a house should be built for us at "the place of the deep waters." The villagers continued to be friendly, and some of them were becoming our friends. But they were also very different from us, and we felt the force of this difference.

One night, the conversation finally turned—uncertainly, via Hawi—to how long we would stay in Yibihilu. Dusk was turning into night, and the men and boys around me became silhouettes with bones in their noses and feathers in their hair. Trophy skulls of pigs and cassowaries swayed from the rafters. A chunk of resin sizzled on the stone lamp. I looked up and saw people and personalities I was beginning to know. But they also appeared alien. Some were covered head to foot with the scaly skin of ringworm. Others had streaks of soot or caked ulcers on their skin or large cracks in the thick calluses that lined their feet. Their toes splayed, as if they had been born to stride along mossy log bridges that we inched across timidly. Even when sitting down, I towered over them. My gawky six-foot white frame stood out against their dark bodies, which averaged five feet four inches at full height.

Their skill and prowess in the forest dwarfed my own. How quickly and silently they could climb a tree, club a lizard, shoot a fish, or ford a stream. I knew that until recently they had eaten the flesh of persons killed as sorcerers. Their polished arrows were propped in the corner. Many layers of their culture remained obscure to me. The joy of our beginning made me question whether my giddiness would change to disillusionment when the novelty of our warm welcome wore off. But the die, it seemed, had already been cast. After undergoing years of scholarly training, journeying halfway around the world, and enduring mosquitoes and leeches—and with our personal and professional identity on the line—how could we turn back? They asked, "How long do you think you will stay?" I heard myself say, "Two years." My head swam as I heard the hubbub around me. But in the best Gebusi tradition of "everything is going to be fine," the discussion quickly turned to where our thatched house was to be built. On this side of the village, or on that one? The following morning, strings were laid on the ground to mark where the walls would be. And our house was built above them.

Note: See Gebusi video clips and commentary on the author's reentrance to Gebusi society in 2013 ("Anthro & Studying Culture") and on Gebusi language in the field ("Language in Practice") on www.bruceknauft.com → Gebusi.

BROADER CONNECTIONS
Fieldwork and Culture

- Cultural anthropologists such as Bruce study culture through **participant-observation.** Extended research over longer periods of time results in long-term or **longitudinal fieldwork.**

- **Gift exchange** and **reciprocity** are important ways that human social interactions are established and reinforced—including with anthropologists in the field. Gebusi employ exchange and reciprocity in food-giving and in gift-exchange names between friends.

- Cultural anthropologists are often distinguished from government administrators, missionaries, or aid workers in that they typically try to participate in local means of reciprocity and exchange. Professionally, cultural anthropologists attempt to observe and learn about diverse peoples rather than actively trying to change their customs, behavior, or beliefs.

- The impact of external influence or **colonialism** is diverse; Gebusi largely appreciated Australian colonial presence, but the neighboring Bedamini people, who killed many Gebusi in raids, resisted and resented it.

- Many peoples of the world have been influenced by external threat and pressure either from outside their country or nation (**external colonialism** or **imperialism**) or from inside it (**internal colonialism** or **nationalist domination**).

- Among Gebusi and other peoples, **culture** may be defined as a shared and public system of **meanings, beliefs, and values.**

- **Cultural change** not only alters practices and beliefs but can reinvent them in new ways over time (the **reinvention of culture** or the reinvention of tradition). Gebusi culture intensified in part because Australians pacified their tribal enemies while introducing them to modern goods such as steel knives and axes.

- Most peoples assert **cultural values** that they emphasize and share as a positive belief system or **cultural ideology.** Among Gebusi, deep cultural values are reflected in *kog-wa-yay*—the "good company" of togetherness, friendly talking, and exuberant or playful cheering or yelling.

- *Kogwayay* among Gebusi can be seen as a **key symbol** in Gebusi culture—a cultural concept or emphasis that is widely shared, prominent, emotionally powerful, and frequently demonstrated.

- In many societies, positive cultural values are complemented by troubling or challenging features of social domination, conflict, or disorder that are downplayed or papered over. Among Gebusi these include **gender domination** of men by women and the **scapegoating** of people through accusations of **sorcery.**

- Cultural anthropologists often undertake ethnographic fieldwork that is at turns both enjoyable and challenging or difficult. This is true both in remote areas, such as the Papua New Guinea rainforest, and in highly developed areas, including anthropological fieldwork in modern cities in Western or non-Western countries.

Chapter 2

Rhythms of Survival

Boyl slung her load of leaves to the ground while the other women staggered into the village and followed suit. The foliage had been stripped from sago palms, folded, and then loaded onto their backs in net bags supported by tumplines across their foreheads. These leaves would form the bulk of our house, as they do all Gebusi dwellings. We hardly guessed that a house made mostly of leaves could shelter us from up to 14 feet of rain each year along with temperatures topping 100 degrees. But they could. The long leaves are carefully pinned to wooden strips about five feet long. Hundreds of these extensive leaf strips are lashed closely together, like shingles, to the beams of the house. For the roof of the village longhouse, which measured 74 by 34 feet, the many many thousands of leaves easily weighed several tons. The bulk of the dwelling was its massive roof, which peaked some 25 feet high and sloped over windowless walls until it almost touched the ground.

We were amazed to see our own house take shape. Yuway and the other men scampered over its wooden frame like skilled acrobats, hoisting log supports and the heavy ridgepole. Without measuring tape, plumb line, or any materials other than wood, leaves, and vines, they built the roof and all of the house like a first-rate construction crew. Lack of formal training was overcome with practical ingenuity and intimate knowledge of forest materials. Their indigenous numbers were just three: "one" (*hele*), "two" (*bena*), and "two plus one" (*bene bwar hele bwar*). Anything greater

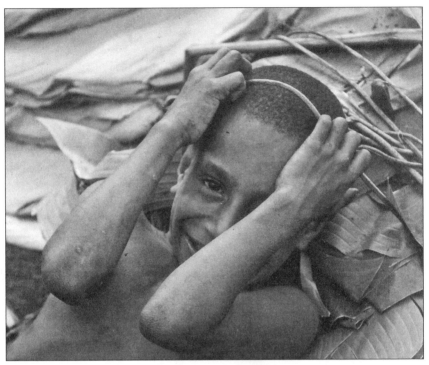

Boy with a bundle of tied leaves, 1998.

than that was simply "many" (*bihina*). Counting was as irrelevant to the Gebusi as their physical skills were finely honed. As ad hoc engineers, they were quite astounding.

This is not to say that arithmetic is unknown in other non-Western cultures. Like the ancient Babylonians, the Kapauku people of West New Guinea developed a base-60 number system, which they use to count items into the thousands for fun. But one group's chosen passion is another's apathy. Although the Gebusi shortchanged their numerals, they had a rich vocabulary for a seemingly endless variety of plants, vines, and trees, each of which had special properties and uses.

If culture humanizes the physical environment, the Gebusi longhouse has been their biggest accomplishment of material culture. Being the main gathering place for the 52 residents of Yibihilu, the "house long" (*masam sak*) was their tangible sign of village cooperation, physical prowess, and collective labor. Materially minded anthropologists describe culture as "adaptive" because human creativity and symbolic diversity have allowed us to survive in so many different physical environments—from the arctic to desert to the tropics—and practically everywhere in between. Whereas animals are more limited by genetic or "instinctual" behaviors, we humans add enormous capacity for learning and for making our efforts collective through language. Culture allows us to adapt to the world far beyond the constraints of our body and physiology.

Given the prominence of the Gebusi longhouse, it surprised us at first that it was often empty. The longhouse was the permanent residence of just two extended families who, like all Gebusi, often left for treks in the forest. Others lived in smaller houses nearby. But the longhouse had been built by the community at large and functioned as an evening gathering place and site of community celebrations and ceremonies. Although humming with energy when the village was full of people, the central dwelling gave way to the surrounding forest as activity dispersed during the bulk of most days. Hawi goes off with a group of young men to spear fish. Boyl and her husband depart to collect bananas from a distant garden and to see if tubers are ready to harvest. Young girls leave with their adult sisters to forage for fresh bamboo shoots, rummage in the nest of a wild bush hen for eggs, or scoop under rocks in the stream for freshwater prawns. Along the way, they keep a keen eye out for a stray bush rat or snake that could be clubbed with a stick or sliced with a knife. Men carry bows and arrows and look for signs of a wild pig, a sleeping lizard, a possum on a low-lying branch, or a cassowary—a large, flightless bird that looks similar to an ostrich. Even a good-sized tarantula can be seized for the cooking fire. Gebusi eat practically anything that moves.

By late afternoon, those within reasonable distance return to the village for an evening meal and general conversation. The atmosphere is languid and friendly as families congregate. Men sit together and share large bamboo tube pipes filled with powerful home-grown tobacco. Women chat as they stoke the hearth and cook the bananas. Back in the forest, some families are too far away to return for the night; they make a temporary camp and sleep in a makeshift shelter or lean-to. Imba and his wife, Walab, walk for a day to distant clan land, accompanied by their siblings and children. The men in the group chop down and split open a stately sago palm; then the women pound its interior pith into flour. Deep in the forest, it can take women two weeks or more to process the sago and leach its fiber into weighty bundles of caked flour. Meanwhile, the whole group lives in the forest. Imba and his male kin hunt and forage; the children play together or set off with a group of adults to gather breadfruit or Tahitian chestnuts from stands of trees. The mini-community sleeps in a temporary shelter of poles and sticks topped with sago leaf thatch to keep out the rain. When the sago palm is completely processed, the fruits of the women's labor are bundled in bark, wrapped in leaves, and slung on their backs in big net bags. Women haul them to the river and load them onto canoes, or they carry them by land to the settlement. For weeks on end, the heavy parcels will supply starchy flour that is easily cooked on the fire.

Beyond its food, the rainforest is ripe with meaning. Hogayo lingers by an old settlement where his father was born; Oyam stops to drink from a stream that belongs to her mother's family line. Memories are associated with each stand of trees, creek, small hillock, or patch of old garden land. As the Gebusi walk through the forest they relive past experiences and remember what the forest has provided their kin, their ancestors, and themselves. They rediscover how the trees have grown, when their fruits will be ripe, what animals have left traces nearby, and when the area should be revisited to reap one or another natural harvest. The forest is not simply "land"; it is a living cornucopia with meaning and nuance in each nook and wrinkle. Gebusi describe their lands with fondness and nostalgia. They name individual places and luxuriate in their tranquil distinctions. When Gebusi sing at dances and séances, many of their most haunting songs recall places in the forest.

Between daily trips and more extended ones, the residents of Yibihilu spent almost half their nights—45%, to be precise—in the forest or at another settlement. In earlier days, they could easily scatter to the bush if they thought enemies were on the prowl. It's no surprise, then, that the early Australian patrol officers struggled to locate Gebusi in the forest. Partly out of frustration, they called the local population "nomads"; indeed, they named the whole region the Nomad Sub-District and their local outstation the Nomad Patrol Post. In fact, though, they were mistaken. Anthropologists define nomads as people who have no permanent residence—people who shift their settlement every few weeks to forage and hunt, or to tend their livestock. Sedentary peoples, by contrast, build durable houses and live in long-lasting settlements. Certainly, the Gebusi longhouse qualifies as a long-lasting residence; even in precolonial times, it lasted for several years. Though Gebusi travel widely across their lands, they are "sedentary" and live primarily in a durable settlement.

Though Gebusi flirt with being "semi" nomadic, they benefit greatly from growing food in regular gardens. Most of these are within a one- or two-hour trip from the main settlement. Game animals aren't plentiful in the Gebusi's portion of the rainforest—mostly wild pigs and cassowaries—and though Gebusi eat and enjoy smaller forest creatures, these don't supply many calories day-to-day. So Gebusi could not survive effectively as foragers without the plantains and other foods of their gardens.

The biggest task, at least for the men, is felling the trees. Though most families maintain small gardens, large ones are also cleared as a communal project. After several weeks at Yibihilu, we went to see how this was done. We left in high spirits, men whooping and children frolicking; it was going to be a big garden. Our 20-minute walk to the site felt more like a festive stroll than a work brigade.

With the rest of the men, I took turns chopping trees and resting by the makeshift cooking fires while chatting, munching bananas, and smoking Gebusi tobacco. To my surprise, Yuway told me not to chop any of the trees all the way; each time, I was stopped halfway through. The other men were doing the same. Perplexed, I asked why—but became only more confused when Yuway made dramatic pantomimes of noise and crashing. After two more hours of "half-work," to my bafflement, hardly a single tree had been felled. Our work pace dwindled until only a handful of men were left at one end of the large plot. There, they attacked a particularly large and majestic piece of timber—while the rest of us were waved off to the far margins of the area. Everyone said I should not, under any circumstances, wander back onto the garden site. Knowing that the Gebusi had strong spiritual ties to their land, including its tree spirits—I thought the plot might now be under a sacred taboo until rites were made to supplicate the spirit of the tallest tree before it was felled.

But I was wrong. The enormous tree began to creak and groan from the continuing blows of the senior men's axes. Though towering above its leafy rivals, a thick skein of vines and foliage knitted them all together. It tottered briefly, then thundered down with an amazing crash. As it fell, its force exploded in domino fashion across the entire acre of half-cut timber. Hefty trunks were suddenly toppled and flung in all directions, like telephone poles ripped up by a falling master pylon. It was frightful, wonderful, and awe-ful—an arboreal tornado. Then it was over, as quickly as it had started. All that remained were the whoops of the men, a blizzard of leaves fluttering to the ground, and a mass of fallen trunks and limbs. I was stunned and had to sit down.

Regaining my bearings, my confusion persisted. To be sure, the trees had been felled with surprisingly little effort. But now their fallen bulk smothered the garden beneath. How could it be planted, much less cultivated? Yuway and the others were unconcerned. They showed me that banana suckers and root crop seedlings had been stuck in the ground days before. When the trees had been standing, I hadn't noticed them. Though a few of these plantings were now crushed by fallen limbs, the vast majority were simply sheltered from the blaze of the day and the pelting of rains—by the fallen branches now hovering above them. Without this covering, the new garden would have wilted in the tropical sun or been washed away by torrential storms. As the foliage of the felled trees decomposed, the crops beneath sprouted through these fertilizing remains until strong enough to grow unshielded. Though the garden now looked like a chaos of fallen trees, it was actually a finely honed system of indigenous cultivation. Anthropologist Edward Schieffelin gave it a fitting name: "felling the trees on top of the crop."

As the Gebusi starch staple, plantains require almost no weeding, grow quickly, and don't bear fruit until the caloric pods have grown beyond the reach of hungry animals. As such, Gebusi avoid the hard work of having to fence their gardens. And by picking the fruit *before* it is fully ripe, they prevent marauding birds or bats from eating it. Instead, the bananas are softened by throwing them directly on the fire. Retrieved with wooden cooking tongs, they are scraped of their charred skin and eaten straightaway.

As their plantains suggest, Gebusi grow food without much work. Letting gardens lie fallow for years before recutting and replanting them qualifies Gebusi food-raising as "horticulture." By contrast, "agriculture" would require more labor per unit of land—irrigation, strong fertilizing, plowing, fencing, and/or terracing. Though these techniques increase the land's yield—and the number of people it can support—they exact a higher price in human work or mechanized intervention. Gebusi relax happily at the other end of this spectrum. Because they have plenty of land, they avoid the effort of repeatedly cultivating any one plot. After a few years, the rainforest reclaims its terrain, first with tall grass, then shrubs, and finally trees—each providing nutrients that enrich the clay soil. Ideally, the grandson of the original gardener comes back to the plot and recultivates both its social and its nutritional essence. Gebusi cycles of regeneration and growth are hence spiritual and cultural as well as ecological and demographic: the rejuvenation of land, food, people, and spiritual connection. Because land is plentiful, it is easily lent to friends as well as kin, extending and intensifying social and spiritual networks.

Across generations, Gebusi have raised ample food even though their part of the rainforest is not that bountiful. And in the process, they don't seem to have strained themselves unduly. Certainly, Gebusi endure stints of intense labor. Women carry heavy loads through the rainforest, and they transport firewood, food, and even their babies in net bags slung on their backs. Though men may also bear these burdens, women provide the ultimate "carrying capacity." Even for women, however, many hours on most days drift by in relaxation—conversing, eating, and playing with children. And men have even more time for social pursuits. Their palavers extend for hours

Sefomay, an adult Gebusi woman, carrying two net bags and her son, Moka, who wears his own net bag, 1981.

into the evening. Every week and a half or so, they additionally convene an all-night spirit séance. After this extended songfest, they typically sleep for half of the following day. Added to these are ritual feasts and dances that energize the entire settlement about once a month.

Marshall Sahlins called simple human cultures "original affluent societies." Though their technology and material culture are often rudimentary, people are still able to spend hours each day socializing or lazing about. Although obtaining food and providing shelter require work, this effort ebbs and flows in harmony with the environment rather than as a struggle against nature. From the icy arctic to the parched deserts of Australia, simple human societies have survived with plenty of time to spare. By contrast, the advanced technology of modern societies has arguably reduced rather than increased our leisure time. On most nights, the Gebusi get a good nine hours or more of sleep. Here in the US, I am often lucky to get seven. Each of our intended labor-saving devices brings new demands for productive work.

If Gebusi throw the frenzied pace of modern living into relief, they also have their own afflictions. Their deeper struggle has not been so much to acquire food as to fight off illness and, as discussed later, to endure human violence. But the Gebusi's biggest enemies have ultimately been small. Mosquitoes bring the scourge of malaria. Parasitic worms cause chronic and draining illness. Diseases such as tuberculosis and introduced influenza wreak havoc. In the hot, humid climate, cuts and scrapes easily fester and form putrid skin ulcers. All these ailments sap energy and could be combatted by better nutrition. But traditional Gebusi were at pains to improve their diet. Their staples of plantains and sago brim with starch but provide little protein. Forest animals are hard to find and kill, and hunting more frequently in the deep forest would expose Gebusi to yet more mosquitoes and malaria—and greater risk of accident and injury. Malnutrition was hence a problem, and young children often had the tiny limbs and distended "sago belly" of a high-starch but low-protein diet. Ultimately, the "affluence" of Gebusi leisure has itself been an adaptation to their environment: it is better to conserve energy and relax than to work harder and improve nutrition only marginally.

We can illustrate this by pig-raising. Gebusi love to eat pork. But keeping pigs would require fencing and then feeding them every day. So they take the easy way out. When the opportunity arises, Gebusi capture wild piglets in the forest. They feed them leftover food, carry them around in little net bags, and tame them to some extent. But as the pigs grow bigger, Gebusi turn them loose. The critters live in the forest on their own but still come back to Gebusi for occasional handouts of food. As such, the pigs are neither wild nor domestic but somewhere in between. For a major feast, Gebusi lure fully grown and semi-wild pigs back to the village with pieces of banana or sago, which they leave by the pig's tracks in the forest—a bit like the trail of Hansel and Gretel, in reverse. Following the trail of food, the pigs find their way unwittingly back to the village, where they can be slaughtered fresh on the spot. Keeping pigs semi-domesticated doesn't allow Gebusi to raise very many of them—barely one for each extended family. But it does provide both a reliable source of meat for special occasions and a way to avoid the work of fencing and feeding pigs, and even of having to carry a heavy slaughtered pig back to the village.

This illustrates a larger point. Anthropologists often class societies according to their mode of livelihood or subsistence, their style of residence, and their type of economy and politics. But these categories are not rigid in practice—and people like the Gebusi often defy them. Gebusi subsist through gardening as well as foraging and hunting—they are "horticulturalists," but their practices also include "foraging." In residence, their lifestyle is mobile and almost "semi-nomadic," yet they build durable houses and are "sedentary." They efficiently raise pigs, but the animals are "semi-domesticated." In terms of leadership, Gebusi have neither the aggression and status-competition of so-called big-men (often associated with the political form of "tribes") nor the completely decentralized leadership typically associated with "band" societies of foragers. Personally, I like the fact that Gebusi are "in-betweeners." Like many peoples when considered closely, they crosscut many of our concepts and classifications. Such terms remain important for general comprehension—and they typically loom large in the chapters and glossaries of anthropology textbooks. This is useful for conveying broad comparisons and contrasts between cultures. But it doesn't plumb how a society or culture is put together in actual practice. It is in part for this reason that individual case study ethnographies, such as this present one concerning the Gebusi, provide a useful complement to textbook overviews. While comparative anthropology or "ethnology" gives us categories for global understanding, "ethnography" depicts a single society in greater and richer human detail.

However one slices it, the diverse ways that people pursue their livelihoods and organize their society is a testament to human creativity and to the power of culture as a means of adaptation. I am continually struck by how people not just survive but find meaning and purpose across different environments, including in the intense modernity of our digital 21st century. If the task for many of us is now to find balance between labor and leisure, between work and life, the examples of other peoples and cultures, including the Gebusi but also those in modern cities in different world areas, are useful to consider—a full arc of human possibilities and potentials we can learn from. As economic and ecological challenges grow more serious, we can benefit from considering the great resilience and creativity of human adaptations.

For their own part, and amid their many challenges, Gebusi have basked in their environment. A storm blows in and doesn't let up for hours. Rain pelts and pockmarks the village, carving gullies and little canyons in the central clearing. Streams swell and rivers roil and flood, their clay banks becoming muddy slides to any who would traverse them. Plans are canceled. But Gebusi simply take the day off. Toasty in their houses, men light up their pipes and chat while women play with children, toss plantains on the fire, or thread more inches on the large net bags they are making. Someone tells a story or a myth. Plans unfold for a coming feast. Those returning through the downpour make fun of how wet and muddy they got. Sometimes they defy the rain, whooping loudly and marching through it proudly.

When a dry spell descends and the rivers shrink, men make plans for spearing or poisoning fish. The low, clear water exposes their prey, making them easier to catch. Hawi was one of the best fishermen. His favorite stalking place was above the rapids in a quiet pool of the Kum River, where he swam underwater, jabbing at his targets with a pronged spike. One day, he speared the biggest fish of all, 20 pounds or more. To the people of Yibihilu, taking this giant prize was like winning the Super Bowl. Energy swelled with cries of joy and amazement. Beyond good fortune or skill, the spearing of the huge fish affirmed the beneficence of the river, the harmony of the villagers with their forest spirits, and the goodness of the village.

Portions of fish were shared with each inhabitant of Yibihilu, the "place of the deep waters." To this day, Hawi has always been my "fish," my *dio*, based on the fish he shared with me that afternoon. That night, Swamin held one of his biggest and most dramatic séances. His spirits sang how the monster fish had willingly given itself up to Hawi to feed and support the village. The spirits, the environment, and the Gebusi themselves were harmoniously linked in a grand cycle of life.

While the Gebusi seemed to luxuriate in their environment, it was hard for us to follow their lead. Daily physical routines proved a major challenge. Ailments and illness became inevitable over the course of two years: headaches and chills from malaria; digestive disorders; intestinal worms; skin lesions, boils, and rashes; and jungle rot that thrives in your body's most private parts. Our lives were made bearable by the small arsenal of medications we brought, both for ourselves and for Gebusi. But not being doctors, it was often hard to know what to do or how we could help our Gebusi friends. However, the people of Yibihilu were our best role models. They accepted infirmity when it came and made the best of life while it lasted. Tabway was afflicted with a putrefying ulcer in her thigh. Her leg would shudder in torment but her face was calm and even showed a soft smile. Sefomay's foot was permanently and painfully swollen to twice its normal size. She would joke that her "leg was rotten"—but her spirit was not.

Sickness and death visited Gebusi at every season of life. Malaria, pneumonia, filariasis or "elephantiasis," tuberculosis, influenza, and diarrhea were at once causal and contributing factors. Gebusi were distressed by microbes, parasites, clogged lungs, contaminated blood, and swollen spleens. By the time they reached what we would call middle age, most of them were physically wizened. Almost all adults had had at least one near-death illness. Sickness dovetailed with poor nutrition; weaker bodies struggled to fight infection. Of girls who lived to be five, only one in three survived to age 40. For boys of similar age, only one in about six lived into their fifth decade.

If Gebusi could not cheat death, they savored life while it lasted. They enjoyed simple pleasures, smiled often, laughed easily, and celebrated when they could. Notwithstanding their crusades against sorcery, there was little they could do to reduce their own physical risk—either from disease or from one another. The deaths that we witnessed were met with quietude and acceptance, the warm hands of friends giving way to piercing wails only at the end.

Gebusi ailments put our own in perspective. On a daily basis, our two biggest challenges were heat and insects. Such "little" things are almost embarrassing to admit, but chronic discomforts loom as large in fieldwork as they are typically neglected in scholarly accounts. If heat and humidity turned our papers limp and our shoes green with mold, we easily felt the same way. The following extract is edited from my fieldnotes:

> When humidity and temperature both exceed 98.6, you can't be cool. Though I sit in the shade of my house, calming myself, my throbbing head fuels sweat. I stay absolutely still, motionless, eyes closed. Sweat beads, then dribbles from my brow, chest, and thighs. I splash with water from my basin, but sweat just replaces it. I lie down in my sleeping room, a bit darker, and take off all my clothes, every stitch. I kneel on the floor beside my sleeping net (since fractions of confinement make a difference).
>
> The three-point stance is my naked attempt to relax in the heat. Lying down creates hot contact between my skin and what I am laying on; a puddle of sweat quickly appears. So my best posture keeps an illusion of repose, with the smallest possible part of my body touching the floor, as much as possible in languid air. My three points of contact are the tip of my big toes, kneecaps, and elbows, reducing my area of contact to a few scant inches. When I get it right, my head can hang an inch or two off the floor without having support. My mind calms, so does my skin. The sweat still collects across my cheeks and drips from my nose. It splats onto the floor, but softly, slowly. After ten minutes, I'm as serene as I can be. Relaxation is key, since heat makes friends with anxiety and stress. Yesterday I misplaced my notebook—and my frustration quickly steamed my glasses! My three-point stance won't cure the heat. But it makes it easier to live with.

For their part, the Gebusi hardly minded either temperature or humidity. They often kept cooking fires smoldering in their houses, which have no chimneys. The heat and smoke dispersed mosquitoes and drove away insects that would otherwise infest the roof of the house. But we had been raised in northern parts of the US and couldn't tolerate the added heat of a continual fire in our house. So we opted for less fire—and got more bugs. Insects were a whole dimension of fieldwork. We couldn't ignore them:

> They are everywhere; even sitting in a canoe in the middle of the river, the creepies and crawlies land on you. Some are really strange looking, sporting weird colors and wild-flight torsos and ways of moving that come from another world. Magnified by a thousand, they would be perfect in a Hollywood alien thriller. But most of them are innocuous; you just pick or brush them off and move on.
>
> There are several exceptions. Oversize grasshoppers give a startle when they land on you suddenly. Five-inch spiders raise my adrenaline when I find them sharing our outhouse. Cockroaches are everywhere. Hundreds of the big ones live in our cardboard cartons and eat the labels off our precious tins of food. But the mosquitoes I hardly even count as insects because they are more insidious. Not just because there are so many of them, nor because they fly into our thatched house without pause or restriction. It's the malaria and elephantiasis they bring. They wait like cowards until dusk before taunting you with their mock fragility. They lilt in squadrons on low power but somehow float just beyond your grasp, waiting like lunar modules to hit your pay dirt. Swatting hard only flits them away to a yet choicer landing place. "One small bite for one mosquito, one giant risk for mankind."
>
> There is a special insult to getting several bites. How many did you really receive in the dimness? Was it only two? Or six? Is that another new one now, just beside the others? Did you really take your antimalarial pill (none of which are completely effective)? The best thing is to go inside the mosquito net—and that very quickly, because nothing is worse than having mosquitoes inside your net. But we can't live under a mosquito net from six at night till six in the morning; we have to eat and wash, write our notes, and of course, be with Gebusi. The evening should be the most enjoyable part of the day, but that's when "mossies" come out the most. Going to the bathroom remains the worst. Mosquitoes love the bottom of the latrine—and fly up in droves whenever something comes down the hole. They attack our most vulnerable parts when we are most exposed. Talk about a bite in the butt!

If heat and insects were our daily scourge, the Gebusi kept our irritations in perspective. Despite their much graver ailments, their vibrant lives

pulled us beyond the orbit of our own concerns. Call it cultural gravity—
the ability of others' lives to sweep you up and draw you in against all odds
and to your own surprise. This is the deepest part of fieldwork, the part
that makes you grow. We joked with the Gebusi, shared with them, took
part in their activities, and became part of their world. Reciprocally, they
seemed to enjoy us, accepted our idiosyncrasies, and included us in their
activities as much as they could. In professional terms, this is what is often
described as the primary fieldwork method in cultural anthropology: participant-observation.

Professionally, my biggest challenge was learning the Gebusi language.
There was no way to do this beforehand, so I had taken training in how to
learn an unknown and unwritten language without help from translators.
In the field, bit by slow, painful bit, I recognized and spoke sounds that
were meaningful in Gebusi—what linguists call "phonemes"—that do not
exist in English. I compiled lists of Gebusi words and phrases—and puzzled over their meanings. In all these tasks, Yuway was my patient, insightful, and pleasant helper. Over weeks and months and eventually years, he
and I became special friends. He even helped me tackle the complexities of
Gebusi tense and grammar, which were the worst. Gebusi pile meanings
into verbs while leaving out nouns and other phrases. For instance, the
question "Would he have killed me?" is spoken in Gebusi as a single verb,
"kill" (*golo*), which is then modified by a string of suffixes to indicate a
presumed subject, a presumed object, conditional tense, causative action,
and interrogative aspect. The whole sentence is one word: *golo-hi-lay-ba*.

Fortunately, we knew from the start that learning the language would be
our most difficult task. After a few weeks, we could communicate in broken
Gebusi. But only after many months could we meaningfully comprehend
what Gebusi were saying to one another—not in the simple, slowed-down
language they used with us, but in the idioms, quick pacing, and assumptions they used with each other. My advisor told us not to get too discouraged. He suggested if we focused on language learning for the first six
months, we would be okay. He also said our language abilities would continue to improve and two-thirds of our understanding would likely emerge
during the last third of our fieldwork. He was right: we had to be patient.

Along the way, we developed our own rhythms of daily adaptation. Fieldwork is at heart its own brand of optimal foraging. As the Gebusi shifted activities to gain the most from their surroundings, we tried to do the same. But as professionals, our desire to participate, to observe, and to record our experiences became a continual dance between "living with" and "writing up." Days during fieldwork blended language learning, observation, note-taking, interviews, writing, and reflection—amid the constant intensity of public social scrutiny. I was continually surprised at how long it took me to type up my notes and organize them into topical themes. Even when not much was going on, I seemed to be behind in my work. It became painfully obvious that fieldwork was not a process of quickly discovering "the truth."

My learning with Gebusi emerged gradually through a blur of confusing experiences and competing interpretations. I found repeatedly that my language skills were inadequate, my interpretations misleading, and my assumptions wrong. I remember during our first weeks pointing to various objects with my index finger and asking in simple Gebusi, "What is it?" (*ke ka-ba*). But no matter what I pointed to, the answer I got was always the same, "*dob.*" I was royally perplexed. But the mystery was explained when I learned the meaning of *dob*. *Dob* was the finger I was pointing with! Understanding was always a process of learning from our mistakes. We began at the lowest rung, asking nonsensical questions like "Is your son a girl?" But just as quickly, we learned to laugh at our foibles. It helped a lot that Gebusi laughed so good-naturedly along with us, just as they did at their own mistakes and problems.

As time went on and comprehension improved, I came to see cultural anthropology as a kind of dialogue—a conversation between Gebusi meanings and our own understandings. The trick was to have each side of this cultural equation make sense to the other. This process was rooted in participation and observation, but it continued afterward in writing and reflection. Writing ethnography is almost invariably a process of trying to explain events and actions that were, at the time, confusing if not opaque.

Fieldwork braided us ever more deeply with the Gebusi. A balance between give-and-take became key in our lives and our work: the ability to admit error and try yet again, to receive as well as to give, to be acted upon as well as to act. For this, Gebusi have been wonderful teachers. Reciprocity has always been the heart of their social life. As we gradually realized, balanced reciprocity infused most aspects of Gebusi culture, including their relation with their environment, their distribution of food, their ritual celebrations, their marriage patterns, their connections with the spirit world, and even their patterns of death and killing. The ideal of balanced reciprocity was one of the most personally and professionally important things I have learned from the Gebusi. Apart from their gendered divisions, they were egalitarian to a fault, and they reinforced this norm by constantly striving to give rather than just take.

> The big feast was yesterday; today, our friends are happily eating the celebration's remains. Since my own household contributed fish and rice to the collective effort, people now want to repay me.
>
> A member of each major family came this morning and presented me with a bird egg. I was deeply touched. Most memorable was five-year-old Kawe, who has become my "biscuit" exchange-name friend. I saw him coming from across the village. With the confident stride and smile of a grown-up, he looked at me from twenty yards away and walked over directly, never shifting his gaze. Stopping in front of me, he flashed his cutest tooth-missing grin, extended his little hand that held his egg, placed the egg in my palm, turned around, and walked back proudly, neither uttering a word nor looking back. I will not forget it.

Update: What has happened to Gebusi health and livelihood since 1980? Their subsistence base has both persisted and "exploded," and in the best sense of the latter term. By the mid-1990s, as you will see in Part Two, Gebusi were raising a whole host of new and intensified crops to sell for money at the Nomad market. But by the mid-2000s and dramatically since 2010, the bottom has fallen out of this market—and in the absence of a cash economy, Gebusi have returned to traditional means of subsistence. In the bargain, however, the new foods they have learned to raise— pineapple, pumpkins, squash, corn, peanuts, and nutritious root crops like sweet potatoes, which are now themselves a major starch staple—have stayed with them. As a result, Gebusi now have a far more varied and nutritious diet than they did before. Though not entirely a thing of the past, malnutrition is far less evident than it used to be.

A further benefit is the continued absence of Bedamini raiding, which allows Gebusi to be much more secure and stable in residence and organization. Villages are now fewer but larger, and much more permanent than before, lasting decades. In ways I hadn't fully appreciated, the shifting residences of Gebusi life had been, at least in part, a strategy to avoid being targets for Bedamini attacks. With this threat gone, people settled down, became less anxious, and traveled to garden lands more freely and in smaller groups. This trend has intensified over the years, allowing Gebusi to exploit their land more flexibly without fearing for their lives. At the same time, collective life in the village is more populous than before, including in large meeting houses, built with traditional materials, that function like the old residential longhouse.

Material investment in heavy-construction items like hand-hewn canoes has also increased. This is significant since Gebusi now cultivate large gardens along long stretches of riverbank, from which they can easily transport themselves, supplies, and food back and forth. Indeed, to make greater use of navigable watercourses, including for fishing, Gebusi have gradually tended to move downstream and to live near rivers. In the bargain, they have become more significantly a "canoe people" than they were in 1980.

In all, then, the remarkable patterns of Gebusi subsistence have not only persisted but intensified to the present. This enables and supports a much larger Gebusi population than before—up from about 450 in 1982 to more than 1,000. And yet, happily, Gebusi continue to have plenty of extra land to sustain their livelihood; their subsistence regime is not only home-grown but truly sustainable. In a modern world of ecological stress and environmental destruction, Gebusi provide a fine example of how careful local management of land, resources, and people can provide "rhythms of survival" that draw deeply upon cultural traditions to chart a rich and sustainable future in the 21st century.

Note: See field video clips of Gebusi subsistence livelihood ("Livelihoods") in 2013 on www.bruceknauft.com → Gebusi.

BROADER CONNECTIONS
Subsistence, Health, and Language

- Gebusi have lived in a pristine or primary **rainforest** area in the country of Papua New Guinea (PNG).

- Though Gebusi travel flexibly and might even be considered seminomads, they live in permanent villages and thus are **sedentary.**

- Gebusi are partly **foragers**—they **hunt and gather wild food**—in addition to being **horticulturalists** who raise food in gardens. Their gardening shifts flexibly and does not require the intense labor that would otherwise be associated with **agriculture.**

- Gebusi illustrate **cultural adaptation**—social adaptation by cultural means. This allows human groups to survive and to thrive in diverse and challenging environments.

- Simple human societies like the Gebusi have leisure to the extent that Marshall Sahlins has called them **"Original Affluent Societies."**

- Like many remote or poor peoples, Gebusi endure severe **health challenges,** including malaria, childhood malnutrition, elephantiasis (filariasis), tuberculosis, worm (helminthic) diseases, and influenza.

- Gebusi had low life expectancy, with death striking at any age. But with better **nutrition** from introduced crops, their health and longevity have increased.

- Gebusi have also benefitted from greater residential and social stability associated with absence of Bedamini raids.

- Like many anthropologists, Bruce's biggest cultural challenge in fieldwork was learning the Gebusi **language.**

- Gebusi language included culturally recognized sounds or **phonemes** that are not distinguished or "heard" as different sounds in English.

- **Morphemes** are the smallest units of meaning in language. In the Gebusi language, morphemes included the many prefixes, suffixes, and "infixes" of Gebusi verbs—including the three components of *kog-wa-yay.*

- Bruce took many **fieldnotes** as events were happening. Writing these up and configuring them supported his ethnographic write-up or **ethnography.**

- As in many or most societies, establishing **social reciprocity** was personally and professionally indispensable to long-term fieldwork among Gebusi.

- Drawing upon their cultural past, Gebusi have intensified and expanded their traditional **subsistence regime** to develop a **sustainable livelihood** that effectively supports a growing population in the 21st century.

Chapter 3

Lives of Death

It is hard to watch a baby die. Its scrawny body cries until its wails lose force and leave a ghostly little corpse. It was also hard on us that Gebusi men didn't seem to mind. During our first five weeks in the field, we saw one baby die and then another. As the mother wailed, her women kin gathered in support. But the men continued joking and smoking in the longhouse, and the boys played gaily in the village clearing. Only the baby's father stayed close by, and this with an air of detached waiting, until the small body could be quickly buried. Managing babies and managing death were women's work; if women bore the day-to-day challenge and joy of caring for new life, they also bore the sting of its death. I visited the mother in each case to lend support. But both times, being a man in women's space, I felt the most courteous thing I could do was to leave. The father of the second infant, Owaya, said the baby was dying "just because"—but then added that maybe a woman from Wasobi sent sorcery to kill it. Gebusi at that time attributed all natural deaths to sorcery. But they really only investigated the deaths of adults and older children.

Until infants are about seven months old, when their first teeth emerge, Gebusi don't think of them as fully human. Before then, they're thought to lack a full human spirit and aren't even named. Many infants only flirt with life; 38% of them died in their first year. It was almost as if the community was protecting itself from identifying too closely with so many young lives ending so quickly. But this distance is not shared by the mother, red-eyed and weeping, or by her closest female kin. I was confused at heart; it was my first real lesson in the cultural divergence between Gebusi emotions and my own.

Just three weeks after the second infant died, a third death hit the village: Dugawe killed himself. Unlike the infant deaths, which were taken as "normal," this one shocked the community. No one could remember a man having killed himself. Although we didn't foresee it at the time, Dugawe's death drew us into a whirling cultural vortex. Confusing events and experiences flew by; we struggled to piece them together. People we knew and liked suddenly did things we could not believe. In retracing this path—its twists and turns, and my own confusions—I came to know much about Gebusi life and death, the importance of kinship in their society, and exactly how, during fieldwork, one tries to make sense of a foreign culture.

I didn't believe Yuway and Silap at first when they told me the news; they seemed so nonchalant. But within minutes we rushed to the forest to retrieve the corpse. When we arrived, Dugawe's wife and two other women were weeping by the body. Silap brushed them aside and wailed loudly; Dugawe had been Silap's extended "brother-in-law" (*gol*) and "initiation-mate" (*sam*). His closeness to Dugawe reflected the fact that Gebusi settlements bring together men—and women—across different family lines.

As Silap finished wailing, the women came back to resume their crying. They called to Dugawe, telling him how sorry they were about his death and how much they wanted him back. Meanwhile, Silap retired to smoke tobacco with Yuway and waited for other men to arrive. None of them seemed upset, much less distraught, as they discussed how to take Dugawe's body back to the village. Wondering why he had killed himself, I went with others to inspect the body.

Dugawe had been a strong, handsome man, but now his face was pale and slack, already beginning to swell in the tropical heat. I looked for signs of foul play. Perhaps his death was a murder disguised as a suicide. But the only sign of struggle was a mark on the front of his faded T-shirt; something had poked and scratched down its fabric for a couple of inches. The shirt was not punctured, however, and nothing had pierced Dugawe's skin. To the men, though, the tiny scratch exposed a large canvas of anger and shame.

It turned out that Dugawe had fought earlier that day with his wife, Sialim. During the scuffle, she had held an arrow, thrust it toward him, and scratched his shirt. Their fight had been about a sexual affair that was generally acknowledged between Sialim and a young man, Sagawa. Publicly cuckolded, Dugawe had been furious. He had wanted to kill his wayward wife, and perhaps her lover as well. But Silap and others had discouraged him from doing this. Incensed but lacking other recourse, Dugawe had fought with his wife. He was further shamed by her scratching his shirt, his prized possession. When she went off to fetch water, the men said, he took tubes of poison he had previously made to kill fish in the stream and, in a fit of rage, drank them all. Empty tubes with the smell of the deadly toxin were found nearby. Dugawe had died a writhing death after poisoning himself in anger against his wife. But he was so much bigger and stronger than she. Why was his anger so self-directed?

It was all confusing. For the moment, all I could do was try to keep up with events as the men lashed Dugawe's body to a stretcher and marched it briskly back to Yibihilu. Seemingly by chance, two women converged on us in the forest from another direction. They were extended "mothers" of Dugawe who had come to view his body. Seeing his corpse, and his wayward wife behind us, they virtually exploded. Screaming, they tore straight into Sialim. She turned to avoid them, but the lead woman walloped her on the back with a steel ax, blunt side forward. This was followed by another heavy blow. The woman then turned and threw herself on Dugawe's corpse, pawing it and crying in great screaming sobs, as if her emotion would wake it up. The second woman then resumed the first one's attack, screeching at full pitch and shoving Sialim with a pointed stick as if she were going to drive it right through her. Silap and Yuway rushed in to hold her back while another man wrestled Dugawe's closest "mother" away from the corpse. The rest of the men quickly picked up the body and raced with it down the trail and out of sight. Yuway, Silap, and I followed closely, with the women coming more slowly behind.

When we arrived at Yibihilu, Dugawe's body was laid in state in his family house, just 25 yards from our own. A crowd of women wailed loudly while others arrived in short order. Many of them pummeled and berated Sialim, who hunched and whimpered but could not run away

Woman grieving the death of her husband, 1981.

without neglecting her duty to mourn her dead husband. Our neighbor, Owaya, emerged waving a firebrand in her face and shouted, "*Si-nay*!" I later learned this meant, "We're going to cook and eat you!"—which is what Gebusi traditionally did to persons executed as sorcerers. She gasped, whimpered, and shuffled further away.

Inside the house, we gathered with the women weeping over the corpse. Some of them flailed hysterically. After a few minutes, the atmosphere seemed to calm. But then a man with blackened face and body lunged suddenly through the doorway. Screaming, he cocked an arrow in his bow, drew it to full strength, and released the bowstring with a sharp snap. In my shock, I didn't realize he still held the arrow with the other fingers of his shooting hand—he had snapped the bowstring without firing the arrow. Yelling, he then repeated his diatribe—plucking his bow individually at each of us in the house. Silap then rushed in and interposed himself. With calming words, outstretched hands, and a wan smile, he gingerly and gradually placated the intruder. As the two of them moved outside, I saw 20-plus warriors from other settlements massing. Almost as quickly, the men of Yibihilu also gathered, but as peacemakers rather than antagonists. Armed with stoked tobacco pipes, they snapped fingers and extended repeated hits of powerful tobacco to each visitor. Quickly, this smoking melted the tension like a cool drizzle against the heat of the day. After a short while, the visitors retired to the longhouse and then rested on sleeping mats. Those of us from Yibihilu scurried to cook bananas and present them in hospitality.

Only an hour later, a constable arrived from Nomad Station. Silap and other men had taken the rare step of sending word to the Nomad Station about Dugawe's death. Why? Apparently, villagers had worried that authorities might receive a different tale of Dugawe's death from another source. After a long conversation through several interpreters, the constable finally wrote a brief entry in his police book: "Reason of death: Suicide caused by his wife fooling around." Though the constable's inquiry was completed, discussion about Sialim continued. Given the anger against her, it was decided that she should go with the officer back to Nomad and stay there for her own protection. The main events of the day were then over; the piercing wails of women haunted the night.

The following morning, Dugawe's body was grossly bloated. His swollen limbs oozed corpse fluid, and his peeling skin exposed putrid yellow-green flesh. His belly and even his genitals had swelled with the gases of decomposition. The stench was unforgettable; it burned up my nose, down my throat, and into my brain. Equally powerful were the actions of Dugawe's female kin. With unearthly sobs, they draped themselves physically over the corpse, lovingly massaged its slime, and drew back its skin. They rubbed their arms and legs with the ooze of the body. Corpse fluid on one's skin is a tangible sign of grief, of physical as well as emotional connection to the deceased—making one's own body like the corpse. Seeing this, Dugawe's departing soul was said to know how much they cared for him and ease his anger at having died, at least a little.

The men of Yibihilu dug Dugawe's grave by his house, and the women rolled his corpse onto Silap's back. As he strained and stood up under the weight, the body's arms flung out dramatically to both sides. The women shrieked. Men rushed to steady the corpse and help Silap place it in the grave. Dugawe's possessions—his bamboo pipe, bow and arrows, and so on—were quickly arranged in the grave by his female kin. Bark was placed over the corpse, and then the hole was filled in. Just as directly, the men retired to the longhouse to rest. The closest female relatives threw themselves on the mounded grave and wailed.

Prior to fieldwork, the only dead body I had seen was the sedate face of a friend of my parents at an open-casket funeral. Now I was shocked and repulsed by the events surrounding Dugawe's death. It seemed hideous that his corpse was allowed to decay and that our women friends wallowed in its stench. But I also began to see that this raw transformation—of a human being into a decomposed natural object—was an emotionally and physically honest acceptance of death. Dugawe's disfigurement showed me the fact of his death like nothing else could do. His demise was not hidden, not made pretty, not covered up in attempts to "spare grief." Were Gebusi customs improper? Or, was my own culture's tendency to sanitize and downplay the truth of death off-kilter?

I ultimately found that the dramatic actions of Gebusi women with corpses puzzled me less than the more reserved conduct of Gebusi men. As they went to the longhouse to smoke, joke, and drink bowls of root intoxicant, they acted as if nothing was wrong. When I heard that a visiting spirit medium would hold a séance, I thought he would commune with Dugawe's spirit and inquire about his death. Instead, the séance was a songfest of ribald entertainment. Why? The men said Dugawe's spirit was too angry to talk, and in the meantime, since they were all together, they might as well have a good time.

It was all bewildering. Which details concerning Dugawe's death were relevant, and which were superficial? How did Gebusi funeral practices and sorcery beliefs influence their social relationships and their emotional lives? I tried to connect the dots, but even as the picture stayed fuzzy, additional questions arose. What did Dugawe's sexual and marital problems with Sialim reveal about Gebusi gender relations? How typical, or anomalous, were the events of Dugawe's death in Gebusi society? As I struggled for answers, further events both sharpened my questions and posed new ones. Gradually, the events following Dugawe's death unfolded into a sorcery investigation—an inquiry into who had "killed" him. Its twists and turns helped me answer the questions I had, but not in the ways I expected. In retrospect, I realize this trail of discovery reveals much about the practice of ethnography itself as well as about the customs and beliefs of Gebusi.

With benefit of hindsight, anthropologists are charged with making sense of diverse societies and culture. Experience becomes fieldwork, and fieldwork becomes ethnographic writing. But how does this occur? For me in the field, it was challenging. No Gebusi gave me an overall narrative of Dugawe's death, its aftermath, or the events that preceded it. Rather, the story emerged from disparate and fragmentary events and observations, pieced together after the fact.

Though the big funeral feast for Dugawe took place just two days after his burial, it ended up being a sideshow to events that occurred weeks later. And by the time this sorcery investigation resumed, my opinion of Sialim had changed. At first, I thought she had acted irresponsibly. She had carried on a sexual affair with a young man named Sagawa, and she had apparently shamed her husband into killing himself. But additional facts painted a different picture. As Eileen found out from the women, Dugawe had previously killed not only his first wife but also his own small son. These murders had been so awful that villagers had informed the police, and Dugawe had served a five-year term at the Western Province prison. To my knowledge, no other Gebusi had ever been incarcerated there—or has been since.

With his prison term over, Dugawe had returned to the Gebusi and married Sialim, who had recently been widowed by the death of Dugawe's "brother." Gebusi widows often end up marrying a clan brother of their dead husband. This custom is common in a range of societies; anthropologists call it marriage by "levirate." Such marriages can keep a woman—her residence, her labor, and her children—within the clan of the deceased husband. Women themselves may desire this. Knowing Dugawe's history, however, Sialim did not want to marry him. As newlyweds, they fought, and he frequently beat her. On one occasion, she showed her bruises to police at the Nomad Station, and, knowing his violent history, they put him in jail. While he was there, Sialim took up with Sagawa, her young lover. Perhaps she hoped her new relationship would become a de facto marriage. But Dugawe was discharged earlier than expected. Enraged, he wanted to kill Sialim and Sagawa. But Silap and other men persuaded him this would only give him a longer prison term than he had already endured. Amid this tension, Dugawe took up again with Sialim. But after their fight, he killed himself.

From a Western feminist perspective, Sialim could hardly be blamed. She had been saddled with a murderous spouse and an abusive marriage. She had tried to find refuge, sought solace with another partner, and then stood up for herself when Dugawe beat her. What villagers took as a sign of travesty—her fighting with her husband and scratching his shirt with an arrow—could have been a desperate attempt at self-defense. However,

Sialim was rebuked not only by the men of Yibihilu but especially by
Dugawe's female kin. She had gone outside the community, gotten her
husband jailed, and cheated on him. Making matters worse, her romantic
affair was with an uninitiated young man.

What was I to think? I could criticize the Gebusi for condoning violent
sexism. But it was also true that Sialim had violated standards of marital
fidelity deeply held by Gebusi men and women. I felt sandwiched between
these views. At least it was fortunate for her own sake that Sialim had gone
temporarily to Nomad.

As I later realized, Gebusi sorcery inquisitions typically did not take
place until well after the burial. The main exception was if the corpse,
while lying in state, itself "signaled" the sorcerer. A suspected sorcerer
might be enjoined by the community to shake the decomposing corpse
while crying out his or her own grief. If at that unlucky moment the
corpse gave a "sign"—spilling cadaveric fluid, "moaning" from gases in its
lungs, or bulging or bursting its eyes (from the pressure of decomposition
gases in the braincase), the suspect could be axed to death on the spot. If
the corpse's "verdict" was clear, little retribution would be taken against
the killers, even by the victim's closest kin. But this had not happened with
Dugawe's corpse. So the men of Yibihilu had soothed the anger of
Dugawe's visiting relatives by extending hospitality—snapping fingers,
sharing tobacco, giving food, and holding an entertaining séance.

Friends told me that further inquiry into Dugawe's death shouldn't
take place in the heat of the moment but should be undertaken more
objectively and slowly—somewhat like a murder investigation in Western
societies. For Gebusi, however, the investigation was to identify the sorcerer who had killed Dugawe by magical means. In their belief, *all* human
deaths were caused by people—either through sorcery or through violence. Even a man who had fallen out of a coconut tree and broken his
back had been killed by a sorcerer—who had forced him to lose his grip.
For Dugawe's death, Gebusi took it as self-evident that a sorcerer had
made Dugawe crazy enough to kill himself.

Five weeks after his funeral, the real inquiry into Dugawe's death began.
In a nod to neutrality, the inquest séances were conducted by a spirit

medium who had hardly known him. But when these were inconclusive, further investigation was led by our clever friend Swamin, the main spirit medium of Yibihilu. By this time, I knew Gebusi sorcery had two main types. *Bogay* constitutes what ethnographers call "parcel sorcery"—sickness sent by manipulating a parcel of the victim's leavings. By contrast, *ogowili* qualifies as "assault sorcery," a cannibal attack by magical warriors. For Gebusi, *bogay* explained the torment of a long lethal illness, while *ogowili* explained deaths that were quick and sudden as well as those caused by accident—and suicide. In reality, we found no evidence that Gebusi actually practiced either type of sorcery, but their belief seemed unshakable.

In Dugawe's case, death was caused by *ogowili*. Although *ogowili* are male, Sialim could be guilty of Dugawe's death if she had had sex with an *ogowili* (such as Sagawa, her lover) and induced him to drive her husband crazy. In his séances, however, Swamin's spirits redirected this suspicion. Rather than accuse Sialim, the spirits described how *ogowili* warriors had descended on Dugawe from a distant settlement while Sialim was away fetching water. Though the sorcerers had disguised the evidence and covered their tracks, Swamin's spirits assured the assembled men that signs of their attack could still be found near to where his death had occurred. Further, the *ogowili* could be tracked back to the sorcerers' own settlement, where they could, in principle, be attacked in human form to avenge Dugawe. But to track assault sorcerers through the forest, Gebusi needed help from their spirits.

At about five o'clock in the morning, as Swamin's séance ended, the men of Yibihilu readied themselves to search for the assault sorcerers responsible for Dugawe's death. Uncertain what was going to happen next, I pulled on my boots and grabbed my flashlight. The men were carrying bows and arrows, and some had painted their faces black, as warriors. Eventually, we approached Abwiswimaym, the forest place where Dugawe had drunk poison. The mood was tense as we searched for the ghostly form of assault sorcerers ahead. Quiet and anxious, the men sought cover, pointed their arrows, and advanced warily on their spectral enemy. I pinched my arm to remind myself that we were not likely to find an actual person but rather evidence of a magical attack. After a while, however, the area was declared safe; the assault sorcerers had left.

Next, we searched for the magically transformed remains of the sorcerers' attack. With Swamin's spirits guiding us, we found an odd-looking stick that was said to be the "bush knife" that the sorcerers had used to cut Dugawe open. An indentation in the ground was the "footprint" of an *ogowili*. A discolored patch of dirt was Dugawe's "blood," which poured out during the attack. As incredulous as I was, the men around me seemed completely convinced. The very power of assault sorcerers rests in their ability to disguise their attacks and use magic to make the results seem normal. We then tried to track *ogowili* back to their distant settlement. But Swamin's spirits lost the trail as we waded up a stream. As such, we could not determine exactly where the sorcerers were from, or their identity. But the investigation did validate that Dugawe had been killed by an assault sorcerer from a distant village. It being impossible to discover more, no further action was taken.

I thought this would be the end of Dugawe's story, but in Gebusi society, as in our own, poignant events often cast a longer shadow. The verdict of Swamin's spirits provided a reprieve for Sialim, who had not been implicated. During the next seven months, she spent more and more time with Swamin's household. Eventually, she willingly consented to marry him— over the entreaties and objections of her young lover, Sagawa. Strong and robust for a middle-aged man, Swamin had been a widower. During our final year of fieldwork, he and Sialim seemed to be happily married.

Though this would have been a good Hollywood ending, it was not the one we ultimately came away with. It turned out that about a year before our arrival, Swamin had killed Sialim's own mother. The old woman, named Mokoyl, had been named as the parcel sorcerer responsible for the

A very ill man
from Yibihilu,
1981.

death of Swamin's first wife. At the time, Mokoyl tried to prove her innocence by conducting a bird egg divination—cooking eggs placed inside a
large mound of sago starch. Unfortunately, the eggs were badly undercooked. When Mokoyl had given Swamin one of the eggs to eat—as she
was expected to do—he had vomited. This was taken as a sign that Swamin's dead wife was clutching his throat, refusing Mokoyl's food and con-
firming her guilt. A few weeks afterward, about a year before we began our
fieldwork, Swamin tracked Mokoyl alone in the forest and split her skull
with a bush knife. As the spiritual evidence had confirmed Mokoyl's guilt,
most in the community agreed she had been guilty and deserved to die.
Her body was summarily buried in the forest, but villagers from another
settlement, knowing she had been killed as a sorceress, dug up and cooked
and ate parts of the body before it decomposed. In doing so, they indicated
their own support for the killing. Government officers never discovered
what happened.

Adding this last powerful episode to the preceding events, what conclusions can we draw about Dugawe's death—and the process of "doing
ethnography"? As is typically the case for anthropologists, my "methods of
inquiry" included participant-observation, formal interviews, casual conversations, translations of recordings (in this case, including Gebusi spirit
séances), and life histories of Gebusi as backed up by genealogies and histories concerning residence, marriage, and mortality in the community. It
was important to cross-check this information, particularly the events that
predated our arrival, to ensure my details were accurate. To this was added
my daily fieldnotes and reflections—sometimes insightful, but at other
times misguided—concerning what actually happened. Within a few
days—while the information was still fresh—I typed up my fieldnotes and
analyzed them in relation to other information I gathered. Even concerning eye-witness events, my initial awareness was often dim and partial—
strong in feeling but weak in understanding. An initial event like Dugawe's
death, dramatic as it was, was just one end of a tangled skein. It sucked me
into a thicket of crisscrossed meanings and histories. Figuring it out, writing it down, and getting a larger picture was quite a task—the "work" of
fieldwork.

Expanding this process, of which Dugawe's death is but a single example, life among Gebusi was a continual stream of dramas big and small.
These linked Gebusi together—and us to them—while gradually revealing
general patterns of Gebusi life. I found myself living in an intricate soap
opera—truth more surprising than fiction. Lovers, killers, spouses, coresi-
dents, friends, and relatives all had their parts in this rich and occasionally
toxic brew. No wonder that coming together in collective good company
was so important to Gebusi—or that it was such an accomplishment!

What is participant-observation in such a world? And how can a field-
worker keep a sense of ethics and wits about him or her in the process? For
Dugawe's death, I observed and to some extent participated in the
retrieval of his body, his funeral and burial, and the spirit séances and sorcery investigations that followed. However, I did not want to participate in
an attack on a suspected sorcerer. We tried to facilitate Sialim's departure
to a safer place when sentiments against her were highest. This said, we
worried that more severe violence might occur. Later in our fieldwork,
when our understanding was better, an older woman in the village was
accused of being a parcel sorcerer. In this case, we were able to act like kin
supporters and side with the woman's family when she was forced to test
her innocence by cooking a divination sago. Fortunately, no violent action
was taken against her, but she nonetheless had to move out of the village
with her closest kin. As this indicates, cultural anthropologists often court
risk and uncertainty as they decide what to observe and how and when to
engage in the "participant-observation" of fieldwork. As discussed later,
ethics in fieldwork are always important. This is true for the very reason
that, amid fieldwork's surprises, it's not always clear how to handle situa-
tions that are difficult, delicate, or dangerous.

Between events observed, those that could be reliably reconstructed,
and those we could participate in with good conscience, what larger patterns emerge concerning Dugawe's death, its history, and its legacy? What
can we say about Gebusi culture generally by drawing out this story?

Let's review. We began with a description of Dugawe's suicide, the
attacks on Sialim, the decomposition of his corpse, and the aggressive
mourning and burial of his body. Then came the surprisingly festive
events of the funeral feast that commemorated him. This was followed by
a month of waiting, and then, after other aborted attempts, Swamin's
revealing death inquest séance. This recast the death as an attack by assault

sorcerers from a distant settlement. A hunt in the forest for the culprits proved inconclusive. Eventually, Dugawe's spirit was declared appeased and his widow, Sialim, was exonerated. Several months later, Sialim and Swamin were married. Rounding out this history were events occurring before our own fieldwork. These included Dugawe's killing of his first wife and son; Swamin's killing of Sialim's mother; the jailing of Dugawe for having beaten Sialim; and Sialim's sexual affair with Sagawa.

This web illustrates how major Gebusi events, such as Dugawe's death, link causes and conditions that stretch forward and backward in time. Topics that may seem disparate—sickness and death, marriage, sex, sorcery, homicide, and suicide—become connected. A single event such as Dugawe's suicide thus exposes many issues: emotional dynamics among Gebusi, relations between men and women, the importance of spirits and spirit mediums, the impact of government prison, and even the role of subsistence practices such as fish poisoning. In lived experience, these features resonate and twine together. As such, the anthropological concepts and categories we may use to illuminate this story—sorcery, divination, ritual antagonism, levirate, spirit mediumship or shamanism, spirit séance, accusation or execution, and so on—are like convenient handholds on a mountainside rather than the mountain itself.

What does Dugawe's story tell us about the Gebusi? Concerning sorcery and gender relations, the events surrounding his death illustrate—as I otherwise confirmed more generally—that:

1. Gebusi women take primary responsibility for mourning and for emotionally identifying with the person who has died. Men investigate the death and take action against those deemed responsible as sorcerers.

2. Gebusi visitors' burials and funeral feasts express antagonism, but this aggression is undercut by the hosts' hospitality. Deeper anger is usually not expressed until proper inquests and divinations have been arranged.

3. Gebusi have believed that all adult deaths from sickness, accident, or suicide are caused by male assault sorcerers (*ogowili*) or by male

or female parcel sorcerers (*bogay*). Of the two, suspects for parcel sorcery (such as Sialim's mother) are more likely to be executed.

4. There is virtually no evidence that the Gebusi actually practice sorcery, though they believe firmly in its existence. Gebusi sorcery is a form of scapegoating. The identity of sorcerers is "confirmed" by elaborate spirit inquests and divinations.

5. Male spirit mediums play a key role in Gebusi sorcery accusations. The opinion of spirits during all-night séances has been especially influential for finding and interpreting "evidence" of sorcery.

6. Though spirit mediums should be neutral parties, the outcome of the sorcery inquest may benefit the spirit medium who conducts them. In Dugawe's case, Swamin's spirits directed antagonism away from Sialim as his own future wife.

7. After sorcery inquests are completed, social relations are often reestablished between the families involved—even if an accused sorcerer has been attacked or killed. After Sialim's mother was executed, her relatives made peace with the killers. Sialim herself continued to live in the Yibihilu community after both her mother's killing and her husband's suicide. Indeed, she ended up marrying her mother's killer!

8. Sickness, death, sorcery, and marriage—events that may seem spontaneous, idiosyncratic, and even bizarre—often link in a cycle of reciprocity and balance over time. In Dugawe's case, Sialim was attacked in reciprocity for his suicide. The earlier death of Swamin's wife was balanced by Swamin's killing of Mokoyl and then by the "replacing" of his deceased wife by Swamin's marriage to her daughter, Sialim.

In ethnographic writing—and in anthropology textbooks—one often finds statements to the effect that "People in society X do or believe Y." But in most if not all cases, such statements collapse and compress a tangled web of ethnographic information. As generalizations, such statements can be useful and are not "wrong." But in lived experience, they admit many exceptions and provide only a glimpse of human experience and diversity.

During fieldwork, gradually increasing awareness of the issues surrounding Dugawe's death further sharpened the questions posed above.

How typical were the events surrounding his death? How did these events reflect trajectories of change over time? Dugawe's death was in some ways both normal and exceptional, both traditional and new for Gebusi. On the one hand, the burial practices, antagonistic displays, sorcery inquests, and spiritual divinations that surrounded his death were "typical" for Gebusi during the 1970s and 1980s. On the other hand, certain features of Dugawe's case were exceptional. His was the only male suicide in almost 400 adult Gebusi deaths documented. He was also the only Gebusi known to have killed his wife or his child. Not coincidentally, he was the only Gebusi who had served a lengthy prison term. Quite possibly, Dugawe's experiences in prison and then at the Nomad jail increased his stress upon being released. As such, his unique experiences may well have contributed to his unexpected demise.

Sialim's actions were also unique; I know of no Gebusi woman before or since who managed to have her husband jailed for beating her. She was also exceptional in conducting an open sexual affair while her husband was still alive. These features—Dugawe's unusual violence and Sialim's forceful response—heightened or exaggerated features of male–female opposition in Gebusi culture. Their particular result relates as well to the legacy of Australian colonialism and the presence of Papua New Guinean constables at Nomad Station. Without these influences, Dugawe would not have been imprisoned or jailed for beating Sialim.

And yet, these new developments blended seamlessly with general patterns of Gebusi culture. This includes the marriage of Sialim to Swamin, which completed a cycle of balanced exchange both in death and in life: the death of Swamin's first wife was avenged by the killing of Sialim's mother and then structurally "balanced" by Swamin's marriage to Sialim herself. She willingly accepted and in some ways pursued this result. Did she really care for Swamin? Was she grateful to his spirits for helping to save her? Or was he simply a convenient protector? Did Sialim dispute the execution of her own mother, or did she accept it as legitimate—as Gebusi sometimes do? Perhaps all of these were true to some extent. Though it may seem odd or shocking that a woman could marry her mother's killer, it is not uncommon for people in many cultures to live with those who have harmed them or their relatives. In the US, one finds many cases of child abuse or spousal abuse in which the victim accepts and even defends the person who has abused them.

Finally, the events surrounding Dugawe's death are distinctive and even unique in time. That they reflect general patterns in Gebusi culture does not mean they reflect Gebusi culture now. As we will see in later chapters (and as amazing as this would have been to me during my first fieldwork), Gebusi have to a large extent now given up their beliefs and practices concerning sorcery accusation. Though we want to draw conclusions from our work, these can change, sometimes dramatically. Rather than downplaying or limiting this awareness, anthropologists are dedicated to understanding human diversity as it changes over time.

Events such as Dugawe's death and its aftermath challenged me to the hilt. They also yielded insights that were crucial to my understanding of death and dying, gender relations, scapegoating, and the power of human affiliation in the face of violence and suffering. Most ethnographers try to find generalities while valuing the uniqueness of the people they study. They seek to appreciate cultures while exposing their values and also their blind spots. In the mix, we try to balance our engagement with our own feelings and values. Like most ethnographers, I both succeeded and failed in all these respects. But the attempt has been well worth the effort.

Update: The principal people in this story—Swamin, Sialim, Sagawa, and Silap—are now all deceased. And with the passing of their generation, much of the Gebusi's inquisition against sorcery has also died, as we shall see. This is not due to police presence or even to the advent of Christianity, both of which have increased but then declined in recent decades. Rather, this is due to the realization and growing awareness and decisions of Gebusi themselves. Amid this change, however, larger patterns of balance and interconnection that are illustrated by Dugawe's death and its legacy remain very much alive. Gebusi continue to live with drama and emotional gusto that pulses, complements, and reciprocates over time.

So, too, making sense of unexpected dramas, piecing together events and fragments like broken potsherds, continues for me to the present. In 2013, during my most recent visit, an unexpected dispute broke out over an ax. I had given this as a general gift, but it was claimed by one senior man and his lineage. Out of nowhere, tempers flared and fighting was threatened between different factions. But then, the situation settled down, adversaries shook hands, and all went back to normal, as if nothing had happened. Awash in confusion, I still have to piece together the ongoing puzzle of Gebusi as it changes over time. Unexpected events still take careful reflection and working out, and the story eventually becomes clear—if that's possible—in retrospect. Above all, however, the richness of the attempt is still worth the effort.

Against these continuities, some aspects of Gebusi "Lives of Death" have really changed. Better nutrition, residential security, midwives, and inoculation of infants (even in the absence of a health clinic) allow many more babies to survive. Given Gebusi's population increase, one might now be tempted to assert, in contrast to before, "Lives of Life!" Sayu, our charismatic toddler of 1980, now has seven surviving children, the latest of which was born when I was with him in 2013. Suicide is still an anomaly—no cases are known to have occurred since Dugawe's. As we shall see later, divinations with a decomposing corpse and sorcery divinations more generally are now a thing of the past. Current practices of Gebusi dying and burial are neither as emotional nor as violently dangerous as they used to be. Gebusi still treat death with poignant and visceral engagement. It still fuels their cycles of marriage, reciprocity, and replacement. But does so less violently than before, with less "extremity" and seemingly more "balance."

BROADER CONNECTIONS
Life Stories, Social Life, and "Doing Ethnography"

- Like many cultural anthropologists, Bruce's fieldwork **methods** among Gebusi included **participant-observation,** structured **interviews,** informal conversations, unstructured interviews, **oral histories** (including life histories, event histories, residence histories, and dispute histories), **genealogies,** census and residential surveys, and **verbatim text transcriptions and translations** from recordings, including of Gebusi speeches, music, and spirit séances.

- Anthropological **ethics** and the **protection of human subjects** are important to cultural anthropologists. These include the principle of "do no harm" and, especially under conditions of danger or uncertainty, reduce risk and increase benefit to local people.

- Anthropologists need to be self-aware and **reflexive,** especially under conditions of danger or threat, to minimize the risk of their actions to others.

- The cultural construction of the Gebusi **life cycle** included pronounced beliefs about infant identity and becoming human, maturation and adulthood (see Chapter 6), the cultural construction of **disease** and death as caused by sorcery, and dramatic practices concerning **death** and the treatment of corpses.

- Gebusi **gender relations** include male dominance and sometimes gender violence—including by Dugawe and other members of the community against Sialim.

- Gebusi have believed in **sorcery** of two major types: *bogay*, or parcel sorcery, based on belief in imitative magic, and *ogowili*, or assault sorcery, based on magical attack by warriors against the victim.

- Gebusi sorcery inquests rely on spiritual guidance through **shamanism** (or spirit mediumship) and various kinds of divination.

- Gebusi sorcery accusations illustrate the cultural projection of **stigma** and social control through **scapegoating.**

- The **anthropology of violence** and conflict provides a complement to emphasized cultural values, such as Gebusi's emphasis on good company.

- **Ethnography** proceeds in the field by piecing together and analyzing disparate information, a process that continues for Bruce to the present.

- Gebusi patterns of **death and dying** have changed since the 1980s: fewer babies die, corpses are buried without divination, sorcery accusations have declined, violence is less, and the population has grown. However, general patterns of balance and reciprocity across death, marriage, and exchange continue to the present.

Chapter 4

Getting Along
with Kin and Killers

To follow the play, you need to know the characters. If the play is in sports, you need to know what sport it is, the teams, and the rules. For me, lives in Yibihilu were somewhere between a dramatic play and an intense sport. The sport analogy may be a stretch, because the "game" was to manage one's relationship with others in the community, not to defeat a rival team. Indeed, when men and boys played soccer (which patrol officers had introduced), Gebusi preferred the game to end in a tie rather than one team winning and the other losing. In daily life, as on the field, Gebusi were organized into groups. And to know what was going on, you had to know the groups and their rules of engagement. Suddenly a dispute would break out. One group would start swinging clubs against another, which retaliated in like fashion—while a third cluster stood between them as peacekeepers, trying to break things up. It all happened quickly; we couldn't tell why people sorted out as they did. The same was true more generally—groups of people would casually depart to forage in the forest, give and receive gifts of food at feasts, or present costume decorations to initiates. Why did some people act together as opposed to others? And why had some people been killed in the community while most others remained friends?

Kinsmen marching to funeral dispute, 1981.

In all societies, kinship and marriage are important. And if there is one topic that has been cornered by anthropology more than by any of the other social sciences, it is kinship and marriage. On the surface, kinship is simple. Each of us has a family. We know our parents, our brothers and sisters; we know what marriage is, who our cousins are, and so on. But things are less obvious when we consider other cultures—or even when we consider our own more closely.

In Gebusi society and many others, if you ask people what group they belong to, they will tell you the name of their clan. A clan is a named and permanent social group whose members pass down membership through descent from one generation to the next. Clan members should generally not marry each other, as they claim to descend from a common blood ancestor. We say "claim" because clan members often can't trace the actual genealogical linkage between them. Gebusi clan membership is passed down through the male line—like last names being passed down in most Western societies. So we call Gebusi descent groups "patriclans." Within these, some subgroups can demonstrate unbroken links of actual genea-logical connection, and these are called patri*lineages*. By contrast, most people in the US don't belong to a clan, a lineage, or, indeed, to *any* con-tinuing descent group. This is because our "families" aren't permanently named; they shift over generations. Among Gebusi, patriclan members call each other "brother," "sister," "father," "father's sister," "grandparent," and so on, depending on their sex and generation—even though to us most of them are "cousins," "uncles," "aunts," and so on.

Ties of lineage or clanship are crucial for forming alliances with—and oppositions against—other groups. When Sialim's first husband died, she was expected to marry Dugawe, the deceased man's patriclan "brother." This "marriage by levirate" kept her—and her daughter from her first marriage—within the same clan as before. We can graphically show this by using standard kinship symbols: a triangle for a man, a circle for a woman, an equal sign for marriage, a slash to indicate someone died, a vertical line for descent, a horizontal line for siblingship, and a slash across a horizontal line to indicate that kinship cannot be completely demonstrated (see Figures 4.1 and 4.2).

If we want to be more complete, we can add Dugawe's first marriage and the children of the two marriages. We can indicate persons who died

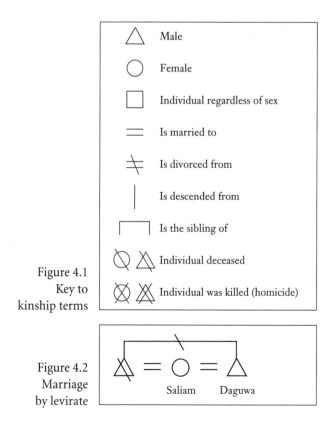

Figure 4.1
Key to
kinship terms

Figure 4.2
Marriage
by levirate

Saliam   Daguwa

from homicide with an X rather than a slash, and we can show the order of each person's marriages with numbered boxes (see Figure 4.3).

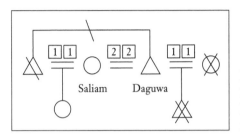

Saliam   Daguwa

Figure 4.3
Families from
leviratic
marriage

Though kinship diagrams take some getting used to, they are important to understand social relations in small-scale communities. They also alert us to things we might otherwise miss. For instance, Figure 4.3 reminds us that the marriage between Sialim and Dugawe was actually the second one for each of them. It also shows that Sialim had a surviving daughter from her first marriage, that Dugawe's first wife and son were killed, and that Sialim and Dugawe's own marriage did not produce any children.

Because Gebusi trace descent through the male line, connections of "brotherhood" and "sisterhood" pertain only as long as ancestry goes through fathers (see Figure 4.4). For us in the US, by contrast, the people we consider "cousins" are traced equally on our mother's and father's sides. But for Gebusi, a cousin on your father's side is a "brother" or a "sister," whereas a cousin on the mother's side is not a clan member and can even be marriageable.

Does this seem complicated? It certainly was for me! In college, I thought kinship and calculus were similar: I knew they were important, but I couldn't really see the point—and I wasn't very good at them. But across the globe, cultures use hundreds of ways to align relatives, assign who is "really" related to whom, establish rules and patterns of marriage, and structure alliances and oppositions between groups. And when during fieldwork your friends are dating, marrying, fighting, giving gifts to one another, and so on, you can't figure it out *except* through kinship.

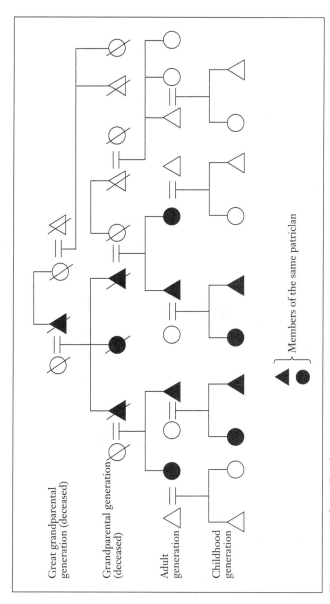

Figure 4.4   Gebusi clanship

For instance, Gebusi marriages are ideally paired between clans or lineages. If a "sister" of the husband also marries a clan "brother" of the bride, neither side gives up a woman without getting one back. This may sound strange, as if women were exchanged like pawns. But among Gebusi, sister-exchange is more interesting and surprising than this.

First, Gebusi take the ideal of marital balance loosely. Because they have complicated ways of extending "siblingship" beyond even the patriclan, they sometimes find creative ways to define a woman as a kind of sister. Second, the bride-to-be has veto power in most marriages. If a Gebusi woman really objects to marrying a certain man, her wishes usually hold sway. Alternately, a teenage girl and a young man may fall in love even though there's little chance that a "sister" of the young man could marry a "brother" of the young woman. These "unreciprocated" unions provoke strong objections from the young woman's fathers and brothers. But the young couple can prevail if the woman is strong willed or runs away with her new husband. Though the parents or brothers of the woman get upset and might beat her if they find her, many of these romantic unions endure and are ultimately accepted as marriages.

As in all human cultures, marriage between certain Gebusi relatives is completely prohibited, including between a mother and her son. But other rules about who is marriageable are wildly diverse, including how large or small the group is that is "exogamous"—that you have to marry outside of. In Western societies, marriage is not legally prohibited except within the nuclear family and sometimes between very close cousins; the whole rest of society is in principle an open field for marriage. Until recently, however, you couldn't marry someone of the same sex. And during a large span of American history, it was illegal for a white person to marry someone of African-American descent: you had to marry within your racial group.

Among Gebusi, you generally have to marry someone outside your clan (which averages 18 persons in size) plus one or two additional "brother" clans. Adding in a few other restrictions, about two-thirds of the village was potentially marriageable to the average young person in Yibihilu. In fact, most Gebusi do find their marriage partners within the village, or in a hamlet close by. As such, Gebusi communities are largely "endogamous."

Community endogamy among Gebusi combines with sister-exchange marriage, and vice versa. If a young woman likes her own brother and his new wife—not to mention the new wife's brother, her own potential spouse—then she looks forward to completing the marriage exchange. The two couples will typically live together as a joint family, and such family units tend to be strong and cooperative. Ultimately, however, Gebusi sister-exchange is "preferred" rather than required. Perhaps a bit like eHarmony pairs up couples today, Gebusi parents can "suggest" a prospective partner but seldom mandate one. In fact, just over half of Gebusi first marriages (52%) were sister-exchanges. Most of the remainder were "romantic unions" that did not follow rules of sister-exchange.

Taken as a whole, Gebusi villages bubble with kin relations traced variously through mothers, fathers, brother- and sisterhood, and intermarriage. The 52 residents of Yibihilu identified with 13 different clans. The men of the village belonged to seven clans and 11 different patrilineages, and about one-third of them were totally unrelated to each other. As such, Gebusi villages are "multiclan" rather than clustering around men of a single patriclan. This helps explain just why Gebusi place such a high value on *kogwayay*, on collective good company: their ethic of friendship knits the village together and helps it stay integrated and cooperative across diverse lines of kinship, and non-kinship!

Having summarized Gebusi social organization, we can now put it to use. In particular, we can ask what patterns emerge from kinship that combines very small lineages, preferential sister-exchange marriage, community endogamy, and residence based on diverse ties of kinship, marriage, and friendship. As we have seen, only half of first Gebusi marriages are balanced through sister-exchange. This creates a problem, because Gebusi lack effective ways to recompense a lineage or clan that loses a sister or daughter in marriage. In some parts of Melanesia, Africa, and Asia, a woman in marriage can be "paid for" by valuable gifts. These payments to the bride's kin are sometimes called "brideprice." Many anthropologists prefer the term "bridewealth," though, because the transaction is not a human purchase but the opening round of wealth exchange that may last for years between the kin of in-laws linked by the marriage.

Among Gebusi, however, bridewealth or brideprice was negligible; when there is no return marriage, there is also no payment to mollify the bride's kin for her loss to their group. So what happens? Though this causes

Antagonists at a funeral make peace by passing a tobacco pipe over the deceased's grave, 1981.

resentment, Gebusi tend to sweep it under their cultural rug. Most in-laws claim they accept marital imbalance and get along well. And in-laws coreside just as often when the marriage that links them is unreciprocated as when it is balanced through sister-exchange. Given their cultural emphasis on good company, it is not easy for Gebusi to admit or address this tension.

Here is where issues of kinship, residence, and social etiquette get particularly useful and interesting: they help explain how Gebusi have had such a high rate of violence and killing associated with sorcery accusations. Important here is that Gebusi sorcery accusations are especially likely between kin groups linked by a marriage that has not been reciprocated. Gebusi themselves don't emphasize this, and even when a community member is accused of being a sorcerer, the closest relatives of the accused typically say nothing. They may even continue joking so as not to lose public face. Instead, as shown in Chapter 3, tangible "evidence" should be used to verify or dispel the accusation, including perhaps a "sign" by the corpse, a packet of "skin and blood" identified by a spirit medium, or divination food that the suspect has undercooked. To Gebusi, these signs are physical evidence, like fingerprints on a smoking gun. Why was the sorcerer accused or attacked? Because, Gebusi say, the evidence shows him or her to be guilty! Such evidence is widely convincing to the community.

This is where social organization becomes important: beyond what Gebusi think and say, it provides evidence that I myself find to be compelling. We all know that people sometimes say one thing and do another. In

American society, marriage may be promised "till death do us part"—but almost half of all marriages in the US end in divorce. This is an important statistical fact even though it captures neither the joy of a good marriage nor the pain of a bad one.

Anthropologists have often debated which is better—a close-up portrait that is rich with people's own views, or objective views that are more detached but also more encompassing. Is a statistical depiction more scientific or more dehumanizing? My own sense is both views are needed as an effective complement and counterbalance to each other. Zooming in, anthropologists sometimes foreground the rich detail of individual lives and experiences. But at other times, they draw back—as in the present chapter—to look more dispassionately and statistically at a bigger picture.

Among Gebusi, I gained a society-wide view by collecting census material, residence histories, and kinship diagrams. By charting the genealogies of 18 clans—as far back as they could be remembered—I documented all the causes and frequencies of death, and double-checked the results with other Gebusi. It was tedious work, but Gebusi were interested in the details and usually proud to present them correctly.

So how do we know that Gebusi who are related via marriage often accuse one another of sorcery, even though Gebusi themselves don't say this? Because statistics reveal that persons related by marriage are more than three times as likely to accuse one another of sorcery than expected by chance. In father-in-law/son-in-law relations, the rate of sorcery accusation is a whopping 15 times greater than would be expected. In sorcery accusations across a marital link, over 70% of the time, the marriage was never reciprocated. In structural terms, this makes sense. Gebusi marriage is based on "person-for-person" exchange. If the woman is not replaced by another woman in marriage, she can be replaced by the taking of another life. More generally, the life of the sorcerer is taken "in exchange" for the death of the person who died of sickness. The lack of exchange for a woman in life thus increases the chance of violent revenge between two patrilineages when one of their members dies from illness.

Killings of Gebusi were remarkably frequent. Of all adult deaths, almost one-third were homicides (129 of 394, or 32.7%). This toll of violence is greater even than that of the Yanomami, the so-called fierce people of the Amazon rainforest. On a per capita basis, the rate at which Gebusi were killed exceeds the carnage of the bloodiest human war in history—World War II in Europe, including the Holocaust. Not all Gebusi killings were individual executions of sorcery suspects, but the majority were—61%. Another 21% were the result of Bedamini raids, in which large numbers of Gebusi could be killed simultaneously. Only 5.5% of violent Gebusi deaths resulted from battles or fights between massed groups of Gebusi warriors.

Gebusi adults of both sexes and almost all age categories could be killed as sorcerers. But those most likely to be accused and executed were senior men and women. By contrast, children have never been accused of sorcery; in Gebusi belief, they are not old enough to know how to perform it. Additionally, young women were almost completely immune from Gebusi sorcery accusation. This makes sense from a society-wide perspective, since young women are crucial to a society's reproductive survival. Though no less excusable in our own moral and ethical terms, the killing of men and of older women has less direct impact on reproduction. Enormous numbers of European men were killed during World War I, but the population was replenished quickly because many young women were available for childbearing. For Gebusi, relative immunity of young women from sorcery execution meant that the homicide rate, high as it was, did not prevent collective survival. Gebusi lived in good company even as they killed persons suspected of sorcery.

How have Gebusi viewed their own killings? This issue is important because sorcery execution was common within communities—the same group that was supposed to be bonded in good company! To Gebusi, however, violence is the exception that proves the rule: the community could continue in good company just *because* those who had been malicious within it had been found out and eliminated. Among the remainder, good company, was, in fact the general rule. Outside the narrow context of sorcery inquests, most Gebusi were good-natured and friendly. Even persons whose close relatives had been executed as sorcerers often lived with, and could be friends with, the families of the killers—as was the case with Sialim, who married the man who had killed her mother. Even when they wanted revenge, the men of the sorcerer's patrilineage were few in number—not numerous enough to prevail against the rest of the multi-clan community. For most Gebusi, it wasn't murder to execute sorcerers. Rather, it was a proper way to dispense with persons who were believed to have used killing to compromise community good company.

Beyond my deep concern for those who were accused—after all, to me they were completely innocent—of what significance is Gebusi sorcery and violence? For one thing, sorcery accusations reveal the role of culture in constructing or creating stigma. Cultural beliefs can powerfully validate discrimination and legitimize the scapegoating of innocent persons. This justification can be abetted by structural tensions of social organization, kinship, and demography that lie outside daily awareness. Given this, a scientific understanding of structural tensions within a society—beyond the ideas and beliefs of the people themselves—is particularly important to complement and counterbalance the positive views and rich values held within cultures.

In American society, tensions in family structure that result from class inequality, unemployment, racism, and gendered inequality clearly inform patterns of violence, drug use, alcoholism, and domestic abuse. By understanding how inequality works among peoples such as the Gebusi, we may see more clearly how larger patterns of discrimination operate in other societies, including our own. Western cultural values of equality concerning race, gender, ethnicity, nationality, and religion are strongly assumed in discourses of human rights, freedom, and democracy. Amid this positive emphasis, which is important and should not be minimized, we also need to unearth patterns of inequality and discrimination that persist in fact.

As with Gebusi, we may confuse how we would like society to function with how it operates in reality. Just as we can believe in marriage despite a significant rate of divorce, we may believe in sexual, racial, and cultural equality and yet find that women are not paid as much as men for doing similar work, or that foreigners or racial or ethnic minorities are relegated disproportionately to low levels of income and status. In the mix, it is easy to neglect patterns of kinship and social organization that are important to ethnic or foreign-born minorities because their networks of affiliation are not well understood by Americans—and may remain outside legal recognition. In various ways, then, cultural beliefs and their discrepancy with actual behavior can be as strong in our own society—and as linked to the organization of kinship and gender—as we may discover them to be in others.

Cultural anthropologists often look to other cultures and then reexamine their own beliefs and actions. Beyond the value of understanding kinship, community organization, and their relation to conflict or violence in other societies, awareness of these patterns prompts us to look more closely and critically at the challenges faced in our own society.

Update: If Gebusi show us much about cultural difference, their patterns of violence and sorcery show us at least as much, if not more, by their changes over time. Since 1989, as far as I know, not a single Gebusi has been killed, either through sorcery execution or otherwise. As we will see in Part Two, the causes for this reduction are complex, including the demise of spirit séances, divinations, and collective sorcery accusations; changes in burial customs; and an emergent and self-defined Gebusi sense of what it means to be "modern." As we shall also see, the coming of Christianity to the Gebusi has been an important part of these changes, though not exactly in the ways we might expect. The Gebusi's conversion to Christianity was at their own desire and instigation. The pastors had no idea how important Gebusi shamanism, séances, and divinations were to sorcery inquests and the killing of suspects. And for a number of years there have been no police to deter violence. As such, the continued reduction of Gebusi killing has stemmed in large part from their own decisions about how to develop and change over time. Though sorcery suspicions are not entirely a thing of the past for Gebusi, they now tend to be vestigial beliefs and grumblings that do not result in public accusation or killing. To me—given how central, deep, and richly engrained Gebusi sorcery practices used to be—this seems quite amazing.

Comparatively, this is quite striking: one of the highest rates of homicide yet documented in the ethnographic record—a rate that had long persisted—has been reduced and then continued at zero for a quarter of a century. This is not only very good news, but a striking larger commentary on the ability of human societies to reduce their level of violence. From a Western perspective as well, this should not come as a surprise: the rate of killing that was so horrifically high during World War II has dropped to world-historic lows, and stayed there for decades, in the very European countries that had been most deeply involved in this slaughter.

Two other Gebusi "updates" can also be noted. First, senior women and men live longer than before, both because they are no longer subject to sorcery attack and because their nutrition is better than it was before. In contrast to my early days among Gebusi, many older men and women now live long enough to enjoy grandchildren and to remain productive members of their family and community.

The final point concerns Gebusi social organization. Of all the dimensions of Gebusi social life that have changed over the years, their system of kinship and social structure seems the most enduring and constant. Though the structure and size of their settlements have changed, Gebusi patterns of clanship, coresidence, and kinship continue, including most parts of their marriage system. This raises a key question: if tensions in Gebusi social structure informed their previous high level of violence, how are these tensions now managed and defused? Though I have some hunches about this, I can't yet pretend to have an adequate answer. But I hope to investigate this further—during my next visit with the Gebusi!

Note: See Gebusi video clips and commentary on Gebusi kinship relations ("Social organization") in 2013 on www.bruceknauft.com → Gebusi.

BROADER CONNECTIONS
Kinship, Marriage, and Social Organization

- Gebusi social relations are hard to understand without making **kinship diagrams** in standard notation.
- Gebusi **clans**, groups of persons "putatively" related by blood descent, average 18 persons and are traced through male descent (patriclans).
- Gebusi **lineages** of those with demonstrated male descent (patrilineages) contain only a few persons each.
- Gebusi clans are named, endure through time, have collective rights and obligations, and are thus **corporate descent groups.**
- Gebusi usually marry outside their clan, which means the clan is generally **exogamous.**

- Gebusi generally marry within their longhouse and associated hamlet community, which means the community is largely **endogamous**.

- Gebusi marriage by **levirate** (leviratic marriage) occurs when a woman marries a clan brother of her deceased husband. This maintains the association of the woman with the deceased husband's clan—as it did when Sialim first married Dugawe.

- In Gebusi and many other societies, kinship terms are often extended to a larger group of people as **classificatory kinship**.

- The Gebusi desire to balance the marriage of women between lineages or clans reflects a cultural emphasis in **marriage** on **sister-exchange marriage.**

- "Tit-for-Tat" exchange, which can be termed **direct reciprocity**, is evident in Gebusi sister-exchange marriage and also in the execution of alleged sorcery suspects in reciprocity for the death by sickness of the sorcerer's supposed victim.

- Unlike many ethnic groups in New Guinea, Gebusi place little emphasis on material transactions such as **bridewealth** (or "**brideprice**") that compensate a kin group for the out-marriage of their women.

- Among Gebusi, underlying resentment in unreciprocated marriages informed violent accusations of **sorcery.**

- Gebusi sorcery accusations led to one of the highest rates of **homicide** yet recorded. More recently and just as dramatically, however, Gebusi homicide has since reduced to zero and stayed there for the past 25 years. As in Europe after World War II, this shows the degree to which human aggression and violence can be lessened through cultural self-control.

- Comprehensive understanding of a culture combines "**experience-near**" with more "**experience-far**" perspectives (per **Clifford Geertz**). These have also been described as "**emic**" versus "**etic**" views of culture, or "insider" versus "outsider" perspectives.

- Combining insider and outsider views of culture helps balance our appreciation of cultural values with an understanding of **structural inequality** between subgroups or classes of people.

- Continuity of basic features of **kinship and social organization** has been perhaps the most enduring aspect of Gebusi and many other societies over time.

Chapter 5

Spirits, Sex, and Celebration

Gebusi gender, sex, and spirituality differ greatly from Western customs; they push our envelope of understanding. Though Gebusi have embraced alternative sexuality, especially for men, this isn't to say that their practices have been a model of tolerance, much less of gender equality. But neither is it to say they have nothing to teach us. Amid tensions and challenges, exposure to Gebusi sexual culture was a rich part of my fieldwork. Although I thought I was tolerant to begin with, I came away with a greater respect for sexual diversity than I could have imagined. I also became more aware of gender discrimination than I had been before. If sex is often a delicate topic, it is also an important one, and one that needs to be studied with sensitivity.

I was first confronted with Gebusi sexual culture at events that included ritual feasts, dances, storytelling, and spirit séances. Here is an example of joking among three adult men:

> YABA [TO DOGON]:   *Go over there and sleep with the women. Build your "fire" over there.* [Go over and have sex with them.]
>
> SWAMIN [TO YABA]:   *If he goes over there and lies down, where are you* [Yaba] *going to put your "forehead"* [phallus] *to sleep?! You'll just have to go over and lay your "forehead" on* his [Dogon's] *grass skirt!!*

YABA [TO DOGON]:   *You're wearing a big grass skirt* [for me to lie on].

DOGON [TO YABA]:   [You do and] *I'll pull off your loincloth!!*

YABA [TO DOGON]:   *And you'll sleep there* [in my crotch]*!!*

[Whooping and laughter from the other men.]

DOGON [TO YABA]:   *No! I'll give your loincloth to the women and take off their clothes for you* [so you can take the female role]*!!*

[More laughter from the men.]

SWAMIN: *The younger men must be getting tired from ladling out all their "kava"* [semen]*! I'll ladle out mine with a thrust!!* [Kicks out his foot.]

[General laughter.]

DOGON [TO YABA]:   *Can you give some to me??*

YABA [TO DOGON]:   *We'll have to lay down "forehead"* [phallus] *as a gift-exchange name!*

YABA AND DOGON [LEANING THEIR HEADS TOGETHER]:   *YAY!!*

[Laughter and yelling.]

Simmering in everyday life, male joking found its greatest outlet at festivities and celebrations. Jokesters didn't have to be related to each other; in fact, it was best if they were not. Dogon and Yaba were unrelated and didn't live in the same community; not being otherwise connected, they were all the more in "good company" for being able to joke together. These connections were made easier by men who were related to both jokesters. In the present case, this role was taken by Swamin, who was a community coresident and distant in-law of Yaba and a maternal relative of—but not coresident with—Dogon. At the time, all three men were widowers in their early 30s. What about the content of their bawdy jibes? Were Yaba and Dogon really apt to have sex together or use "phallus" as their gift-exchange name? No; their joking reflected nonsexual friendship. Most Gebusi sexual joking, some of it quite physical, flirts with possibilities that aren't consummated. Thinking back, the same was true of the locker-room pranks played by members of my high school soccer team in Connecticut. In a similar way, much Gebusi horseplay is what could be called "homosocial" rather than "homosexual."

Given this, I wasn't sure at first if Gebusi males ever engaged each other sexually. A young man might shout, "Friend, your phallus was stroked, and it came up!" But beneath the surface, how much was orgasmic fire and how much was playful smoke? I suspected that male trysts took place near the outhouse at night during séances and festive dances. To find out if this was true, I sat near the appropriate longhouse exit at séances so I could see who went out and if they hooked up. But I felt uncomfortable doing so, as if I was being a voyeur. Yet, I didn't want to project male–male sex onto Gebusi if it wasn't the case, and other anthropologists would want to know if it was. My Gebusi friends seemed unable to talk about the subject in a serious way, as any sober query just became another joke. Ultimately, I did see pairs of males at ritual feasts slip out toward the outhouse, cavort with each other in the night shadows, and return visibly relaxed a few minutes later. But these pairings were not between principal joking partners. Rather, they tended to be between a teenage boy and a young initiated man.

Hawi later verified for me that the teenager manipulates the phallus of his elder counterpart and orally consumes the semen. And it turned out that insemination had an important cultural function: it supplied the uninitiated bachelor male life force for his masculine development. Unlike girls, who were believed to mature without intervention, boys were "grown" in part by the masculine life force in the form of semen. Hawi also verified that, as a rule, men who had been married for a significant time—like Swamin, Yaba, and Dogon—did not tryst with each other, however mightily they may joke about it. In effect, they relived their earlier virility through sexual banter.

Armed with this knowledge, and being married at the time, I felt comfortable accepting and participating in male jests. Then one day, I went to a séance held by Swamin at a distant bush hamlet. The singing warmed up and exceeded even its normal heated pitch. In song, a "playmate" spirit woman hovered atop the house, showed her private parts, and cried to have sex with Gebusi men. Pandemonium broke out as men screamed their sexual desire. Doliay straddled a housepost and yanked it back and forth between his legs until the whole building shook. Hawi bellowed that he had to "let go" and shot his arrow through the roof thatch "up into" the spirit woman. Egged on, the younger men and teenage boys paired up and started leaving for trysts in the darkness to "relieve their frustration."

It was then that Mora stroked my arm and leaned his head close to me, "Why don't you and I also go off together?" He rubbed his fist up and down over the index finger of his other hand, motioning that I would be the one satisfied. I shouldn't have been surprised; Gebusi men had become open with me about their sexuality. After my shock, I thought I recovered rather well. I smiled back at Mora: "I'm really sorry, but, well, I'm already married. So I can't go off with you; it would be taboo for me." But I was as unprepared for his reply as I had been for his overture: "Don't worry. Didn't anyone tell you? We break those rules all the time! Let's go!!"

I broke out in a sweat. I was not about to join Mora for a sexual encounter. But what would happen to the men's trust in me—their willingness to include me in their ritual world? Would Mora be insulted or slighted? Would my status as a welcome observer be compromised? The men were already gearing up for the elaborate rituals and secret practices of the male initiation. Would I be excluded from learning the keystone customs of private male culture? I already knew that insemination had cosmic and spiritual significance. The Gebusi word for initiation, *wa kawala*, means literally, "boy become big"—and this "bigness" was promoted by ingesting male semen.

I tried to suppress my anxiety as I answered Mora. I told him that going off with a young man for sex simply wasn't my custom, my personal *kogwayay*. I said that back where I came from, some men did have sex with young men like him, but others did not—and I was in the latter group. So, I apologized, I could not go off with him.

Anthropologists are sometimes chided for generalizing about the people they study—for instance, that "Gebusi practice sister-exchange marriage" or that "Gebusi men have sex with each other." Such generalizations cover up much variation. When Mora replied to me, he seemed to underscore this point. "That's okay," he said. "Some of us have sex with each other a lot, but others don't do it much." And with that, the séance went on as before. Relieved, I continued my role as observer and shadow participant—trying to sing, ask questions, record the proceedings, and joke, if anything, even more good-naturedly than before.

As it turned out, Mora's reply was truer than I first realized. Though Gebusi teenagers do, in principle, increase their growth by consuming men's semen, their own growing sexuality is not so easily bottled up. Sometimes, the initiates-to-be found sexual release with each other. This was especially true of Hawi and Doliay. We have encountered Hawi before—my initial helper and uncertain translator, accomplished fisherman, and energetic young bachelor. Among the soon-to-be-initiated young men, Doliay was his closest comrade. Though he was the shortest of the initiates, topping out at just four feet ten inches, Doliay was a vacuum-packed firecracker. Intense, funny, industrious, smart, and completely undaunted, he was also a little Atlas, as if his lost stature had congealed into strength.

During the months prior to the initiation, Hawi and Doliay were a hilarious pair. At séances, they would rush out together and saunter back a few minutes later, happily spent. Reclaiming their energy, they would then stand together and jive, as everyone laughed, reaching for each other's crotches while guarding against a similar riposte. Like other men, they never indulged in public nudity or open sexuality. But they swelled with bravado and boasted that, as they had each other as sexual partners, they would never get married.

According to academic views of insemination or "ritual homosexuality" in New Guinea, boys who receive semen are said to be discouraged or prohibited from themselves having sexual release prior to initiation—lest they deplete the male essence they have been accumulating. Rituals of manhood were assumed to be trials of self-discipline, with boys being sexually as well as socially subservient to older initiated men. But Gebusi defied these assumptions.

What is more, Hawi and especially Doliay were drawn to Gebusi women as well as to each other. Before the initiation, Doliay was caught having sex with Nelep. When her husband entered the house from a night-time gathering, Doliay's shadowy figure bolted from Nelep's sleeping quarters, leapt out a side door, and fled into the night. The implications were scandalous. A teenager and not yet initiated, Doliay was some 15 years younger than Nelep. Their encounter had probably been as brief as it had been illicit. But clan genealogies were dotted with cases in which an unguarded widow or middle-aged woman had become pregnant by a younger man. Nelep's husband, Wasep, beat her, but not as severely as most men would have done. Saddled with skin bruises and a scalp laceration, Nelep cried and whimpered in the public clearing. She recovered and reentered village life without further incident, apparently having paid the price for her indiscretion.

For his part, Doliay fled to another settlement until tempers cooled. Upon his return, he was not beaten—the Gebusi double standard remained in effect—but was chastised to the point that it appeared he

Woman in costume singing, 1998.   Festive man at an initiation feast, 1998.

might not be initiated. Denying initiation is a severe sanction for young men who flout the rules against having illicit sex with women. Sagawa had already been precluded from initiation because of his affair with Sialim and her husband's subsequent suicide. However, even those teenage boys who had to forego initiation were still able to become fully adult men.

Some cultures, including our own, fuel the same desires they also forbid. As such, it was ultimately not surprising that Gebusi men's fantasies of illicit sex with women sometimes became reality. Indeed, this tension was the central theme of Gebusi folktales. In these, a lone handsome bachelor was typically enticed by an equally solitary, and gorgeous, young woman. Brought together by forces beyond their control (such as the death of their parents) the couple had to live on their own and cooperate though they were unmarried and not related. The strong attraction of the couple with no one around to prohibit them from having sex provided the dramatic centerpiece of the tales. Though on the surface the couple exercised restraint—despite titillating opportunities to do otherwise—for the male audience the tales were anything but heroic or restraining. Rather, the plot served as a foil for them to joke with gusto. Listeners would make loud exclamations: "If it had been me, I couldn't have waited; I would have had sex with her again and again!" Indeed, it was the tension between the exemplary actions of the hero in the story and the contrary declarations of the male audience that made the stories so entertaining. Morality tales on the surface, they were in fact a forum for projecting illicit male fantasies.

What about Gebusi women? Wives cared little if their husbands had sex with teenage boys or with young initiated men. But they were furious if their husbands seemed attracted to other women. During spirit séances and storytellings, women listened to men's antics from their side of the sago leaf wall that separated them from the men's area. Sometimes, they responded with their own smiles and suppressed joking. As Eileen wrote, "Gebusi women regard sexuality as a positive force in the formation of marriage—as long as such relationships are based on reciprocal sexual longing."

Given the general Gebusi emphasis on sexual desire—both heterosexual and homosexual among men—did Gebusi women have their own lesbian relations? Though older and younger women are known to have had sexual relations among the Kamula, a group to the Gebusi's southeast, there is little traditional evidence of lesbianism from anywhere else in New Guinea. Has sex between women been rare in the region—or has it merely been unreported by male anthropologists, from whom it has been hidden? With tactful diplomacy and in private, Eileen asked women whom she knew and trusted if Gebusi women had sex with one another. Their responses were uniformly negative, ranging from incredulity to disgust: "No." "Certainly not." "How could one even do that?" "Is that really something that women do where you come from?"

In social reality as well as in male fantasy, Gebusi men are enticed by women's sexuality. During male séances, spirit women had to be kept happy and interested by Gebusi men's joking in order for the singing to continue and reach a successful conclusion. Fickle and capricious, a spirit woman could leave the body of the spirit medium and end the séance prematurely if she felt unappreciated and unaroused by the Gebusi male audience. In addition to cutting short the entertainment, this precluded the instrumental goal of the occasion, such as curing a sickness, identifying a sorcerer, or divining the location of lost pigs. Contrary to my initial confusion, the "functional" and the "entertainment" sides of Gebusi spirit séances were not opposed—they were directly linked.

As much as they really wanted to, Gebusi men couldn't have sex with spirit women—since they lived in the world of the spirits! The big exception here was the Gebusi spirit medium or shaman. In his dreams and at séances, his own spirit experienced the spirit world "for real." Over time, in fact, he came to have a spirit world wife, spirit children, and a whole set of spirit world friends and relatives. Among these, it was the beautiful unmarried spirit women who sang through the medium's body and joked salaciously with Gebusi men. The male spirit children of the spirit medium were also important, since it was they who would speak through his body at the end of the séance, near dawn, and provide the major verdict or conclusion to the spirits' investigation. During the night, however, the bulk of the medium's songs were sassy tales sung by spirit women. Progressively, their blurred identities became an idealized fantasy of unbridled female libido for Gebusi men.

Having traversed a full circle—from men's sex with each other back to their attraction for women—we can better understand Gebusi men's bisexuality. Gebusi dances are rife with sexual allure. The dominant features of the male dancer—his red body paint, feathers, black eye-banding, and hopping dance steps—are strongly associated with the red bird-of-paradise. And this, for Gebusi, is the preeminent form taken by young spirit *women*. In essence, the male dancer impersonates a very beautiful and seductive young woman. Male audience members voice great attraction to this male-cum-female presence. Gebusi women also accentuate the cross-gender imagery; they accompany the man's dance by sitting offstage and singing haunting songs of women's loneliness and sexual desire. As the men in the audience look at the dancer, hear the women's singing, and pine for the beautiful spirit woman, they joke about having sex with women— at the same time that they redirect their arousal as homoerotic horseplay with each another. Male sexual desire for women is thus both heightened and redirected selectively onto men and teenage boys. In parallel fashion, in spirit séances, the impersonation of the female spirit woman by the male shaman becomes the target both for men's heterosexual arousal and for redirecting this attraction onto other men, that is, homosexually.

In Gebusi worldview, the notion of "longing" (*fafadagim-da*) directly connects same-sex and cross-sex desire through the redirection of sexual frustration. For a man to cry out, "*Ay fafadagim-da!*" is to proclaim, "I'm frustrated," "I'm sexually pent up for anyone," and also "I'm aggressive and angry enough to act!" That erotic arousal conveys aggression and even anger seems politically incorrect from a Western perspective, but makes perfect sense to Gebusi. The spirit woman is alone in the forest; she wants a man but cannot be approached by real Gebusi men. So, too, the dancer at feasts and the young maiden in Gebusi narratives are beautiful but unreachable, alluring but frustrating. It makes men angry as well as playful that they can't attain this object of erotic desire. During the dance itself, the more humorous side of this aggressiveness is emphasized. But in spirit séances for sorcery, the rough edge of aroused anger, fueled by the spirit women's allure, has a more sinister side: the enraged revenge against loneliness and loss that are provoked by sickness and death in the community. This is also *fafadagim-da*. Hence, it is no contradiction for Gebusi that their spirit séances arouse both sexual desire and the possibility of homicidal revenge against sorcery suspects. Gebusi connections between sex and violence that at first seemed bizarre later made complete cultural sense.

What does the kaleidoscope of Gebusi eroticism tell us about human sexuality more generally? First, it underscores the variability of sex and gender across cultures. Gebusi men have culturally heightened their heterosexual frustration and yet bonded with each other in same-sex relations. Though Gebusi men might have been considered "bisexual" in an overall sense, their orientations ultimately wreak havoc with Western categories such as "homosexual," "heterosexual," and even "bisexual." On the one hand, men had an overall heterosexual "orientation." On the other, they could also have sexual relations with other men—though usually not also with women as well in the same frame of time. Gebusi women, for their part, easily accepted men's sexual relations with each other but bristled at the idea of men having sex with women outside of marriage. And they found the idea of same-sex relations between women to be quite unthinkable.

Man in costume for the Yibihilu
initiation, 1981.

If we consider human diversity on a global scale, we can appreciate how rich, variable, and often paradoxical sexual activity can be. Anthropologists such as Gilbert Herdt have documented the enormous diversity of human sexuality across world areas, including not just same-sex, cross-sex, and bisexual relations, but a plethora of different sexual lifestyles. Even among the few million inhabitants of indigenous Melanesia, sexual customs have ranged from prolonged male chastity and beliefs in women's depleting impact on men, to fervent love magic and serial sexual intercourse—both heterosexual and homosexual among men—to collect or ingest sexual fluids for a variety of ritual and magical purposes. In many if not most of these same societies, monogamous marriage remained the norm for most adults.

Even among individuals, Gebusi sexual culture revealed much variation. As is clearly evident in American society—and certainly among students on college campuses—sexual behavior can go against not only standards of what is considered proper, but also against a person's own beliefs about what kind of person he or she generally is. If cultural orientations are variable in the realm of gender and sexuality, individual ones can be even more so.

Cultures vary as well in their type and degree of sexual tolerance. Some societies are more accepting of sexual alternatives; others are less so. Gebusi enforced some constraints on sexuality quite vehemently, including beating women suspected of infidelity or flirtatious misconduct. Despite their emphasis on marriage and marital fidelity, Gebusi were relaxed concerning sexual relations between teenage boys and between them and young married men. In one study in the United States, by contrast, 29% of teenagers who identified as gay or lesbian had attempted suicide because of the stigma they endured. A significant proportion of homeless teenagers in my home city of Atlanta are young people who have been kicked out of their homes for pursuing alternative sexual lifestyles.

The anthropology of sexuality and gender has an important role to play in broadening our understanding of sexual alternatives, stigma, and tolerance. I feel fortunate that my Gebusi friends helped me understand the sexual side of their culture—and accepted my own orientation in the bargain.

Update: Over the years, much has changed concerning Gebusi sexuality, including—as we will see in Part Two—sex relations between Gebusi men. During their period of greatest Christianization, Gebusi patterns of male bonding, joking, and camaraderie were greatly reduced. In some ways, however, the larger tenor of men's camaraderie has more recently continued and reemerged. Gebusi men still joke sexually quite physically—and hilariously—with each other. The primary jokesters are still older, unrelated men who are unlikely in fact to have sexual relations with each other. The context and venue for this joking continues to be songs or dances that project fantasies of illicit sex, not with other men, but with young women. And the license afforded men's displays and jokes still far outstrips that allowed or encouraged for women.

However, the actual extent of male–male sexuality is far less than it used to be. In the absence of ritual mandate or institutional encouragement, one might even say that sex between men is now absent altogether—except that it is impossible to know what individuals might do in private without public sanction or knowledge. It should also be noted that per government statute, sexual relations between persons of the same sex, even when it is fully consensual, is officially illegal in Papua New Guinea.

Another major change is that the division between Gebusi men and women is far less strict and formalized or ritualistic than it used to be. For an unrelated woman and man to be talking and socializing was previously considered scandalous—the social equivalent to engaging in sex itself. Today, by contrast, Gebusi men and women interact much more easily and casually, including not only husbands and wives and boys and girls but unrelated men and women in the village. This is not to say that Gebusi gender relations are anywhere near as casual as they are in Western societies. But their change is still striking against the baseline of previous decades.

Overall, the most notable point is perhaps that Gebusi have always considered masculinity and femininity less in terms of whether one has ever had a same-sex encounter than in terms of larger sexual orientation. Gebusi men and women always tended to emphasize heterosexuality, and this is yet more true in the present. More generally, it is increasingly evident through cross-cultural study that a person's sexual *orientation*—and even an individual's self-proclaimed sense of his or her own sexual *identity*—may not be consistent with each and every instance of his or her actual sexual *behavior*. This underscores the importance of not judging or categorizing an individual in an overall sense based on his or her behavior in a given instance. Both in general and in their own view of themselves, it is hard to reduce people to individual instances of sexual acts.

Note: See Gebusi video clips and commentary on Gebusi male–male sexual and social relations ("Sexuality") in 2013 on www.bruceknauft.com → Gebusi.

BROADER CONNECTIONS
Sexuality and Gender

- As Gebusi illustrate, **sexuality** and **gender** are highly variable across cultures.

- Sexuality is an important but delicate topic of anthropological investigation that needs to be considered carefully and respectfully.

- Gebusi practices of **male–male sexuality** and of male transmission of life force as semen from one generation to the next illustrate the **cultural construction** of life cycle reproduction.

- The tendency of Gebusi men to joke energetically about activities they might not actually practice highlights the importance of distinguishing between verbal statement and actual behavior in the study of social action, including concerning **gender relations** and **sexual relations.**

- Bruce's response to Mora's sexual advances illustrates that, for their own personal reasons, cultural anthropologists may choose to stay outside some cultural practices even as they attempt to understand and appreciate them.

- Gebusi illustrate that some societies are more accepting of **alternative sexuality** than others, even within their own country. In Papua New Guinea, as in some countries of sub-Saharan Africa and elsewhere, sexual relations between persons of the same sex are presently illegal even when these relations are based on mutual consent.

- In societies such as the Gebusi and in Melanesia as a world region, practices of alternative sexuality may coexist with **heterosexual marriage.**

- Sexuality is strongly and importantly linked to other features of culture, including, among Gebusi, ritual and religious symbolism, sorcery accusation, and both camaraderie and violence within the community.

- Gender and sexuality are variable by personal preference or predilection within cultures as well as between them.

- As is true of Gebusi and of people generally, **sexual identity**—one's perceived and embraced sexual disposition—may not always be consistent with one's actual **sexual behavior.**

- Understanding sexuality and gender in other cultures, including Gebusi, can help us better understand patterns of individual and **collective diversity** in our own society.

Chapter 6

Ultimate Splendor

Gebusi celebration of life, spirituality, and sexuality came together most fully and completely in the climactic events of the male initiation— the biggest and most elaborate spectacle in Gebusi society. Typically occurring just once in the lifetime of each major settlement, the initiation cycle began with the building of the village's central longhouse. The dwelling provided enough space to house relatives, friends, and visitors from the surrounding settlements during the initiation itself. At Yibihilu, the longhouse was built by six extended families from four different clans whose young men lived in the village and were initiated there. These six young men, one from each family group, ranged from about 16 to 20 years of age: Hawi, Doliay, Yuway, Haymp, Momiay, and Hiali (the younger brother of Salip).

After the investigation of Dugawe's death was put to rest, our friends began preparing in earnest for the initiation. During the next six months, much and then almost all activity in the village focused on the upcoming celebration. For such a small and isolated forest people, the scale, effort, and energy of the preparations were amazing. In October and November, villagers spent several weeks amassing huge piles of firewood to be used for cooking immense quantities of feast food. In December, January, and part of February, families went deep into the forest to cut and process sago palms. After the women pounded and processed the pith into flour, the heavy starch was put in large net bags and hefted in human caravans back

93

to the village. In late February and early March, the men of Yibihilu dispersed into the forest to hunt game, especially wild pigs and cassowaries. At the same time, women went off to process yet more sago.

Finally, it was time for villagers to reassemble. The large pigs of the settlement—one for each of the initiates—were tracked down, lured back to the village, penned in wooden cages, and fed to fatten them further. By late March, the village was again a beehive of activity. Enormous piles of leaves and cooking stones were stacked next to the firewood. Food piles grew larger, including coconuts, greens, nuts, bamboo shoots, kava roots, and dried tobacco leaves. By the end of March, when everything was finally ready, the people of Yibihilu had worked and prepared for half a year. During this time, they had amassed enough food to feed virtually all of the more than 400 Gebusi—with plenty of extra for visitors to carry home.

If food represented the initiation's material foundation, the costumes of the initiates were its artistic centerpiece. As previously mentioned, the Gebusi term for initiation is *wa kawala*, "boy/child become big." This refers simultaneously to the growth of the initiates and to their donning of elaborate costumes at the initiation itself. The costume parts accrued from a far-flung network that spanned the entire tribe. From diverse settlements, people were mobilized to obtain materials and construct the score of elements needed for each initiate's final outfit. The full diversity of the initiates' kin contributed costume parts as gifts. Leading up to the initiation, they painstakingly crafted armbands, leg bands, waistbands, chest bands, feathered headdresses, shell necklaces, and looped earrings; carved and strung long hardwood bows; and shaved elaborate decorative arrows. Rounding out the initiates' gifts were newly made household items such as large, beautifully woven net bags and sago-carrying sacks. But none of the items were displayed, much less given, until the final celebration.

Eventually, the effort of the community, indeed, practically the entire tribe, grew toward a final climax. But how? Gebusi have no centralized leadership to orchestrate such a large undertaking. Part of the answer lies simply in tradition. Based on past experience, households knew the sequence of preparations and the time needed for each. Just as important, they knew how those in other settlements would respond to the delays and complications that invariably arose during months of preparation. Collective discussion bubbled when people returned from the forest and met in the village. Though each extended family was ultimately autonomous, they were eager to trade information, strategize plans and contingencies, and keep track of each other's progress. The people of Yibihilu had already worked together to build their big longhouse. Now they were charged to bring together the grandest features of Gebusi society and culture.

To this end, the spirits of the Gebusi world were enormously helpful. At each stage, a lively séance was held. Hurdles of preparation were addressed and positive resolutions charted. As Swamin described it, the spirits were planning to hold their own initiation at the same time that villagers would be holding theirs. Predictably, then, they were generous with advice and support.

Armed with otherworldly confidence, our friends at Yibihilu planned with excitement and worked with keen anticipation. During months of preparation, they overcame periods of poor hunting, cured persons who were sick, endured two additional deaths and associated sorcery inquests, found and retrieved their pigs that had wandered deep into the forest, and arranged for a full complement of sponsors across settlements for each of the six initiates. Their enthusiasm stoked a rising tide of good company. I had never experienced such a frenzy of friendship, laughter, and enjoyment along with plain old hard work. Everyone—women, children, men, and, of course, the initiates themselves—were swept up in the happy maelstrom. Just when we thought the level of camaraderie was about to level off, it would ratchet up to yet a higher level. The Gebusi continued to surprise us.

As we gradually realized, the festivities leading up to the initiation mirrored the basic structure of Gebusi ritual feats with which we had already become familiar. Elaborately decorated visitors would descend on the village in a show of force and aggression. They would then be appeased by gifts from the hosts—the smoking of tobacco, the drinking of water and kava, and the consumption of piles of food. Hosts and visitors would then celebrate through the night while eating, talking, and generally having a good time. Sometimes, one or more of the visiting men would dance in costume as women sang and men joked lustily. Or an entertaining spirit séance would be arranged. At dawn, when everyone was happily tired, outstanding issues of political contention or dispute would finally be addressed. With so many people from so many kin groups feeling so good, amicable resolutions were all but assured. The visitors would then return home, weary but happy, while the hosts retired for a daytime sleep. During the months prior to the initiation, this same basic pattern of hosting and feasting—and amicably discussing any issues of tension—was used to dedicate the longhouse, commemorate the ear-piercing of younger boys, and observe other celebratory milestones.

Oddly, the feast that formally inaugurated the initiation itself concerned *siay*, a thin forest vine. The associated feast was *siay sagra*—literally, to "straighten the *siay*." Hundreds of strips of this sturdy fiber would later be wrapped around the bark waistbands that the initiates wore as part of their final costumes. Traditionally, the strong waistband had been like a piece of midriff armor, protecting against enemy arrows. The presentation of *siay* to the initiates by their primary sponsors marked an official announcement of the initiation to come. It also established clearly which sponsors from which settlements would be responsible for supplying various costume parts, bows, arrows, and other gifts to each initiate.

In planning for the *siay* feast, the men and boys of Yibihilu had amassed dried meat from hunted animals—while the women and girls processed yet more sago. To only a slightly lesser extent, the sponsors also had been busy with these same tasks—the hunting of game and the processing of sago—to give to the initiate they were sponsoring. When all was ready, each initiate traveled to the settlement of his preeminent sponsor, his *tor*, and formally invited him to the *siay sagra* feast at Yibihilu the following evening. In response, the young man's *tor* presented him with a large roll of cooked sago, which the initiate carried back to Yibihilu. In economic and political terms, the *siay sagra* "sealed the deal in advance of the show." In social and emotional terms, it created a sense of good company among all the settlements that would funnel together to celebrate the initiation.

Two weeks later came the ultimate festivities. These began with what anthropologists call a transitional or "liminal" period for the initiates. In many societies, major life cycle rituals are preceded by an "in-between" period that registers ambiguity between the person's previous position and the new one he or she will occupy. For instance, rituals of status elevation are often prefaced by rites of humility, submission, or teasing—a bit like the hazing of new fraternity members before their admission to the club. For Gebusi initiates, their in-between status was signified by bold stripes of yellow ocher, painted on them from head to toe. The Gebusi word for yellow, *bebagum*, literally means "in the middle of" or "wedged in between." Along with their bright yellow striping, each initiate was festooned with a fringed headband, yellow forearm bands, yellow-painted waistband, nose plug, woven throat band, and a single white egret feather stuck in his hair. As a finishing touch, a broad white leaf was attached to the front of his waistband so it hung down almost to his knees, like a giant penis. A topic of lewd joking and teasing by the men, this phallic leaf was a very public symbol of the initiates' pent-up sexuality. Each of them was costumed identically, down to the smallest detail. As they lined up and stood with proper humility, it seemed their individual identities had fused into a beautiful and yet humble collective whole.

The initiates' biggest trial was to wear the new wigs their sponsors now came to give them. The climactic festivities would shortly follow this ritual of "tying the bark wigs." But first, its painful prologue had to be endured. Wig wearing may not sound traumatic, but the adornment was made from large wads of sodden yellow bark. Tied in bulky bundles to narrow strands of each initiate's hair, the wig pulled down mightily on the wearer's scalp. In fact, the wet bark was so heavy—I estimated 80 pounds for each initiate—that after it was tied to the initiates' hair it had to be supported with a pole held by two helpers, who strained to raise it as each of the young victims, in turn, was ordered to stand up. All the while, the surrounding men crowded around, whooping and joking with abandon. The prime sponsor of each

Yibihilu initiate, Momiay, wearing a heavy bark wig, 1981.

young man then trimmed off the wig's long streamers, reducing its weight on the scalp of the initiate to perhaps "only" 25 pounds.

Fighting back tears, the silent initiates were ordered to line up and listen to their elders. Senior sponsors of each initiate then came forward and lectured him on Gebusi values of generosity and virtue: "Always be generous with your kinsmen and in-laws, however long they live." "Don't be stingy with your food. Always give yourself the least." "When you come across your uncle's garden and see he has some nice food, never just take it." "If you ever steal, you will be rotten and no one will like you." "Whenever guests come, you must always snap their fingers firmly and warmly." "Never hide your tobacco away; always share your smoke with anyone who visits." Predictably, the greatest admonitions concerned sex: "You can never, ever chase after another man's wife." "Never flirt with your uncle's woman." "When you see a female 'bird' alone in the forest, you can't just go and 'shoot' it because you think you are 'hungry.'" "Don't you ever pry open the 'cooking tongs' [legs] of a village woman."

Although the sponsors started out seriously, their diatribes quickly lost steam; after a few minutes, their speeches labored to sustain their stern invective. When the sponsors finally got to their warnings about sex, the men and even the uninitiated boys could barely suppress their chuckles and smiles. Then, with loud cries of "SUI-SUI-SUI," the sponsors shooed the initiates outside to fetch water from the spring, ten minutes away. Amid whoops and hollers, men and boys accompanied the initiates, who carried water tubes and strained to walk while wearing their wigs.

This trip to the watering hole turned out to be the prime occasion for revealing male secrets. In some New Guinea societies, elaborate restrictions surround the transmission of sacred male knowledge. In some cases, this information is doled out piecemeal over years. Measured against such standards, the Gebusi were amazingly carefree. While approaching the spring, men spoke in only slightly lowered tones about the various foods that the new men, once initiated, would not be allowed to eat. Red pandanus could not be eaten because it formed red paste, like menstrual blood. Slimy forest greens could not be eaten because, when they were cooked, they oozed like a woman's genitalia. River lobsters couldn't be eaten because they once pinched a woman in her upper thigh, which made them turn red. On and on went the list—until I tallied 23 food items that would now be taboo to the initiates. In each case, the reason for the prohibition was the same: the food had some association, however circuitous, with women's primary sexual organs. As I later found out, initiated men were not supposed to eat these foods until fathering their first or second child. But most of the taboos were observed only loosely in practice. I was told that a hungry man might easily break his food taboos when out in the forest, especially if experience had taught him there was little harm in doing so. And though the list of dietary proscriptions seemed long, almost none of the items were frequent sources of protein.

As for additional male knowledge, there seemed to be none. At first I thought Gebusi must have had deeper male mysteries for me to discover. But I gradually came to recognize that the best-kept secret was the one I had overlooked: Gebusi men simply had few initiation secrets. Male sexual encounters with other men had not been hidden from women, and the initiates had taken no pains to hide their trysts. As for the telling of food taboos at the watering hole, the reactions of the younger boys were revealing. Though men urged the boys to stay away and to cover their ears—lest premature knowledge stunt their growth—most of them edged closer. Some even cupped their hands *behind* their ears rather than over them, to better hear the secrets. No one seemed concerned. In fact, the telling of "secrets" was mostly an occasion of male laughter and bravado. Some men proclaimed they would gladly die from breaking food taboos and by having illicit sex with women. Like their myths and séances, Gebusi male secrets were more a source of ribaldry than of sober declaration. Ultimately, the same was also true of the initiates' biggest trauma—the wearing of their bark wigs. Though the wigs were painful, the initiates quickly learned to manage them by hunching their weight onto their shoulders. By 2:00 P.M., Hawi had cut off his wig entirely. When I asked him why, he claimed it prevented him from preparing sago for the upcoming feast. By evening, only Yuway and Doliay still wore their wigs, and both of these were gone the following morning.

In some Melanesian societies, traditional rites of manhood were genuinely brutal. And they sometimes began when boys were only six or seven years of age. Ordeals might include nose bleeding, penis bleeding, tongue bleeding, cane swallowing and vomiting, body scarification, and being beaten, berated, rubbed with stinging nettles, and forced to live in seclusion, in their own excrement, without food or water. In some societies, new initiates were threatened with violent punishment, including death, if they violated taboos or revealed male secrets to women. In contrast to these extremes, the Gebusi initiation was thankfully mild. Older men said their rites of manhood had always been this way—more a celebration than a trial of suffering. The same was true of some other groups in Papua New Guinea, including the Purari, who, as it also happened, were vigilant head-hunters. Once again, cultural diversity was surprising and remarkable.

After wearing their bark wigs, our young friends enjoyed one last night of sleep—as much as they could get, amid their excitement—for several days to come. The following morning, after being repainted in yellow stripes (but without their bark wigs), they left to revisit their main sponsors. I decided to go with Hawi to Swamin's little hamlet at Sowabih-ilu. There we found ourselves crammed into a mini-longhouse with 50 other people who had come there from settlements farther afield. A similar gathering was held simultaneously at the settlement of each initiate's main sponsor, coalescing most of the tribe at staging points the night before finally coming together at Yibihilu.

After a festive midnight hike back to the main village, lit by the moon, I awoke to find smoke from a score of blazing cook fires fingering up to shred the fog and greet the morning. The whoops of those stoking the fires soon mingled with the squeals of dying pigs, which stood in their cages and were shot full of arrows by gleeful men. Singed and splayed to cook on top of the sago, the six large pigs—one for each initiate—would provide the most lavish meal since the last initiation had taken place in a neighboring community several years before. By mid-afternoon, the six initiates were finally ready to become truly "big"—to don their crowning costumes. We thronged around and escorted them out to the nearby forest, where they could be dressed. The atmosphere was too festive to be exclusive, and in addition to the young boys, some of the women who had woven parts of the initiates' costumes also came along.

Thoroughly cleansed of any lingering yellow paint, each initiate was painstakingly dressed as an electrifying red bird-of-paradise. The sponsors and helpers of each initiate took primary charge, painting with meticulous precision. Then they scrupulously dressed the initiates with the ever-so-carefully-made gifts of feathered headdresses, waistbands, shells, arm-bands, leg bands, woven chest bands, nose plugs, looped earrings, and more. The closest parallel, it seemed to me (although I had never actually witnessed it!) was the careful dressing of a traditional American bride prior to her wedding. The analogy wasn't completely far-fetched in that the initiation served, in its own way, as a kind of male wedding. Each young man would now be suddenly and imminently marriageable. All but one of the initiates would, in fact, be married within a few months. The additional gifts that the initiates received were a virtual trousseau to begin married life. In contrast to the initiation itself, the marriages that would follow—to women whose identity was not yet known—were strikingly unceremonial. As we later discovered, marriage itself was a tense affair characterized by worried courtship and adult irritation. Marriages were generally devoid of festive gift giving, costumed dancing, or public celebration. It was initiation, not marriage, that involved the cooking and distribution of the village pigs and the publicly celebrated transition to virile adulthood.

If Gebusi initiation was like a marriage without women, the initiates themselves were tantamount to brides. The bright red paint that graced them from head to toe was the ultimate feminine color. Its association with crimson menstrual blood grew deeper as the various food taboos were retold to the initiates during their decoration. In the process, a large new phallic leaf was attached to hang down between their legs. Even more than the standard dance outfit, the initiation costume was the purest expression of the beauty, allure, and sexuality of the red bird-of-paradise—a spirit woman. But before they could be formally displayed and celebrated, the initiates had to be completely costumed and publicly paraded back to the village. Given the importance of this task, the initiates' sponsors refused to hurry despite the beginnings of an afternoon drizzle. Huddled under trees and with bystanders holding palm fronds to protect them, the initiates gradually emerged in final splendor. Each painted stripe, leg band, armband, and headdress feather was perfectly aligned and exactly identical on each of the initiates. I was deeply moved to see my young friends—Yuway, Hawi, Doliay, and the rest, whom I had come to know so well—so wonderfully transformed. Their grandeur was sublime.

Against this aura, the rain fell harder. The costuming was now complete, but a grand procession back to the village had become impossible. So we retired with the initiates to their family houses on the periphery of the village, waiting for the storm to pass. Unfortunately, it did not. Instead, the rain grew stronger and stronger. We sat and sat as minutes became hours, from late afternoon into evening, and from evening into night. It was an incredible, pelting rain, and it was completely unpredicted.

Even as dawn broke, the water continued to thunder. The smooth village clearing had become a torrent of mud.

There were plenty of ironies. If the storm had held off for just another 15 minutes (or if the sponsors had been a touch quicker with their decorations), the triumphal procession could have quickly taken place. We would all then have been happily together under the sheltering roof of the main longhouse. The visitors would have descended with great whoops to "confront" the initiates and have had their "anger" dispelled by the silent beauty of their immovable presence. Food would then have been served and eaten, and dances by the visiting men would have continued until morning. In short, everything would have gone according to plan. Now, however, the initiates, their sponsors, and the rest of us had stayed sitting up all night waiting for the rain to stop. Things were worse for the throngs of visitors. Festooned for their own grand entrances, they had retreated to the forest and huddled in makeshift lean-tos in a futile attempt to keep dry. Neither they nor we had had anything to eat. Everyone was very tired, wet, and hungry.

Why couldn't the initiates simply be led under cover to the longhouse, so visitors could enter and the food be served? The answer was consistent: "Because the initiates' red paint would run down their bodies." Beyond the importance of the triumphal procession, it was unthinkable to Gebusi that the beautiful red of the initiates, the congealed symbol of femininity that framed their masculinity, could be allowed to dissolve and drip down their skin. The specter of red liquid oozing down their carefully appointed bodies seemed tantamount to male menstruation—the destruction of masculinity rather than its crowning achievement. So we waited and waited for the rain to end.

To my amazement, almost no one got visibly upset. The main exception was Silap, who cursed angrily and chastised whatever ghost was raining so literally on his parade. Everyone else eased into a kind of meditative doze, neither anxious nor despondent, but serene and trusting that all would work out. Despite the months of preparation and the sheer scale of the event—its social, spiritual, and material significance—the response to the storm was vintage Gebusi: quiet acceptance in the face of reality that couldn't be changed. When the rain finally broke, by midmorning, my compatriots managed a few whoops of relief and anticipation. Cooking fires were now restoked and foods reheated. I checked our rain gauge. It was filled to 93 millimeters—just shy of four inches. This ended up being the fourth-biggest single rainfall during our entire two-year stay—and the biggest within a month on either side of the initiation. Villagers shrugged it off as part of their unpredictable weather: "That's just the way it is."

The six initiates were finally lined up in front of the central longhouse. Shoulder to shoulder, they were individually brilliant but yet more stunning as a collective whole. Uniting the aesthetic and the physical, they literally embodied the full power of Gebusi society—its material culture, its networks of kinship and friendship across space, its symbolism and beauty, and its deep identification with spirituality and sexuality. Together, the initiates crystallized the sublime growth, gift giving, and forbearance of Gebusi as a whole.

Into this electrifying vista, visiting men now rushed with abandon—a human stampede of celebratory aggression. Painted warriors bellowed and screamed. They sprinted through the mud and plucked their bows, spiraling in tightening circles around the initiates in happy displays of mock antagonism, wave after wave, group after group. One man was carried in naked—covered head to foot in mud. His tongue hung out, and a huge fake phallus was tied to his waist. At least for the moment, he was a bloated corpse covered in cadaveric fluid—and indicting everyone around him as a sorcerer. As might have been guessed, even this gruesome display did not unsettle the initiates, who stood their ground with serenity even as children scattered from the "corpse" with ambivalent screams. Excited adults just smiled.

Yibihilu initiates lined up in full costume, 1981.

Eventually the attacks subsided and the feasting and celebration began in earnest. Festivities started with seemingly endless rounds of finger snapping, smoke sharing, kava drinking, and, especially, food giving. With thunderous whoops and hollers, the identity of an initiate's sponsor or other recipient was shouted. Representatives from each of the six initiates' families then rushed to press a mound of food upon the besieged but pleased recipient. Special pleasure was taken in "force feeding" key visitors with great globs of dripping pig fat—pushing it to their faces until they had taken at least one or two gooey bites.

By midafternoon, it was the visitors' turn to reciprocate gifts to the initiates—especially prized hardwood bows and sheaves of elaborate arrows. Many of the male sponsors dramatically plucked the bow they had carved before handing it to their initiate, showing him how strong it was. Previously allowed to use only unpainted arrows for hunting, the initiates could now use painted and people-killing arrows in ritual display and, if needed, in warfare. Exhausted as they were, however, the initiates could hardly do more than stand. Even that became difficult, and by evening, they resorted to propping themselves up while sitting lest they topple over in sleep and smear their costumes. As part of their proud ordeal, they had not talked, eaten, or slept for two days.

Seemingly oblivious to their plight, everyone else was now revved up for a full night of partying—eating, smoking, and drinking numerous bowls of kava root intoxicant. Jokes flew as thick and fast as the rain of the previous night. By now, the whole longhouse was packed wall to wall, with just a small space in the middle for the dancers. The yellow light of bamboo torches cast a golden glow across the faces and costumes. The outfits of the male visitors were as spectacular and creative as they were plentiful—bird-of-paradise and cassowary headdresses, face and body painting in innumerable patterns and combinations, bone and bamboo nose plugs and beads, leaf wreaths, and woven chest bands and armbands. Women were also festooned: almost all of them had fresh grass skirts, bead or seed necklaces, and woven chest bands and armbands. Many also wore headdresses of fringed fiber strips and long egret feathers.

Beyond the usual male dancing, a special dance involved several young women wearing their own red body paint, black eye banding, and red bird-of-paradise headdresses. During the plaintive songs of the women's chorus, the female dancers lilted up and down as they faced their male counterparts. Each held a long, thin rattle that she thrust up and down in front while pulsing to his pounding drum. The sexual charge of these pairings was impossible to miss. The men in the audience went wild, while the women joked and laughed from their own sitting places. A few women could be seen joking and flirting directly with men. It was as if, for a single night, the erotic mirth of the spirit woman had become acceptable for real Gebusi women as well as for men. The night was swept up in festive abandon. We will always remember its intensity.

The morning after was just that. As the visitors left, those from the host village crashed and slept, and so did we. While Gebusi had been busy partying, we had undergone our own initiation. Pumped by adrenalin and coffee, we had primed ourselves to observe and record what we had waited months to see—and what we knew we might not see again. Unlike the Gebusi, we didn't know what was going to happen next or when or how it would unfold. We worried that we would miss important events. I remembered the story of a well-known anthropologist who, working alone, fell asleep from fatigue at the height of a male initiation rite, and missed a key sequence of color-coded costumes that he could never reconstruct. But in our case, we were cajoled good-naturedly by the Gebusi not only to be present but to participate as fellow residents of Yibihilu. This included our happily accepted offer to give rice and tinned fish as food, to help host visitors, and to serve as secondary sponsors for the initiates. When men gave the initiates bows and arrows, I gave them each several prized shotgun cartridges—"Western arrows"—for the hunting shotgun we had given to Yibihilu and which they cherished for providing them extra meat. We also gave each initiate a pair of bright blue satin gym trunks that we had bought during a field break. These gifts were wildly popular and widely talked about, as it was (and remains) difficult for the Gebusi to obtain such items in the rainforest. In return, the families of the initiates gave us pork and sago. To each of the initiates, we became *tor*, sponsor.

That morning, however, all we could think of was sleep. But just when we thought the initiation was over, an additional climax erupted. In early afternoon, we were awakened by loud noises and stumbled out of bed to see what they were. The initiates were herded out of the village, their costumes

Women lined with male initiates at the concluding ceremony, 1981.

retouched, and then paraded back in. This time, though, they were joined by two unmarried young women who stood alongside them in costumes that were, in body paint and feathers, virtually identical to their own. Together, the six young men and two young women linked fingers and stood in a single line. They bobbed up and down in unison as Tosi, the senior woman of the community, came forth to address them. Going down their line, she gently hit each of them with a sheaf of special leaves and chanted that they would henceforth be strong in heart, in breath, and in spirit. She said to each that he or she would have the inner energy of a buzzing hornet. Then she told them to be kind to and protective of others in the village. Finally, she declared for each the name of a young child to whom they were unrelated but whom they were charged to help and protect. With that, she turned and walked away. The initiation was over.

Thinking we had seen everything the night before, we wrestled anew to make sense of this wonderful ending. Although women had been off-stage for many of the initiation's formal events, a senior woman had now conducted its final ceremony. Young women had dressed up and danced the previous night, but now two women dressed up like the initiates and were linked with them physically. The beautiful red bird-of-paradise had finally enveloped real Gebusi women. If this had been implicit in the previous night's dancing and joking, it was now formally proclaimed. What had seemed like—and in many ways was—a rite of male initiation was now a ritual celebration of male *and* female adulthood. The boundless imagery of spirit women, so dominantly appropriated by men, was finally accorded and publicly acclaimed for Gebusi women as well. It was almost as if, in its final moment of ritual celebration, Gebusi culture transcended its own deepest gender division.

This theme grew stronger that same night. Though the initiation was over, the young men and women were now adults—and free to dance on their own. Still dressed in their red initiation costumes, the male initiates added the feathered halo of the standard dance costume and danced for the first time with drums. Moreover, they danced in pairs with the young women who had stood alongside them at the initiation's benediction. Like their linkage earlier in the day, their ritual union encompassed the male–female beauty of Gebusi as a whole.

Given these final events, we wondered how much we should rethink our understanding of the initiation. Was it a *male* initiation—or not? As before, the intricacies of Gebusi made our simple questions deliciously difficult. On the one hand, young Gebusi women were painted similarly to the young men, lined up with them, danced with them, and were charged along with them during the final ceremony to protect a young child. Their maturity and sexuality were on obvious display alongside the young men. In social terms, their costume elements, though not quite as elaborate or copious as the young men's, linked them to kin networks that had given or loaned them these items.

On the other hand, unlike their male counterparts, the young women were not inseminated or otherwise sexually initiated. They were not subject to painful trials testing their stamina, and they did not receive bows and arrows or major stocks of ritual or domestic items. They did not have pigs killed for them, did not have important gifts of food given in their name, and were not enjoined to observe special food taboos. They did not establish lifelong relations of initiation-mate and initiate-sponsor with others in the community. Unlike the young men, whether a given young woman would get dressed up in a red bird-of-paradise costume was decided only at the last minute by the young women themselves. In contrast, the costumes, build-up rituals, and gift giving for the young men had been planned months ahead of time and were central aspects of the celebration.

In a way, the inclusion of women as important but secondary actors paralleled other aspects of Gebusi life. And yet, their inclusion in the final ceremony not just symbolized but embodied their central symbolic importance along with the men. If the initiation symbolized the height of Gebusi male culture, it also extolled women and the Gebusi as a whole.

Spirituality, sexuality, materiality, kinship, friendship, and gender: they all came together with joy and happiness. Against all odds and impediments, against all sicknesses, deaths, and frustrations, the Gebusi somehow came together to celebrate their collective good company. It was a unity I had never seen or felt.

During our waning time of fieldwork with Gebusi after the festivities ended, I began to reflect more deeply on the strength of their culture. For all of the differences and extremes of their ways of life, I learned positive human values and forms of happiness that were quite unprecedented and uplifting for me. As much as I wanted and needed to return to the US, it was hard to contemplate leaving my Gebusi friends and their culture. I knew that adapting again to the scheduled and atomized features of American life would be difficult and that I would deeply miss the friends and the life I was leaving behind.

If the avenues of modern life splinter us into separate domains—work versus play, public versus private, religious versus secular, and so on—here was a so-called simple society that managed to unite them all in full celebration. To me, it was a testament to human spirit that Gebusi could create so much that was positive, beautiful, fun, and meaningful amid lives that were so difficult and tenuous. This is the way I like to remember them from that period: triumphantly asserting the richness and joy of their humanity.

Update: What has happened to Gebusi initiations—will they ever come back? In the community that has descended from Yibihilu, the last full initiation took place in 2003. To this day, when asked, people say with a glint and a gleam, "Maybe, maybe . . ." "Who knows?" "We'll just have to see!" For me, the fact that initiations resurfaced at all following the 1990s was a surprise. Among other things, the residential structure of Gebusi settlements has changed, the need for young men to become "warriors" has become a thing of the past, and, as mentioned, the symbolic division between men and women, though still present, is not as charged as it previously was. But the ideals of collective celebration are still alive and well among Gebusi. They still enjoy and gravitate to large, festive, and, sometimes, richly costumed gatherings. Whether these will again congeal around the centralizing theme of red bird-of-paradise men and women coming to virile adulthood—uniting Gebusi and all their culture as one—remains to be seen.

In 2013, I found at least one hint of possibility. The large community of Yehebi, which neighbors the descendents of Yibihilu, still features an enormously large longhouse. In the rafters of the house I found fresh jawbone trophies of wild pigs killed with traditional bow and arrow. Near them, hanging on a wood railing, was a large new rack of crayfish claw rattles—used in traditional dancing. Customary festivities appear to be alive and well at Yehebi. Knowledge of initiations is not entirely gone. Perhaps they will be rekindled in the future—or reinvented in a new guise.

BROADER CONNECTIONS
Ritual Initiation and Life-Cycle Transitions

- Gebusi initiation is a rite of adulthood, a rite of status elevation, and a so-called **life-crisis ritual** by which young men, and to some extent young women, become full adult members of society.

- In most societies, major celebrations express and integrate core cultural values. Rich with religious symbolism and cultural expression, Gebusi initiation brings together sexual, social, economic, and political dimensions of their society and asserts and affirms their **cultural value** of "good company" (*kog-wa-yay*).

- Consistent with the transition stages of **rites of passage**, Gebusi initiation involves (1) preparatory rites and ceremonies that result in **separation** of initiates as a group; (2) a **liminal** or "in-between" period of category transition for initiates, and (3) climactic rites of social celebration and **reintegration.**

- **Ritual initiation** into adulthood can be severe or brutal in some societies, but among Gebusi it is mild-to-moderate, including the temporary wearing of heavy bark wigs by male initiates.

- The red bird-of-paradise emerges as a core symbol or key symbol in Gebusi ceremonial life. As a **polysemic symbol**—a symbol with many meanings—the red bird-of-paradise is literally embodied on the men, and, ultimately, on women.

- Gebusi initiation is consistent with the classic perspective of social scientist **Émile Durkheim**, who suggested that **religion reflects society**—it projects the social features of society into a spiritual realm. Among Gebusi, the spirits are believed to have their own dances, and their own initiation, at the same time that the Gebusi do. The symbolism of the spirit world, and especially of the red bird-of-paradise spirit woman, is embodied by the initiates in their costuming.

- As well as being observers, Bruce and his wife were participants in the initiation through gift giving to visitors, and they also became a kind of sponsor (*tor*) to the initiates.

- The final rite of the initiation revealed that the Gebusi celebration of fertility and adulthood encompassed women as well as men. In this sense the initiation was a collective **fertility rite.** Though women's gift giving and rites were not as elaborate as men's, the initiation symbolized and socially enacted the unity and growth of Gebusi as a whole.

- Gebusi continue to greatly enjoy festive celebrations. Whether they will continue to organize and enact initiations remains to be seen.

Young people in Gasumi Corners, 1998. →

Part Two

1998

Chapter 7

Time for Change
Yuway's Sacred Decision

> I feel like a neophyte all over again. Though at best not humiliating, fieldwork is always a humbling experience, and in a good sort of way. Arrows barbed at anthropology cast its knowledge as imperialist, gained at the expense rather than for the benefit of other people. But the gawky interloper is usually cut well down to size by the time he or she gets beyond the confines of the hotels, the taxis, and the urban elite to the place in question. Human leveling is ethnography's strength.
>
> — Fieldnotes, June 1998

Leave in 1982, come back in 1998—experience culture as a time machine to the future. Sixteen years is a long time for the Gebusi. So, too, for me, and also for cultural anthropology. While a whole generation of Gebusi was getting older and producing children, I went from young adulthood to middle age in Atlanta. My son went from conception to high school. The world also changed. Market economies, modern ideas, and nationalist development spread to the farthest nooks of the globe. Cultural anthropology changed as well. If my first fieldwork reflected anthropology's long-standing interest in distant societies, Gebusi now engaged my newer interest in change and transformation. Ethnography is as real and important as the lives it encounters, regardless of their context. For Gebusi, traditional interests in kinship, social organization, ritual, and exchange now broadened to include a full range of contemporary practices and institutions—markets, churches, schools, governments, nongovernmental organizations, and the mosaic of social and cultural influences that tie people to their nation, their region, and the larger world. To study such developments, cultural anthropology engages increasingly the full ambit of human cultures—from the most remote to the most urban, cosmopolitan, and digital.

External changes had already come to the Gebusi by 1980: steel tools; trade goods such as cloth, salt, soap, and matches; pacification of the neighboring Bedamini; yearly government patrols; and potential presence by Nomad police. Subtler changes also sprouted. By 1980, most Gebusi cut their hair short rather than tying it in dreadlocks. Some men had even sported carefully trimmed sideburns, reminiscent of Australian patrol officers. Yet, there remained a dearth of extensive intrusions such as missionization, wage labor, cash cropping, out-migration, mining, logging, or road connections to other parts of the country.

For millennia, armed traders, state empires, and other wielders of power have crisscrossed the world; commerce has been global for five centuries. From the 19th to the 20th centuries, New Guinea's east half was colonized and owned variously by Germans, British, and Australians—until Papua New Guinea became an independent country in 1975. Though outside influences seemed minor among Gebusi in 1980, I anticipated that these had intensified. And new intrusions often bring troubling new inequities, including unequal possession of money and goods, and domination by outsiders.

As almost no information had reached me from or about Gebusi, I remained in the dark. Some of my colleagues thought that modernization—Christianization, education, migration, and economic development—would have wrought major changes. Others suggested a continuity of cultural values and social practices would keep things largely the same. Even concerning violence, different possible outcomes competed. Had the gradual decline in homicide continued? Or had the continuing absence of Australian officers encouraged more violence, as had happened in other parts of Papua New Guinea?

Added to uncertainties about Gebusi were those about myself. Before I had been a green mid-20s researcher, anthropologist on a shoestring, with little to lose and everything to prove. Youthful ignorance gave me unbridled faith in cultural understanding—crucial against the difficulties if not the impossibility of the task ahead!

A decade and half later, the realism of hindsight made me more anxious. I was going back to people I knew and liked, but I also knew how tough it was to live in the rainforest—and that my body was not as young as it had been before. Now a professor and author of several books, I was an established academic. Against this, I knew new fieldwork would be humbling. Would my sense of being a successful anthropologist crumble like a house of cards? I was concerned as well about leaving my family, and how they would fare if something happened to me. Finally, I had intellectual uncertainties. A middle-aged outlook can lack the openness of a younger mind. How would I square anticipated changes among Gebusi with my appreciation of their traditional culture? Anthropology crackles with debates between those who focus on global change and those who stress cultural continuity. Are societies more strongly influenced by long-standing values or by new transformations?

Amid my doubts, I really wanted to see what had happened to my Gebusi friends, and ultimately this desire trumped my other concerns. So I committed myself to return: I was going back after 16 years, just by myself. I told myself to take whatever I found at face value—to wipe my slate clean of expectations. After months of securing funds, navigating bureaucracy, obtaining visas, buying supplies, reviewing old fieldnotes, and shedding tears of good-bye, I left for Papua New Guinea. After negotiating the national capital of Port Moresby and the provincial town of Kiunga, I finally chartered a single-engine Cessna to Nomad—and landed for a half-year of fieldwork with Gebusi on June 25, 1998. That night, I wrote the following:

> Tonight, this first evening back, I sit here with Sayu and Hawi, who smile brightly as I type on this keyboard. We have just looked at the screen saver, which has amazed them totally. I am caught in a time warp between the pidgin English called *Tok Pisin*, Gebusi language, heat, fatigue, and my wonder and amazement.

First touchdown was a rush. Hawi was the airline agent who met me at the airstrip! He had a gaunt face and a much receding hairline but was still strong and energetic. We hugged, shook hands, and snapped fingers about a dozen times. He told me he lives right at the Nomad Station—and that he has three sons and a baby daughter! Then he had to attend to the paperwork of the flight. I turned around and had the wonder of seeing age jump right before my eyes. One after another Gebusi whom I had known came up to greet me. The grown children were the most incredible. There was Sayu, our little friend about whom we joked that we would adopt and bring back to the States. He is strong, handsome, and smart! He has already become my closest companion and helper among the younger men. He combines his father's quickness and his mother's intelligence, perceptiveness, and friendship—or at least so it seems on my first impression.

Most striking among my adult friends are their hollow faces, withered bodies, and wrinkled skin that I remember as smooth. But happiness in human connection transcends space and time. We embraced and snapped fingers mightily, including the women. Gazing into the eyes of those whom you know with fond memories from 16 years ago, and who suddenly live again in the present, is totally thrilling and completely unforgettable. In Gebusi legends, reunions and welcomes are so warm and numerous that people's hands are worn bare by snapping fingers heartily and repeatedly. Today, I allowed myself the hubris of feeling the same way. My middle fingers are really sore from the finger snapping that I could not keep myself from continuing even if I had wanted to stop. It is like on my wedding day, when the joy of the event caused an actual soreness of smile muscles that were so irrepressibly stretched as to not help but turn anything in the world to their overpowering good feeling.

Feelings notwithstanding, the day has been hot, and I have a mountain of decisions to make quickly. How many nights will I stay in this unpleasant little house at the Nomad Station? Where will I live after that? How can I build on today's rush of positive feeling? How should I reestablish reciprocity with my Gebusi friends? How will I cook? How many boxes should I unpack? Where are the specific parcels of utensils, sleeping equipment, cloths, toiletries, and so on that I need for this first night? (As expected, there are no real stores at Nomad, so I am glad that I have brought everything with me.) And yet, I simply must take time tonight to write the events of this astonishing day.

1. The author in a welcoming line of Gebusi men snapping fingers, 1980.

2. Girl holding a baby, 1998.

3. Yuway as a young man in festive dress, 1980.

4. Young boy with flowered headband at an initiation feast, 1998.

5. Young woman, Toym, dressed for a Gebusi feast, 1981.

6. Costumed man at Independence Day display, 1998.

7. Traditional dancer at a curing ritual, 2008.

8. Enraptured woman in church, 1998.

9. Schoolgirl in class at Nomad, 1998.

10. Sayu as a bachelor, 1998.

11. Didiga as a bachelor, 1998.

12. Mosomiay [l] and Keda [r] at the Gasumi Corners store, 1998.

13. Yamdaw (Luke) preaching at the Gasumi Catholic Church, 2008.

14. Halowa taking wrapped sago bundles for feast cooking, 2013.

15. Delaw with children, 2013.

16. Mus, now about 60 years old, carrying heavy net bags, 2013.

17. Gasumi villages carrying Bruce's and Latham's trunk boxes from the Honinabi airstrip, 2013.

18. Rainforest morning at Gasumi Corners, 2013.

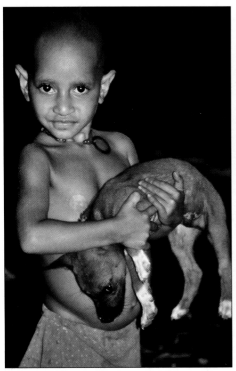

19. Young girl with her dog, 2008.

20. Boy greeting us at the Yehebi longhouse, 2013.

Amid the constant stream of visitors whom I did not want to stop,
I somehow greeted everyone and found that virtually the entire generation of surviving Gebusi from Yibihilu now live in a "corner" of
Nomad just 20 or 25 minutes' walk from the Nomad Station. This is
absolutely perfect, my ideal residential scenario! I should have easy
access to the Nomad Station and its nationalizing influence while
also being able to go with Gebusi back to the forest. Having stowed
my things in the government house by 1:00 P.M., I couldn't resist the
temptation to walk with my friends to their corner settlement and
see for myself the lovely place where I will likely be living. It is all
simply wonderful.

Within minutes, the Gebusi had again astounded me. And the descendants of Yibihilu now boasted a new flock of youngsters as well as children-
become-adults. Within a few days, however, I found that few men of my
own age or older were still alive. Most of those whom I had known as adults
had died, including Silap, Boyl, Swamin, Sialim, Sagawa, Tosi, Wasep, and
Imba. Of the six young men we helped initiate, only three—Hawi, Doliay,
and Yuway—were still living. I mourned the passing of friends even as I
saw their personalities, amazingly, in their children, now pushing toward
their own adulthood. In demographic terms, Gebusi were a new people
and more numerous than before—up from 450 persons to about 615.

Change and turnover notwithstanding, and despite the heat and mosquitoes, it felt wonderful to be back. I was remembered fondly and welcomed joyously. Two children had been named after me in my absence.
Once worn, the glove of friendship always seems to fit. Within a day of my
arrival, Gwabi, who had been 12 years old but now had his own family,
insisted that I live in the big thatched house he had just finishing building
beside his older home in Gasumi Corners. With this as my base of opera-
tions, I became quickly immersed in village life, going both to Nomad and
to the forest, and rediscovering the joys and trials of fieldwork. I had worried about my ability to speak Gebusi after many years, but this came back
to me faster than expected.

In short order, I found that the 122 descendants of Yibihilu and its
surrounding hamlets had fashioned not just a new settlement but a new

way of life. Now living on the outskirts of Nomad Station, they were just a short walk from its airstrip, school, churches, market, ball field, and government offices. No longer nestled in the full rainforest, their settlement was sandwiched between cleared areas that fan out from Nomad Station and the primary timberland that Gebusi previously inhabited. From Gasumi Corners, my friends could still walk to lands deep in the forest, but their lives revolved increasingly around the activities and organizations of Nomad Station. These produced what might be called a new structure of feeling in Gebusi culture. Against this new world, the social life of the rainforest, including our previous settlement at Yibihilu, was gone.

Internally, the new community still retained its kinship connections, including via marriage and maternal ties as well as through clanship. But extended families and even nuclear families now lived separately in small individual houses scattered like islands in an archipelago across three hillocks and a stream. Strikingly, there was no longhouse—no central dwelling place where people gathered. More broadly, the traditional sense of good company—the togetherness, talk, and whooping/joking of Gebusi *kogwayay*—was greatly muted.

Materially, life was much as it had been before. Families had a few additional commodities—perhaps an extra knife, a larger metal pot, or a shovel. But the biggest visible change was their clothing. Before, women were unashamed to walk around bare-breasted; now, they always covered themselves, if only with a ripped blouse. Men invariably wore a shirt and shorts when they went to Nomad. Used clothes were intermittently flown in and sold at low prices at the station, and everyone wore them.

Along with new interests and activities, Gasumi Corners also had a new sense of time. In the relaxed world of the rainforest, rhythms of life had been languid; people could simply not be hurried. There had been little attempt to mark times of day, and there were no words for days of the week, months, or even seasons. We had easily lost track of days if we forgot to check mark them on our calendar. The Gebusi word for "tomorrow," *oil*, was the same as the word for "yesterday." The word for "the day after tomorrow," *bihar*, was the same as the one for "the day before yesterday," and "three days after today," *ehwar*, was the same as "three days before today." Gebusi had used the same word for both their grandparents and their grandchildren (*owa*), and an adult man often called his own son "father" (*mam*). In the cycling of gardens and fallow land, a boy would ideally grow up to cultivate the lands and the trees of his father or grandfather. In short, time and life rolled in a circle. Even male life force was physically recycled from one generation to the next. Things had been ordained to repeat themselves rather than to change.

Now, however, days and even minutes were marked and measured. Everyone seemed to work by deadline to accomplish something that was different from, and hopefully better than, the past. The first Sunday of my stay, I got a taste of this. Sayu had said that church would begin when the sun rose above the trees. Such timing had always been as vague as the morning mist, and events invariably began late. I left early and thought I'd arrive before most others. But along the way, houses were curiously empty. When I got close and heard hymn singing, I realized I was late. Late! The idea had been foreign to Gebusi. But the clock-watching pastor had rung the metal chime, and I had missed the signal in the distance, while everyone else was on time.

Beyond Sunday church services, the new weekly schedule included classes for children at the Nomad School on weekdays, beginning promptly at 8:00 A.M. and lasting until 3:30 P.M. Mindful of time, children from Gasumi Corners left for school by 7:00 A.M.—and got home after 4:00 in the afternoon. Classes were divided into 16 timed periods, some as short as 15 minutes, with transitions marked by the ringing of the school bell.

For adults and especially women, Tuesdays and Fridays from 8:00–10:00 A.M. were market days. Weekend afternoons were carefully scheduled for rugby and soccer matches on the government ball field, particularly for men and boys, who arrived early so as not to miss their starting time. Games were refereed by timekeepers, who sounded a large horn to mark the end of the half and the end of the game. And though most Gebusi could not tell time, all the men seemed to want wristwatches—so they could appear to be acting based on knowledge of the hour.

If time for the Gebusi was increasingly marked and measured, its passage now reflected Gebusi hopes for—and failures of—progress and improvement. For schoolchildren, tests on Friday gauged what they had learned and accomplished that week. Unfortunately, few Gebusi children could finish elementary school, and none were slated for high school in Kiunga. At Nomad market, if food wasn't sold by noon, it had to be taken home or given away. In sports, Gebusi now kept score and played aggressively to win by the final horn. In short, the strivings and shortcomings of new activities were measured against a timeline of hoped-for success. Perhaps nowhere was this more evident, surprisingly, than in spirituality and religion.

Yuway's eyes simply sparkled. "*Koya, koya!*"—"Friend, friend!" We must have gazed at each other, snapped fingers, and joked heartily a dozen times. I had come to his house, just five-minute's walk from my own. Yuway had been my most helpful friend in 1980–82, an all-around good person, and the tallest of the young men we had helped initiate. Shortly afterward, he had become a moon-eyed romantic with his fetching wife-to-be, Warbwi, and we had given him gifts for his marriage. That had been 17 years ago. Here he was again, in the flesh! It was so good to see him. Every few sentences, we smiled and clasped each other again, reassuring ourselves that our reunion was real. We quickly brought each other up to date. He was touched to hear that I now had a son who was full-grown and even taller than I. With subdued pride, he told me that he and Warbwi now had four children: an adolescent boy and girl plus two younger sons. I joked with him that he had been "busier" than I; we both broke into laughter.

As the minutes passed, word spread that we two senior men were having a good jokefest, and this attracted a score of spectators from surrounding houses. Good-natured as he was, I realized that Yuway was getting increasingly embarrassed by our traditional joking. Though I had taken our jests for granted, he started to suppress his grins. From the reactions of others, I sensed that old-time joking, though tolerated from me as a middle-aged man who knew the tradition, was both a spectacle and anachronistic, a bit out of place.

As if to punctuate this perception, Yuway finally told me with a smile that he was an SDA—a member of the Seventh Day Adventist Church. This was Nomad's most stringent Christian denomination. I was naturally intrigued, which led us to a thoughtful discussion of changes in Gebusi religion. Yuway said that when he had arrived in Gasumi Corners from Yibihilu, some ten years before, he had, like most, joined the Catholic Church. The pastor had been solicitous of Gebusi and had even visited their settlements in the bush. When they moved their settlement, villagers relocated it close to the Catholic Church, thinking this would be a strong focus for establishing their new lives. As they got used to singing in church, Yuway said, they sang less with their own spirit mediums. Swamin, their village shaman, started going to church himself and then stopped singing traditional séances altogether. So, too, the other spirit mediums found themselves part of a community that was now singing to a new spirit, to a new God, and stopped their traditional spirit singing. When the Gebusi go to church, they literally, "go to sing" (*gio dula*). Within a few years, the spirit séances that had galvanized Gebusi social life had become history, a thing of the past.

Without spirit mediums, as Yuway explained, people in Gasumi Corners had no real way to contact their traditional spirits; their path of connection was "cut" (*gisaym-da*). No longer could they joke with the spirits, ask their advice about sickness or sorcery, or enlist their opinions or support for fish poisoning, hunting, or the planning of feasts and rituals. Incredibly, the traditional world of Gebusi spirits had just withered away. And with their departure, Gebusi social life also changed. No longer was male camaraderie and its sexual joking central. Those in Gasumi Corners sang to their new God not in dead of night but in the brightness of morning, not with humor but with solemnity, not in lively spiritual conversation but in subservient listening. Apparently the preacher and his God had simply been more powerful than the traditional spirits. Together, they had the prestige and wonder of coming from afar, of promising wealth, success, and accomplishment in a wider world. The Catholic lay pastor lived near Gasumi Corners; he was literate and well educated, wore nice clothes, had a house stocked with supplies and a radio, and flew back and forth to Kiunga. He seemed bent on presenting his way of life and his God as models for Gebusi to follow. They willingly obliged.

Yuway told me that he himself had been one of Gasumi's lay Catholic leaders from 1992 to 1995. (I pinched myself to note how Gebusi now kept track of years.) But after that, he felt more distant from the church.

> "Why did you join the Seventh Day Adventists?" I asked.
>
> "Well, the Catholic Church is kind of 'soft'; I wanted a church that was 'hard.'"
>
> "How's that?" By this point, I was remembering that the Gebusi word for "hard" (*gaf*) also means "strong," "righteous," "angry," and "potentially violent"—as well as "difficult."

"If you are really worshipping God, it shouldn't be a small thing. It should be a big thing. You should really work hard to please God. And you have to be ready by Judgment Day. The Catholics make you work only a little hard. They let people keep lots of customs that God doesn't like—like dancing and smoking tobacco. The SDA Church knows that God doesn't like these and that they are wrong. They make their religion really hard by telling us we can't eat certain things that we like. They make us work a lot in the churchyard, and they make us come for Bible learning as well as their long service on Saturday morning. They have pictures that show just what will happen if you sin—you will burn in hell. With SDA, I know I am really a Christian and that I can go to heaven."

I paused to collect my thoughts. Yuway and my other friends had been so spiritually "Gebusi" before. But his answer revealed the attraction as well as the onus of a fundamentalist Christian faith. His remarks also underscored the distinction between local churches. Catholicism was taken as the "easiest" faith because it had the fewest restrictions. As long as Catholics attended church, worshipped God, avoided fighting, and didn't drink too much kava—their lightly intoxicating root drink, they could be baptized as full Christians by a visiting priest or bishop.

In many world religions—including Islam, Hinduism, and Judaism, as well as various forms of Christianity—fundamentalism has been on the rise. In Nomad Sub-District, including at Gasumi Corners, Christian churches were developed and run by fundamentalist Papua New Guineans who came to proselytize the area from other parts of the country. To me, all the sects had a fundamentalist air, though, as Yuway noted, some were perceived as "harder" than others.

In Gasumi Corners, 59% attended the Catholic Church and 22% the Evangelical Church of Papua New Guinea. Beyond the Catholics' strictures, Evangelicals placed a strong taboo against smoking tobacco and restricted participation in traditional rituals. SDA rules were yet stricter. In fact, Yuway's family was the only one in Gasumi Corners that joined their church. Adding to bans on smoking, drinking, dancing, and observing traditional rituals, SDAs prohibited the eating of pork as well as smooth-skinned fish. This was significant since eating pigs and fish remained prime features of major feasts. SDAs also prohibited any work or gardening on Saturday—their Sabbath, during which church services and Bible study filled most of the day. In principle, "frivolous" entertainment

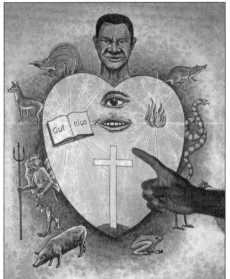 

Nomad Evangelical Church posters, 1998. [left] Enlightened Heart of Man. Inside a golden heart, the fire of the Lord is burning bright; the Bible is open to the "Good News"; the eye and mouth are open to God; and the forces of tradition—such as the red bird-of-paradise and the devil—are extruded outside.
[right] Death of a Sinner. The beer bottle, betel gourd, cards, and chest of traditional wealth indicate the dying man has been a heathen. Tortured by devils, his soul descends to the burning fires of hell.

like playing ball, going to disco, or attending traditional feasts was condemned as irreligious.

Because I knew Yuway to be a caring person, I wondered how his personal beliefs meshed with SDA's reputation for intolerance. He said with all earnestness that he had no anger against those who went to other churches or even those who went to none at all—which included a few in Gasumi Corners. I decided to push him a little: "If someone who is a good person is Catholic or Evangelical, do you think he or she can still go to heaven?"

Yuway thought for a minute, but not too long: "I don't know. Only God knows these things. But for me, I think that someone who is good inside can go to heaven, and it shouldn't matter if they go to one church or another."

"What if they don't go to any church at all?"

"Well, if they are given the chance to believe in Father God but still don't do it, it might be hard for God to see them as a good person and let them into heaven. But it's not for me to say."

I was impressed with his answer. It was then that I remembered the arrows that Yuway had been fashioning when I had come up to greet him. Now they were lying next to him, elaborately carved and ready for painting with bright-red ochre.

"Those are really nice arrows. Aren't they the kind used to sponsor a young man at an initiation?"

"Yes, I'm sponsoring my clan nephew at Taylmi a month or two from now."

"Can you still do that and be an SDA?"

"Well, I myself won't get baptized into SDA until after the initiation. It will be the last time for me to eat pork. And if I go just to see the initiation and not because I believe in its spirits, it's okay."

As I mulled over this last response, the sky opened up as if by divine intervention; suddenly, rain came pelting down. Realizing that it was almost dark—and that the supper fire at my house had yet to be started—I smiled and snapped fingers with Yuway quickly before whooping loudly as I raced up the trail. I was thoroughly drenched by the time I reached home.

Reflecting that evening on the day's events, I was struck how Yuway's remarks resonated with what I was finding from Gebusi who were Catholics or Evangelicals. All three local churches featured a fierce God of fire and brimstone, threatening hell and demanding compliance. All held that Judgment Day could come any time—and that repenting now was key to salvation. All three churches were "hard," though some were "harder" than others. How was it that my friends belonged to these different churches, each of which drew additional members from other diverse communities? While visiting with Yuway that afternoon, his two married brothers, Keda and Halowa, had shown up. It turned out that Keda was a lay leader in the Catholic Church; the previous Sunday, he had translated parts of the pastor's sermon from *Tok Pisin* to Gebusi for the congregation. Halowa, by contrast, was an Evangelical. Each of the three brothers thus belonged to a different church. I found increasingly that Yuway had been right: Gebusi accepted each other's right to choose the sect that suited him best. "Him" is significant here, because most wives attended the church chosen by their husbands. If Christianity saved the soul of the individual rather than the group, so, too, each individual man, at least, could choose his church—and whether to believe in God at all. The Gebusi world of spiritual choices and consequences was no longer governed so strongly by kinship or clanship, but increasingly by a man's choice.

The second thing that struck me was Yuway's plan to give his nephew initiation arrows while himself completing the arduous requirements for SDA baptism. How was this possible? Was Yuway hypocritical? Or was this a classic case of "syncretism," in which two religions blend together? Neither possibility seemed likely to me; I suspected that something else was at issue. It turned out that Gebusi distinguish between witnessing a traditional ritual and actually hosting or performing in one. At a remote settlement like Taylmi—the last big Gebusi village that had not yet gone Christian—one could attend an initiation the same way that one might watch an action video without being a violent or dangerous person; it is viewed as an entertaining drama rather than reflecting one's own lifestyle. Indeed, not succumbing to "pagan ways" while witnessing them could itself be a kind of Christian commitment.

It has often been noted that redemption in Christianity is punctuated by trials and temptations. Preachers at Nomad repeatedly emphasized the dangers of "backsliding" into traditional sin and vice. Though Gebusi willingly submitted themselves to the harangues of the pastor, it was their deviation from Christian thoughts or interests that spurred their desire for atonement—the pang of conscience that begs for moral cleansing. Exposure to and ambivalence about traditional customs was integral to the jawboning process of Gebusi conversion to Christianity. Hopes of salvation seemed directly linked to threats of sin, as if neither could do without the other.

Three weeks later, I experienced this when attending an SDA service with Yuway's family. The pastor's message was bleak. And it became something of a marathon as he exhorted the small congregation for over two hours. Increasingly, they simply hung their heads. That evening, I wrote the following:

The patience and passivity demanded in church—which I noted immediately among the Catholics—are brought to a firmer and sterner level among the Seventh Day Adventists. Today, the long sermon by the SDA preacher was a case in point. He placed great emphasis on the trials of Jesus: his forty days in the wilderness in the hot sun without food or water, his agonizing death on the cross, his suffering for us all. "Our own hardships are small; we should bear them easily and ask for nothing. We should think of Christ—be grateful that He suffered and died for us." The preacher's concluding harangue, which he repeated for a good forty minutes, was similarly somber. Saturday should be a day only for SDA worship. Food and market and other work activities should be finished Friday night. Saturday should be sober and worshipful, morning and night, with no entertainment or even cooking of food. This was the true way to worship God.

Where is the payoff in this scheme? The reward is deferred, but the deadline is now, since Judgment Day can come at any time. Against the austere trials of the present is the glorious image of life after death. Heaven is described as a place full of *bip*, or "cargo," a place where people are endlessly happy, without suffering or sickness. I was reminded of the dramatic cults that some Melanesians developed when they first encountered Western goods. These so-called cargo cults arose as local people attempted to obtain or "produce" European goods through magical rites or by mimicking Western behavior. In their conversion to Christianity, however, Gebusi bypassed such attempts, accepting that wealth and salvation would not

Gebusi women and children during the local Catholic Church service, 2013.

come right away, but only in an afterlife. To attain this, they could ask for little during life on earth. But on the day of reckoning, the ultimate deadline, God would give a reward to those who had truly followed his path.

My field entry concluded as follows:

> Now I can see, at least dimly, Yuway's attraction to this church. It is severe; it stresses the need to be hard and disciplined for God. This is the modern path of dignified compliance in and around the Nomad Station as well as a path for everlasting life. It measures the present not against a happy standard of current success but against trials, and rewards, that were infinitely greater for Jesus. These give reward only later, in the future.

Yuway's choice foregrounds the path that Gebusi were increasingly taking not only in church but also at school, in the market, and even on the ball field: to meet deadlines in the present, wait patiently, and hope for deferred success. All these contexts encouraged an ethic of disciplined action, of being on time and meeting deadlines, and of accepting the authority of outsiders.

The most dramatic case of religious transformation involved Doliay, the youngest and smallest of the six young men whom we had helped initiate. Several years after my first fieldwork, Doliay married Boyl, Sayu's widowed mother. However, Boyl died shortly thereafter. After her death inquest, Doliay confronted the person accused of causing Boyl's death through sorcery—a man named Basowey. Doliay told me that his anger toward Basowey had permeated his thoughts and actions. His revenge took on a surgical and almost Zen-like focus. Though Basowey was almost a foot taller than he, Doliay sought him out and confronted him alone in the forest. He dodged Basowey's arrows and split his head with a bush knife. Then he cut off Basowey's head and left it next to his body in the forest. He then went straightaway to the Catholic compound, told the pastor what he had done, handed him his bush knife, and turned himself in to the Nomad police.

Doliay's killing of Basowey was a watershed. He was sentenced to six years in prison in the national capital city of Port Moresby. No Gebusi had ever traveled so far. But Doliay hardly saw the city. While in prison, he became exceptionally self-disciplined. He learned to speak *Tok Pisin*, converted to Christianity, became a model prisoner, and even became head cook for the warden, who entrusted him with the key to the compound's whole storehouse of food. In 1998, Doliay proudly kept the letter of reference that the warden gave him upon his release. He recalled his jailers with great affection, still wore the shirt that one of them gave him, and named his first son, Willy, after his prison guard friend.

Returning to Gasumi Corners, Doliay became something of an ideal Christian. Unlike those who hung around the pastor's compound in hopes of wheedling a favor or gaining a benefit, Doliay worked for the church with personal commitment. He told me he waited for baptism until returning to Nomad because he wanted to be sure—really sure—that his bad ways were gone, that he felt no more hate in his heart. He felt grateful that God could forgive even as great a sin as his killing of Basowey. He said he would wait with a Christian heart until Judgment Day. I asked Doliay if he wouldn't be tempted to kill another person for sorcery, especially if his

Doliay as an initiate in a yellow costume, 1981.

Doliay, a stalwart member of the Catholic Church, 1998.

beloved son Willy were to die of sickness. His answer was immediate: "No. No way."

> "Why not?"
>
> "It's not for me to take revenge. That's something for the 'Big Fellow' [God] to decide. Besides, the people of Gasumi Corners don't practice sorcery anymore. Even if they wanted to, they would be too scared of what I did to Basowey to send sorcery again. If my son died, it wouldn't be from sorcery!"

Against traditional beliefs, Doliay's view was revolutionary. Before, Gebusi had attributed all fatal illnesses to sorcery. And a man's demand for revenge was greatest when a member of his own family died from sickness.

While Doliay had been in prison, his community had also changed. Incited by the pastors, the villagers redoubled their rejection of violence against suspected sorcerers. The penalty Doliay had been forced to pay—six years in prison, away from all kin—intensified others' reluctance to follow in his footsteps. Basowey's killing became famous as the last sorcery execution, the end of an era. And in its wake, conversion to Christianity swelled rather than diminished. Since then, as far as I know, no Gebusi has ever been killed as a sorcerer—or for any other reason. This is quite amazing: a society with one of the highest rates of homicide ever known has seen it drop to nothing and stay at zero. I confirmed this by cross-checking the circumstances of each death in the extended community since my last visit. To me, this underscores the degree to which human violence is not ingrained or inevitable, but strongly influenced by attitudes and beliefs. And yet, the Gebusi belief in sorcery had been so firm, and their desire to seek vengeance so strong, that I remained skeptical of this good-news story. I was a doubting Thomas—I needed to see in order to believe. Then Uwano died.

A certain depth emerges from the eyes of a man who knows his death throes are starting. Uwano was not old by our standards, probably in his late 40s. Perceptive and a convivial joker, he had been my *arga*, my "bread-fruit" gift-partner, since my first fieldwork. We had always greeted each other heartily. But by the fall of 1998, he was a shell of his former self, having only a tiny reserve of strength to fight his death. When I went to visit him at the Nomad Aid Post on his last night, the swelling that would soon consume his body had already taken his right arm and back. He gazed up with a mixture of knowledge and confusion. He turned and seemed to recognize me; a shadow of a smile flicked his face.

I knew better than to tell him he would get better. I could only kneel down with a helpless smile, look softly into his eyes, and say "*Koya, koya*," (friend, friend) as tenderly as I could. I took his hand in mine and stroked it. It was cold, already dead. He looked at me with that slight shake of head that is the Gebusi expression for, "There's no way; it's impossible." Then he was gone from me, eyes drifting into space. His little frame shook with a small spasm, all that his ravaged body could muster. He did not look back at me as I waited there. After a while, I crept out of the room to talk with his relatives. The stark glow of the fluorescent bulb in that room with no furnishings cast them all in ghostly stillness.

We always project during death, I think—the Gebusi with their beliefs and me with my thoughts of final human connection. And hopefully Uwano, too, reaching out from his doorway on death's divide. He died a few hours later, on October 9, 1998.

I waited instinctively for the sorcery investigations to start. Before it would have been unthinkable for a prominent man to die without a full-blown sorcery inquest. But Uwano's body was carried back to Gasumi Corners for a simple Christian funeral. He was dressed in his best Sunday shirt, head wreathed with leaves, and buried with a graveside service led by a Catholic catechist reading from the Bible.

A few of Uwano's closest relatives grumbled that some sorcerer must have killed him. But there was no spirit séance, no accusation, no attempt to identify a suspect—and no attempt to take revenge. As if to satisfy themselves, the men marched off to one of Uwano's gardens. They pawed around aimlessly in case some obvious sign of sorcery attack could be found. But their search was half-hearted, and they quickly lost interest. As one man said with a shrug, "If a spirit medium were around, we might have a chance of finding something. But there isn't." In effect, they were simply paying their respects to Uwano by visiting the place where they thought he became sick. Not wanting to waste their trip, the men gathered weathered logs near his overgrown garden and shouldered them back to the village for firewood.

In the wake of Uwano's death, Gebusi's descriptions of recent deaths made more sense to me. In case after case, friends had earnestly recounted,

"He-or-she simply died of sickness. We just don't know why. Only God can know. Maybe s/he was killed by sorcery. Or maybe by some other spirit. Maybe Satan was trying to fool us into thinking that it was sorcery. We didn't know. So we just buried the body and had readings from the Bible." Though the dead person's close relatives might suspect sorcery, there was little they could do. Barring solid spiritual evidence, others in the community would not support their suspicions. And if an accusation was launched, it could backfire; the person accused of sorcery could turn the tables and charge the accuser with slander, filing a complaint with the police.

Thinking about all this, I had conflicting views about Gebusi Christianity. On one hand, much of value in Gebusi culture had been lost. The vibrant wonder of traditional beliefs had faded. The poetry, symbolism, and musical awe of their spirit world were almost dead. In their place was a demanding new religion, trumpeted from elsewhere. In the history of colonialism and postcolonialism, including in the global spread of Christianity, pressured or forced conversion has worked hand in hand with powerful forms of social, economic, and political domination. Though Gebusi were thankfully spared coercive intimidation, they nonetheless had become passive recipients of outsiders' spiritual as well as political supervision.

On the other hand, Gebusi's Christian way of life had reduced their extraordinary rate of violence, indeed, bringing it down to zero. Social life was more peaceful than before. Men, women, and even children could walk to Nomad or the nearby forest without fear of attack. Though the great camaraderie of earlier days was gone, so, too, was the threat of lethal violence. Life was tamer in many ways.

What about the experiences of Gebusi women? Previously, they had enjoyed the energy and splendor of the spirit world, but from the sidelines. Although spirit women had been key to the traditional cosmos, Gebusi women themselves were excluded from séances and had little influence in sorcery inquests; men controlled the spirit world and the use of violence. Now, however, women were Christian along with men. The responsibility and the reward of being Christian—of repenting sins and gaining salvation—was individual for both sexes. In the church itself, pews were divided evenly, with women on the left side and men on the right. At the Catholic services, men and women attended in roughly equal numbers, but in SDA and Evangelical services, a decided majority were women. Yet, the church pastors and the primary lay leaders in the community were invariably men. And the authority of "Papa God," as he was called, was both stronger and more patriarchal than that of traditional Gebusi male or female spirits. Sporadically but notably, men in Gasumi Corners would sometimes echo the tone of the preachers or government officials, adopting a lecturing and authoritative tone in their own community. Finally, the number of Gebusi marriages that were acrimonious as opposed to harmonious seemed about the same as before.

Adding to my conflicted feelings about Christianity was another uncertainty: to what extent were the Gebusi's previous beliefs really dead? If only vestigially, the Gebusi still worried about sorcery. In many parts of Melanesia—and in parts of Africa, Asia, Latin America, and even Western countries—belief in sorcery or magic has persisted or reasserted itself. Such beliefs have sometimes melded with Christianity or world religions such as Islam, Buddhism, or Hinduism. In significant areas of Melanesia and Africa, sorcery beliefs play a major role in contemporary disputes and rivalries, including between political leaders. If these customs can continue in modern forms, couldn't Gebusi beliefs come back in new ways?

No matter what happens, however, and even if Christianity is later rejected or disavowed, its influence will have a significant legacy. The hands of time cannot be turned back.

How can we explain changes in Gebusi religion and culture? The complexities of the present wreak havoc with the categories and the richness of the past. The Gebusi cosmos had brimmed spiritually with humans, birds, fish, lizards, and even trees. Spirit mediums or shamans directly accessed the spirit world. Their religion combined animism and shamanism, suggested to be the oldest forms of human religion. Against this deep past, Gebusi have in short order become influenced if not dominated by the world's most widespread and populous world religion: Christianity. Like other world religions such as Islam, Judaism, Hinduism, and Buddhism,

Christianity has been historically associated with state kingdoms or empires, and many of these religions have become more influential across the globe in recent decades, including in fundamentalist guises. Although it once was thought that religions would decline as the world became more modern, the reverse now seems at least as likely. And these changes are often associated with the spread of external influence or domination. At Nomad, government officials were among the strongest proponents of Christianity—and among its strongest leaders. Christianity was taught as a subject in the Nomad school; reciprocally, the teachers often read scripture or gave sermons in church on Sunday. More generally, connections are easily made between the local force of the State, a national or international church, and broader processes of being or becoming modern.

Amid their influence, however, world religions are themselves shaped by the history and beliefs of different cultures. At Nomad, Catholicism, Protestantism, and Seventh Day Adventism are very different from how they are practiced in Western countries, even though all remain strongly Christian. Across the grain of received doctrines or beliefs, people often find ways to assert organic or homemade versions of spiritual and aesthetic expression. One day I found this very forcefully, and quite unexpectedly, in a mode of new expression in Gasumi Corners:

> Today by my house, I had little idea what hit me. The breeze carried a faint melody, beautiful and haunting, apparently from afar. I had never heard anything like it. I went magnetically toward the sound, but I found no houses in its direction. "You want to hear the singing," Kilasui said, and he pointed me down the path. It led from the village to seemingly nowhere, but the music grew louder. It was stunning yet different from the séance songs of old. I wound through the brush to a small fire with breadfruit warming next to it. No one was there, but the music was now full all around me. I looked up. Smiling down like nymphs on high were seven radiant boys smothering each other in soft harmony.
>
> I drew irresistibly up into their tree, its white branches grown as if they knew where each step should be placed. It swayed with my weight, shaking with gentle laughs that echoed the boys themselves. They squealed in delight to have a gawky grown companion, white as their tree, take interest in their singing. Their antics and my own soon brought the attention of other children, some of whom also clambered into the tree and distributed themselves carefully, as if to steady a wobbly ship. Even without their hubbub, our actions could not have

gone unnoticed. I now looked down to see a gathered crowd of women, yet more children, and even Sayu, who grinned up at me through the foliage. Their happiness, mine, and that of the boys made its own harmony, suspended in air with their song.

I had several sublime minutes in that tree—an experience that convinces you to the bone that you've done the right thing to travel so far, to have reached an enjoyment and bonding that transcends culture and that words cannot express. The sky was bluest blue, a cool breeze laced the melody, and I looked out thinking I had captured the innocence and joy of forest peoples that others wrote about so nostalgically in decades past. I cannot fully share or reproduce that nostalgia; there are too many complexities, uncertainties, and problems for that. But those stolen moments of innocence, full and beautiful, when one finds oneself inexplicably a young boy again drawn up in a tree, caressed in a sea of angelic smiles, tender harmony, and rainforest awe, can be neither denied nor suppressed. These are moments that make life not just worth living, but a thousand times over. If music marks the sound of the soul and the wheels of time, the songs of the Gebusi's present are as rich as their spiritual past.

Update: If the arrow of change has not been entirely reversed for Gebusi, its path of "modern" development has surely not been as direct as it appeared in the late 1990s. In some ways, the hopeful singing of the boys in the tree has continued and grown. One of them, along with Sayu and two others, form an exquisite local singing group that has lasted for 15 years. More generally, the dominant strength of Christian presence among Gebusi, though far from gone, has been greatly tempered by the weathering of time. The Catholic Church at Gasumi Corners still functions, but with less energy and enthusiasm than before. Some of the other churches are moribund or struggling, and the Seventh Day Adventists attract no one from Gasumi Corners. Even Yuway gave up his connection with them within a few years.

More generally, the hopes and expectations of Gebusi progress—spiritually, economically, and in education and national development—have been greatly scaled back if not dashed since the late 1990s. These changes are described in Part Three of this book, but the larger point here is that change in a modern world is not a one-way street, much less an arrow of consistent progress. Twists, detours, and U-turns are invariable, as we know full well from the economic retrenchments that affect our own and other Western countries. This does not mean desire and aspiration for progress are extinguished, including among Gebusi, but rather that their intended path is often checkered, convoluted, and sometimes reversed altogether. So, too, this does not indicate that "development" is irrelevant or that changes, such as those embraced by Gebusi in the late 1990s, are without impact. The patterns of the deeper past can never be fully brought back. But neither are they supplanted as completely as it often seems during periods flush with dynamic change.

Gebusi did change remarkably during the 1990s, moving their village, associating with the Nomad Station, and embracing locally modern ways of life as much as they possibly could. Among other things, shamanism, traditional spiritualism, and sorcery violence have never come back among Gebusi—and their homicide rate remains wonderfully at zero. In the mix, they have been changed and influenced by Christianity. But now they are to a much greater extent in charge of their own church. The lay church leaders are still men, but from Gasumi Corners itself, and women continue to have benefited from greater spiritual participation and inclusion. In the mix, no one now seems to want, or to care about, having a wristwatch or keeping track of the hours of the day. In all, Gebusi's awareness and ability to manage outside influences and values, and their ability to combine these with the legacy of their own orientations, is now greater, and more nuanced, than it was before.

BROADER CONNECTIONS
Sociocultural and Religious Change

- **Cultural change** is as old as humanity but it has intensified with **globalization** during the past 500 years and especially since the latter part of the 20th century.

- Just as for many people in remote areas, Gebusi's cultural change has included armed **colonial intrusion** against local peoples (such as the Bedamini) and the introduction of Western **commodities**, including clothing and goods such as metal tools.

- In contrast to colonized peoples in many areas, there is little evidence that Gebusi themselves have been subject to violence from Westerners, land alienation, taxation, forced labor, cash cropping, or labor migration.

- After Gebusi at Yibihilu moved near the Nomad Sub-District Station, they experienced **modern changes** shared by people in many world areas, including adoption of a **world religion** (in this case, **Christianity**), **school,** and a local **market** where items were bought with money.

- **Cultural loss** is common among many peoples. For Gebusi, this included a decline of longhouse living and the loss of shamanism or spirit mediumship, of major sorcery inquests or accusations, and of intense emphasis on *kog-wa-yay* or "good company."

- Becoming **modern** often entails desire for material **progress** over time. A concern with temporal progress was also evident among Gebusi, especially those who believed strongly in Christianity.

- Modern developments are often associated with increasing intrusion by external authority figures. Among Gebusi, these included external church leaders, government officials, police, and, in some ways, the ultimate power of "Papa God."

- Modern development can induce selected positive changes. Among Gebusi at Gasumi Corners, this has included a striking reduction of the rate of killing to zero since 1989.

- Many peoples exhibit resilient or resistant forms of local **expressive culture.** Among Gebusi, this has included local forms of singing developed by boys and young men.

- When a cultural anthropologist returns to the field, as happened to Bruce, his or her connections to local people often expand and become enriched.

- Sociocultural change is not a one-way or consistent process over time. Among Gebusi, more recent changes have reduced the impact of Christianity and of external authorities, though their earlier development continues to have some lasting influence.

Chapter 8

Pennies and Peanuts, Rugby and Radios

Bosap was not happy. The market was winding down, but her piles of bananas and sweet potatoes still lay primped for sale, like wallflowers that everyone saw but nobody wanted. The other women were similarly peeved; their produce was still competing with Bosap's on the sellers' tables. Trying to make light of things—and collect more information in the mix—I tried to view her glass as half full: "You sold at least a little, right? Maybe two or three sales at 10 cents each?" Bad questions, bad timing. Bosap's normally congenial features, already sober, flashed to a scowl. "Not interested," she said, and turned away. She had sold nothing.

So, too, in her life, Bosap had been passed over, though she usually took it all in stride. As she had laughingly said when I talked to her before, "No man wanted to marry me. But then, I didn't want to marry any of them, either!" Among Gebusi, Bosap had the rare distinction of becoming an older woman, now in her mid-50s, without ever having married. When she had been in her 30s, this hadn't stopped her from having a sexual affair with a young initiate. Her pregnancy had created a scandal, but she had carried on with determination. She didn't marry her young lover or any of his older clan-mates (who could have claimed the child and taken Bosap as a second wife). Instead, she raised Kuma herself with the help of her own kin. The pride of her life, Kuma became a strong and decent young man who was now himself almost ready to be married. Over the years I had known her, Bosap had maintained her pleasant disposition and also the conviction to go her own way. Her good-spiritedness was attested by the fact that, even as an "old woman," she had never been suspected of sorcery.

Given her background, I was caught off guard by her response to me at the market. Bad sales were a touchy personal issue, and there were few buyers—mostly government officers and their wives from Nomad Station. Nevertheless, women from Gasumi Corners and elsewhere continued to haul their best produce to market in hopes of selling it. At dawn on Tuesdays and Fridays, they packed their foodstuffs in cavernous net bags and lugged them along the muddy path to the Nomad market. Even on a "good day," many women returned loaded down with the same food they had brought. And prices were low. For the equivalent of 60 cents, one could buy a large bunch of ripe bananas, a pile of shelled Tahitian chestnuts, and a bundle of cooked bamboo shoots. Even at that, few people aside from government workers and pastors had money to spend, and their own wages were small and undependably paid. But local women kept bringing food to market, twice each week. At least their activities gave them a small place in a cash economy.

Wanting to understand this, I tried to ferret out just how much food the women sold, how much they took back or gave away, and how much they earned. As my encounter with Bosap taught me, however, this was

Women from Gasumi Corners selling food at the Nomad market, 1998.

tricky. Women hardly wanted to disclose their many failures and even their few successes—for fear of jealousy. Only a few of them could actually count the combined value of the coins they received, and they shoved their proceeds quickly into tightly wadded bundles. When transactions did occur, they were typically shielded from view; a buyer would have exact change ready, saunter by the table, and quickly sweep the food into a net bag as he handed over the coins and walked away. Prices were standard for each pile of food, so there was no need to bargain or, in many cases, to talk at all.

In typical fieldwork fashion, I discovered this norm by badly breaking it. It was a pleasure to see such good and diverse food for sale, and at my first market, I decided to buy some myself. I went up to a woman selling fresh bamboo shoots and found after pawing through my pockets that my smallest currency was a 2-kina bill. As I handed this to her across the table, I could see the color drain from her face. Though worth only one US dollar, the bill was ten times the price of the shoots I was buying. The poor woman had neither the arithmetic nor the coins to make change. So she was forced to initiate a confusing chain of inquiries that rippled in domino effect through all the people around her. Ten-cent loans and other transfers of coins ricocheted awkwardly through the crowd. After several long and painful minutes, my requisite 90 cents in change was dutifully amassed and counted out for me, as everyone looked on. By this time, I really just wanted to let the unfortunate women simply keep all the change. But two things prevented me. First, I would be badly undermining the standards of the market, which were based on a standard and fixed price for each pile of food. And second, the transaction would advertise to scores of onlookers my ability and intent to pay a 900% premium for all the food that I wanted to buy! So I smiled gamely and apologized pleasantly, trying not to call yet more attention to my gaffe.

How much is a dime worth at a place like Nomad? Cultural meanings, rules, and assumptions—whole worlds of understanding—can underlie the smallest of material transactions. In the US, I walk into a store and don't think twice about buying items from a stranger while other people may see my cost tally on the checkout screen, money given, and, especially, cash given back. This presumes a whole set of market assumptions that Gebusi and their neighbors were just beginning to engage with. But—and this is the more important point—Gebusi men and women were more rather than less motivated to pursue market transactions even though, and in some ways for the very reason that, their knowledge and confidence were undeveloped. Notwithstanding embarrassment, the woman I bought produce from had earned not just my 10 cents but the prestige of selling to an outsider who had money. Of all the bamboo shoot piles, I had chosen hers. She and her kin now owned a 2-kina bill received very publicly. This conveyed value, as I judged from the palaver as I walked away. If I had unwittingly trampled on local etiquette, I had also unwittingly reinforced the idea that monetary exchange is public, impersonal, and prestigious.

Being either a good or a bad ethnographer (sometimes it is hard to know which!), I became increasingly interested in the larger pattern of market transactions. Like the churches, the Nomad school, and the sports league, the Nomad market is an interethnic affair that attracts people from various sides or "corners" of Nomad, each of which has its own ethnic or tribal character. Women from Gasumi Corners formed only a small fraction of those at the interethnic market, but because they were from my own community, I kept them as my focus.

The first and easiest thing to discern was that most sellers were, in fact, women. Counting the sellers from Gasumi Corners on 25 different market days, I found that more than 91% (285 of 313) were female. Some men and boys also came to market, but they seldom sold anything and they tended to stay on the selling area's periphery. Occasionally men would buy a pile of peanuts for a dime—but the center of action, or lack thereof, was the women sellers. All women from Gasumi Corners participated, gathering their best foodstuffs and bringing them to market on average once every ten days. In all, the market was the prime place for village women to conduct business—and be modern. Women also went to church, of course. And girls had become students along with boys at the Nomad Community School. Only at the market, however, were women the central focus of attention. Though they tended to be quiet in public, women at market did visit casually with female kin and relatives, including those from other communities.

How much money did women actually make? I couldn't easily ask them, but I found that I could count the piles of food they initially placed on the selling tables. As the market progressed, I casually strolled the aisles, chatted, and noted down which piles of food had been reduced by sales in what amounts. Since prices were standardized, I could easily then deduce how much each woman had sold by the end of the market. Women who were lucky enough to have sold several items were willing to clarify, if I was unsure, how many were purchased.

During the 25 days that I documented market activity, Gebusi women sold less than half the food that they brought to the market; the rest was carried back home or given away. A woman's average earning per market day was just 20 cents—for selling food weighing several pounds or more. More than 20% of women who brought food to market on a given day sold nothing at all.

The challenge of the women's enterprise was underscored by the inflated price of things that could be bought at Nomad's tiny home-front stores. Benchmark goods were two-pound bags of rice and 12-ounce tins of low-grade fish. Each of these cost the equivalent of $1.50. As such, an average woman's market sales from almost an entire month were wiped out by buying a single small bag of rice or a single tin of fish. Comparing the nutritional value of these against the many hours and calories required to raise local food and haul it to market, the energy cost of women's marketing obviously far outweighed its benefits. Gebusi women's market work was in this sense irrational; why would anyone put such time and effort into an often fruitless enterprise? This question grew more poignant as I saw women from Gasumi Corners continually lugging food to market and waiting aimlessly to sell it.

The onus seemed greatest for two young adolescent girls, Danksop and Waygo, who sat wooden or sighing behind their piles of food for hour

Danksop attempting to sell pineapple and sweet potatoes at the Nomad market, 1998.

after hour. But the answer to my question was one I should have realized all along: in a word, culture. As we ourselves know, there is much more to a purchase—and more to the work that pays for it—than the trade-off between dollars spent and its functional use. Why do we prefer a Ferrari to a Ford, Godiva chocolate to Hershey's, or a ring of gold to one made of tin? Similarly, why do Gebusi prefer a small bag of rice to 15 pounds of potatoes? In both cases, the items of value convey refinement, prestige, and cultural status. If Gebusi marketing seems "irrational," it carries the value and prestige of earning money, of being modern. And it does this for those who are most shut out of the local cash economy: village women. If men obtain occasional paid work—cutting grass on the airstrip, doing odd jobs for government officials, or acting as carriers for visitors on a trek—women earn coins at market.

I realized this in spades when I found my "banker" in Gasumi Corners. Nelep was the cleverest old woman in the settlement. On the way back from the market one day, I joked that though I had money, it was still hard to buy things, as I needed more coins. As the path turned, Nelep quietly motioned me away from the others. "I've got coins," she said. "Come to my house." We then continued to our respective homes. After stowing my things, I walked back to her little dwelling. While doing so, I remembered her personal history, which was as colorful as it was revealing. I knew Nelep well from 1980–82, when she had lived in Yibihilu close to our house. She was then married to the easygoing Wasep and raising two boys. A bold character, she had not only been caught having a sexual affair with the uninitiated Doliay but was the only Gebusi woman we ever knew who had dabbled in the otherwise all-male art of shamanism.

Nelep had endured much since I left in 1982. The cyst on her right wrist had grown larger, making it hard to use her hand. In about 1990, her beloved older son was gored to death by a wild pig, and her grief-stricken husband stopped eating and died just a few weeks later. She was now left with her remaining son and a younger daughter, Kwelam, who was herself seriously ill from a bone deformity in her hip. But Nelep was tough as well as smart—always ready with a witty smirk and an astute solution. She somehow finagled the medical officer at the Nomad Aid Post to have

Kwelam flown to the Kiunga Hospital for an operation—along with Nelep herself. Landing in Kiunga without money or kin, Nelep rummaged in garbage heaps for daily scraps of food. Lacking a blouse, she felt the powerful stigma of going bare-breasted in town, scrounging for rags to cover herself. Amid this abasement, Nelep nursed Kwelam through recovery until they were both flown back to Nomad. Kwelam walked with a limp but was otherwise healthy and indeed one of the happiest girls in the village. Nelep's surviving son, Yamda, assumed pride of place as a respected Catholic lay leader; in 1998, he was newly married with an infant daughter.

As her children grew up successfully, Nelep married the widower Gono—the silent, wiry man who had carried for us during our first expedition to Gebusi-land. By middle-age, however, Gono became crotchety, and he resented his wife's feisty wit and lack of deference. In 1998, he beat Nelep on more than one occasion. As a remarkable stigma, Gono was criticized for his actions by both the men and the women of Gasumi Corners.

Though Nelep still lived in Gono's small house, she kept her affairs to herself—including her earnings from the market, which she squirreled away without telling him. The market money of most wives becomes part of the household economy and, as such, ultimately subject to decisions by men. This said, women took pride in their hard-earned funds and the fact that these could pay for prestigious tins of fish and bags of rice at community feasts, even if these were presented by men. Most Gebusi women were uncomfortable or embarrassed to make significant store purchases on their own in any event.

By dint of personal will, Nelep had kept her earnings for herself and her own children. And she had wisely focused on raising and marketing peanuts, which were the item most widely and regularly sold at the market, even though it was not the splashiest or most expensive product. Week after week, Nelep quietly sold piles of peanuts from her big bag— and over time, her 10-cent sales added up. After we were safely in her house, Nelep smiled wryly and carefully unwrapped several unobtrusive bundles. To my amazement, a mountain of coins tumbled out. She didn't know how much she had earned, but when I counted it up her earnings, she had amassed more than 40 kina, or 20 dollars. This equaled 200 sales at 10 cents each—two years of market sales for the average market woman.

With easy trust, Nelep gave me the bulk of her coins in exchange for two crisp 20-kina bills. Everyone knew that bright red "pigs head" money, as it was called, was the largest and most prestigious currency. That Nelep now had two of these bills seemed to give her a great sense of satisfaction. As she carefully tucked them away, we both knew she could use them to support her children or herself however she wished—and that they were easier to conceal from prying eyes than piles of coins. As for me, I had all the coins that I needed. As I walked home, I tried to carry my stash in my own net bag as unobtrusively as possible. I smiled at the thought that an economy of new money could, at least on rare occasions, benefit both a Gebusi woman and an outsider without compromising the integrity of either. The economy of money in Gasumi Corners was paltry and largely "unproductive." But its economy of culture was strong and important.

My experience with Nelep got me thinking about how women's relations with men were changing. If the Nomad market underscored the hopeful and compromised role of women in a fledgling cash economy, it was complemented by their new role in other spheres. Christian churches had given women a new sense of spiritual participation, even though men were ultimately in charge. Other institutions and activities at Nomad also generated opportunities for women—while also allowing new forms of male dominance, especially in terms of education, sports, and, perhaps surprisingly, theft. But it was difficult for me to talk with women about these developments. For an unrelated man to talk with a Gebusi woman automatically implied sexual interest. Older women like Nelep and Bosap were easier for me to approach as they were no longer considered sexually active. But younger women were a different story. Even for married women in their 30s and 40s, a personal interview was difficult to arrange and even more difficult to carry out. I could talk to a woman if her husband or brother was present. But then the man would reinterpret my questions and answer many of them himself.

The same was true of my attempt to talk to girls at the Nomad Community School; the boys took charge in responding. To be fair, part of the problem involved all the students. Rote learning and copying from the board took a toll on a class of 40, 60, or even 80 pupils sitting cross-legged on the floor or on hardwood benches hour after hour. The children came from several local language groups with their language of instruction being that peculiar dialect of "Papua New Guinea English." After a year or two in school, students could understand this form of English fairly well—but their rote learning left them collectively passive and reluctant to speak. As in church, powerful outsiders controlled the expression of important knowledge. This problem was the worst for the girls. To the teachers, however, the students were like the school's leaky water tank: when something new and good was imparted to them, like the English language, they couldn't retain it but let it seep away.

I got my chance to break this mold when the teachers welcomed me to give guest presentations in their various classes. The kids seemed to love my stories of life in other countries and in the US. But when it came to saying much about themselves—indeed, when it came to saying much of anything—they were tongue-tied. I asked a fifth-grade class to name pictures of things without my first saying the word. Although they knew all the answers, this simple task was painfully difficult, especially for girls. I gave one group of girls three photos of flowers. I knew they knew what they were, and I coaxed them with antics and pleasantries. They beamed as they squirmed, but none of them could get the word out. Finally, I gently leaned close so one of them could whisper very faintly in my ear, "Flowers."

Though girls from Gasumi Corners and other communities increasingly went to school, the gender gap widened with each successive grade, as girls dropped out in higher numbers. Unlike a significant number of boys and young men, no girls from Gasumi Corners had completed elementary school.

Outside school, boys dominate in physical activity through sports. Sports were hardly important to Gebusi in 1980–82—as opposed to ritual fighting and even warfare—but competition on the ball field had since become a modern, more organized and disciplined, and less violent arena of collective male rivalry. Schoolboys from Gasumi Corners avidly played rugby and soccer and later joined community teams that played on the Nomad ball field for much of each weekend. The matches were interethnic occasions at which several hundred spectators might ring the field. In contrast to the dozen or so men's matches each weekend, there was but a single game of women's soccer, and this was played almost entirely by the wives and elder daughters of government officials. Women from Gasumi Corners told me quite earnestly that they would be glad for their daughters to learn how to play soccer. They added that they would themselves be glad to go as spectators if their daughters were playing. But athletic field sports had become a male province, beginning at school during recess. Few girls felt comfortable learning how to play or joining a team.

Ironically, men's dedication to sports was the ultimate solution to my difficulties in talking with Gebusi women. After numerous sun-bleached weekends watching endless matches of rugby and soccer, I got bored. It wasn't that I disliked sports; I had even been a starter for my high school soccer team in the Connecticut state finals. But watching game after game from the sidelines didn't fit my notion of fieldwork with Gebusi. My hours as a spectator did yield some insights. I was impressed by the gentlemanly competition on the field and the caliber of play (which was surprisingly good, even in bare feet). Men in the crowd could interact across community and ethnic lines without constraints of hospitality, etiquette, or reciprocity that otherwise attended visits between settlements. Having noted these patterns, however, I still felt apathetic. So one Sunday afternoon, I just stayed home.

Predictably, the men and boys were all at the Nomad ball games. But quickly I realized this left the women alone back in the village. Away from men and older male children for a few precious hours, women's talk became freer and more relaxed. I found that I could interview women as long as it was a group occasion among them. Indeed, most women were eager to participate in my "talk-work" sessions. It helped that I had brought special trade goods for women that were hard for them to get— especially dresses, bras, and costume jewelry. Shopping for these back in the US, I can still remember the look on the saleswoman's face in the Dollar Store in Atlanta when I heaped 15 inexpensive bras into my shopping basket along with mounds of cheap costume jewelry. Sensing that I should somehow "explain myself," I had said to her, without thinking carefully, that I was buying gifts for my many female friends in the rainforest. Aghast at the implications of my statement, I guiltily guessed what she must be thinking. But it all turned out fine. The sales clerk was Malaysian, and she knew a good bit about rainforest peoples, the difficulty of obtaining trade goods in remote areas, and the politics of gift giving. In fact, she ended up advising me which bras were most likely to fit the short but sometimes well-endowed women of Gasumi Corners. I came away with a fresh understanding about crossing cultural boundaries with women—in Atlanta as well as New Guinea.

Back in Gasumi Corners, the women were drawn to the goods I had brought. I talked with each individually as primary interviewees—listening to the woman's life history and getting her opinions and reflections on various subjects. Particularly with less articulate women, their female kin and friends chimed in with helpful promptings, clarifications, and elaborations. Young women and adolescent girls remained the toughest to talk with. Even when asked by a not-so-young and weirdly acceptable man such as myself, and even with other women present, their responses were often only shuffling feet, embarrassment, and blank looks. Nonetheless, all the women, even the younger ones, maintained their desire to work with me. Partly this was because the other women were also doing it and partly because my background and interest in the community provoked a sense of obligation. But mostly, I think, they wanted the trade goods I gave at the end of the sessions.

A punctuation point to gender change among Gebusi—across developments in church, market, school, sports, and domestic relations—concerned the yearnings of women and men for manufactured commodities and a modern way of life. During the latter part of my fieldwork, I sponsored a contest in which Nomad schoolchildren drew pictures of how they envisaged themselves in the future. I was amazed how eagerly and effectively they took up this task, not to mention the high quality of their drawings. Burgeoning on the pages were full-color pictures of their future selves in modern walks and ways of life. Boys drew themselves as heavy machine operators, pilots, doctors, a rock singer, or a newsman. Girls drew themselves especially as nurses, teachers, or housewives in nice Western dresses. Girls as well as boys drew themselves in highly modern futures. A few actually drew themselves as living in a Christian heaven. By contrast, very few students—just 6% of the boys and 5% of the girls—drew their future selves conducting traditional livelihoods such as gardening, hunting, or fishing.

Notwithstanding their optimism, the students' desires were mostly unrealistic. It seemed highly unlikely that many or perhaps any of them could achieve the future lives they envisaged; the economy of Nomad was too paltry, and education too limited.

What happens to the inflated expectations of young people when their aspirations are dashed? If gender did not divide the modern aspirations of boys and girls at Nomad, one important contrast did emerge. Virtually half the boys envisaged their future as gun-wielding members of the Papua New Guinea Defense Force or the National Police. That boys gravitated to images and roles of forceful power is not surprising. But in a local world where manufactured goods and commodities are increasingly expected— and unavailable—frustrated aspirations can fuel the desire to forcefully possess such items, especially for young men. Theft has been an increasing problem across most of Papua New Guinea. Back at Yibihilu in 1981, people had craved our Western commodities, but we had never feared having them stolen. Living so communally, Gebusi had made a virtue of sharing and respecting each other's property. But things had changed. Villagers were more possessive of Western goods, and money was increasingly important. Activities at Nomad entailed interaction with many strangers—and potential thievery. Families now wanted chains, locks, and metal boxes. In the Nomad police register, theft was the most frequently reported offense—almost twice as common as any other crime—and most of these cases were both made by and targeted against men. Though theft at Nomad was only a small problem compared to Papua New Guinea's larger towns and cities, it was still a focus of real concern.

The biggest case occurred when two boom box radios were stolen from the Nomad Community School. Boom boxes were a major icon of modern identity for young men. They referenced a prestigious world of commodities and accomplishment, of fluent speech in *Tok Pisin* or English, of rock music, and of sexual allure. Boom box radios were also an important sign of modernity for the school, since in addition to playing music and tapes, the boom boxes broadcast national education programs that were timed for presentation in classrooms each morning. As such, the theft of the school boom boxes struck a blow to the sense of progress— and highlighted young men's frustrated desire for prestigious goods. At a large public meeting, officials harangued villagers, criticizing them for letting local boys get away with such an awful crime. To my amazement, they threatened that schoolteachers would not want to live and work at Nomad and that maybe the school itself would have to be shut down. If Nomad was going to be a "bad" place, a place of theft and "backsliding," officials continued, airplanes might stop landing at Nomad airstrip, leaving villagers

Schoolboy Tolowe's drawing of wanting to be a brave policeman who catches young criminals, 1998.

to go back to the way things were. The rhetoric was distinctly Christian, like what I had heard in church; if villagers and young men in particular were going to be deceitful and sin, they would be damned to backwardness. Despite what I thought was over-the-top exaggeration, it was true that given a shortage of teachers and funds, a range of schools in Western Province had been shut down. As in church, some of the villagers hung their heads.

The theft of the radios reflected the hardship of becoming modern in a place like Nomad. The churches, market, and school brought people together in new ways, but they also created an increasingly impersonal world marked by new inequalities—and resentment between those who had more, and those who didn't. Particularly for young men, unable to achieve their modern aspirations, pressure could mount to simply take what they could and reject tedious effort or waiting for an afterlife in heaven.

For Gebusi near Nomad in 1998, local modern developments promised progress. Women, in particular, had more possibilities for participation than they ever had before. Women's lives were expanding at school, in church, and at the market. At the same time, expectations were beginning to confront a lack of realistic ways to attain modern goals—apart from the deferred gratification of Christianity. This was true at school in the higher grades, and at the market for women, including Bosap. But it seemed especially true of young men as they aspired to greater progress. For many of them, traditional masculinity—with its emphasis on initiation, ritual dancing, displays of aggression, sorcery, and violence—had not been replaced with viable ways to be modern. In some cases, these tensions were redirected back onto women—as was the case of Gono beating Nelep, his economically successful wife. For the most part, however, Gebusi men as well as women drew upon deeper cultural values of acceptance to simply absorb their frustrations. In any event, the attractions of Nomad seemed bright with action and possibility—and more interesting for most than life in the deep rainforest. The most palpable sense was of better things to come, even if challenges were great and sometimes insurmountable.

Update: The bustling energy, potential—and subordination and challenge—of local modernity for Gebusi in the late 1990s seem, in hindsight, all the more vivid and striking. On a regular basis, Gebusi would stroll into Nomad just to "take a spin" and see what was going on. The market, school, sports leagues, and government programs were so primed with potential, who could have guessed they would all decline?

Now there is little happening at Nomad; its world has dimmed. The Nomad market, while not completely gone, is but a shadow of its former self. As described in Part Three, money and buyers are now so scarce that few women bother to tote produce to Nomad in a futile attempt to sell it. In a way, this is good or at least economically "rational": when the cost of effort so greatly outstrips the result (even in social status or prestige), interest and commitment can eventually fall off. Even more than the market, the Nomad sports games are now also a thing of the past: the ball field is overgrown, and there have been no games there, or elsewhere in the area, for years. So, too, the Nomad school flirts with low attendance and closure or merging of students across grades: it is just too difficult to keep teachers committed to staying and living at the Nomad Station. And yet, as we shall later see, Gebusi have not given up. In fact, they are a remarkably rejuvenated people.

It is sometimes too easy to assume old traditions die out while modern changes endure. In fact, the sharpness of the new cutting edge may blunt while older patterns reemerge or are revisited in new guises. Consider the impact of "retro" in American pop culture today.

For Gebusi, the past persists in immediate human terms. Though Nelep is now a very aged woman, she has proudly lived to see a whopping nine grandchildren survive. And her surviving son, whom she adores, has become the community leader of the Gasumi Corners St. Paul's Catholic Church.

As with older traditions, the previous influence of life in and around the Nomad Station also has a continuing legacy. As men and women have settled back into a decreasingly modern life, the division and separation between them has continued to soften. Gender relations do not seem as charged or as fraught as they used to be. Though still a challenge, it is now easier to interview women than it was before. In the mix, men as well as women have largely accepted their reduced ability to engage a larger world—and to appreciate their own more fully. Theft is less of a problem than it was before—in part because there are fewer commodities around to covet or steal. And the incidence of beating, both of women and of pets, seems significantly less than it was.

In these regards, the threatening response of officials to the theft of the school radios has proven both ominously correct and completely wrong. Outsiders have indeed given up and left Nomad, including most government officials, teachers, and even the police. Predictably, they have blamed their departure on local conditions and attitudes. But Gebusi and others do not accept this responsibility. In particular, they do not blame themselves as having been sinful or as sliding into "backwardness" from their own shortcomings. Instead, they say, it is the government's own fault that it has gone, that it has "died." In the bargain, though a number of people in Gasumi Corners still go to church, there is neither so much hope of heavenly progress nor fear of hellish decline. Peanuts, pennies, rugby, and radios: like some of Gebusi's older traditions, they now increasingly seem like things of the past—even as they are not fully gone—and might someday come back.

BROADER CONNECTIONS
Markets, Development, and Modern Aspirations

- **Modern institutions** and activities that are common globally, including among Gebusi, include government **school,** public **markets** at which women are prominent, practicing a **world religion,** and organized **sports** for men.

- As is the case with many peoples, modern changes among the Gebusi included increasing interaction with outsiders as well as those from different **ethnic groups.**

- In contrast to indigenous gift exchange, modern **market exchange**—as reflected at the Nomad market—is relatively impersonal and often involves the transaction of goods between strangers by means of money.

- Like women in many world areas, Gebusi women were highly motivated to invest time and effort in market activity. Indeed, their investment was more than what they received back in money. This reflects how modern cultural values and prestige can motivate people to give up traditional practices in hopes of success in a modern cash economy.

- **Female status** among Gebusi, as among many peoples, increased in the sense that women have participated meaningfully in modern institutions and activities such as church, school, and the market. At the same time, **gender dominance** has taken on new dimensions; women's education, church leadership, and economic control are significantly less than that of men.

- As is often the case in developing countries, **education** through formal schooling was important but compromised at Nomad, with large classes and difficulty of educational advancement, especially for girls.

- As reflected in drawings of their anticipated adult selves, children at the Nomad Community School, like in many contexts cross-culturally, desired to have successful modern futures. However, most of these desires were unlikely to be fulfilled.

- As is the case for many peoples, Gebusi activities at school, market, the government, and even church reflected a growing sense of **national identity** and **nation-building.**

- The theft of the school radios at Nomad reflected frustrated economic aspiration, marginality, and stigma of underdevelopment in the context of external authority, control, and power.

- As revealed by Gebusi in 1998 and especially since that time, hopes of modern success are often complemented by challenges, downturns, and periods of decline.

- Like many peoples, Gebusi selectively draw upon or resuscitate longer-standing traditions over time, including during periods of increased stress or challenge.

Chapter 9

Mysterious Romance, Marital Choice

Wayabay was as spare with words as he was decent and direct in his actions. He was clearly troubled, so I asked him in. He hesitated, strong young man that he was, until the force of his question overcame his embarrassment. "Do you have any *adameni*? I would really like some." I had no idea what this was. He stammered and continued on: "*Adameni* is something special. It has to do with an unmarried woman and an unmarried man. When they really like each other and think of coming together." I still had no idea. Whatever *adameni* was, it related to sexual desire between young people. Wayabay was the oldest of the bachelors and was actively trying to find a wife. But what was *adameni*? I wracked my brain. It was clearly important to Wayabay. I was both concerned and curious.

Could Wayabay be asking me for a condom? I knew that he had worked for a trail-clearing crew a few years back and that he had traveled to Kiunga. He had greater knowledge and experience than many. Perhaps he was in a romantic liaison and wanted to protect either himself or the girl. This would explain his embarrassment. I tried, gently, to describe a condom in Gebusi vernacular: "There is this thing that men wear when they have sex. Is this like *adameni*?" Wayabay replied, "Well, I'm not sure." My unease mounted, but I forged ahead: "This is something that a man puts over his 'thing,' his phallus. It stretches like rubber. He puts this rubber thing over his penis before he has sex. He has sex but his 'thing' doesn't touch the woman's 'thing.'"

Now it was Wayabay's turn to be uncomprehending—and mine to be embarrassed. I tried to explain that men can use these rubber coverings when they don't want the woman to get pregnant or when they worry about getting diseases from having sex. All of which sounded no better and, indeed, much worse when spoken in Gebusi. Wayabay shook his head vehemently; *adameni* was definitely NOT a condom.

In despair, we invited Sayu and Didiga into our conversation. Both spoke a smattering of English and had had more schooling than Wayabay. Yes, they said, *adameni* was something for a man. And, yes, it had to do with sex. It also had something do to with *oop*, the generic Gebusi word for "slippery, milky substance" that refers especially to semen. Sex. Men. Semen. I was stymied. Could they be referring to some custom or substance having to do with traditional practices of sex between men? This would certainly explain Wayabay's embarrassment. Perhaps he was having sexual relations with another young man before finding a wife. I took another deep breath. "Does *adameni* have to do with Gebusi traditional sex customs between men?" They looked puzzled. "You know, the sex custom in the initiations, when the adolescent strokes the man's phallus and swallows his semen—so he can grow bigger and achieve more manhood."

Culturally speaking, I had dropped a bomb. Their mouths hung in disbelief, their faces grew ashen. Sayu finally broke the silence: "Did our fathers and boys really do that? In olden times? Did they? Really?!"

Double ouch. Although they had all grown up in a world of male banter and horseplay, none of them, I now realized, had been initiated; the last initiation ceremony had been held before they were old enough. They had never been introduced to sex relations with other men. Given their Christian conversion, it was quite possible they had never been told about the practice. Against their ignorance, I had divulged the reality of a strange sexual practice, a shocking custom that was hard to believe and disgusting to them. I felt awful. But I also felt that I had to be truthful: "Yes, that is the custom that men and initiated teenagers sometimes followed before."

Shaking their heads in disbelief, they stressed, as if it needed emphasis, that *adameni* had nothing to do with sex between men or boys; it was for men with women. What about *oop*? This wasn't semen, they said; it was a thick liquid, but it smelled sweet and tasted good. It was something that a man would dab about his eyes. When a woman looked at him, she would be attracted. Evidently, *adameni* was a love potion. In fact, they asserted, it came from Whites and not from Papua New Guineans, including at the logging camp where Wayabay had worked. *Adameni* came in a bottle and was quite expensive, but Whites said that it really worked. The bottles had a picture of a naked man and woman on the label—just like in the Bible.

Gracious! *Adameni* wasn't a Gebusi word. It was their pronunciation of "Adam and Eve!"—an expensive love potion. Unscrupulous traders peddled it in bottles promising biblical sex and lovely sin—which Wayabay now wanted to attract a wife.

So they asked again, "Do you have any *adameni*? And if not, can you get some?" They all believed in this love potion, almost desperately in Wayabay's case. How to answer? I had already embarrassed both them and myself. For a moment, I thought of boosting Wayabay's confidence by giving him scented skin cream to dab on his cheekbones. But I quickly dismissed this as a bad idea: I had already caused enough confusion for one day! So I said I didn't have any *adameni*. Disappointed but at least in mutual understanding, we finished our conversation and they left.

If Gebusi culture had been hard for me to learn in 1980, I realized that it could still chew up my seasoned understandings with plenty of spit left over. I was still surprised, challenged, and sometimes at sea. During 16 years, Gebusi young men had gone from having sex with one another to apparently not even knowing about the practice. Could this really be? If they hadn't been directly exposed to or told about it, their knowledge would have been hazy, and in a Christian context, excluded. Compare it with our own knowledge of sexual practices among our forebears—including our typical ignorance about types of sexual practice that our own parents may or may not have indulged in. Like many peoples, Gebusi distinguish between things that are explicitly experienced or transmitted and those that are only implied or uncertain. In this sense, Wayabay, Sayu, and Didiga had probably not known about sex between Gebusi men. Until I had told them.

As a 44-year-old, I was one of the older men in the community. It was not uncommon for me to know more about Gebusi family ancestries, based on my early genealogies and life histories, than younger Gebusi did. The gap between young men's knowledge and my own concerning traditional Gebusi sex practices was hence not completely surprising.

Beyond the shock and apparent unawareness of my companions, it was clear, as bachelors, that they were far more concerned about sexual attraction with women than with other men. Before, male–male sex had itself been a prelude to marriage: a young man who had "become big" at the costumed initiation was attractive to women by his very presence; within a few months, all the initiates had found wives and were married. But now this custom was gone, along with much of men's social life. As I was finding out, the same seemed true of women's desire and obligation to marry through sister-exchange. Whereas more than half of women's first marriages had previously satisfied the demands of marital reciprocity, not one of the 16 marriages in the community between 1982 and 1998 was considered a sister-exchange. In short, men could no longer count on the splendor of ritual attraction or obligations of kinship and reciprocity to obtain a wife. Increasingly, young men were on their own; they had to attract a wife through more modern forms of courtship.

Wayabay had not been successful in this regard. He was several years past the age of normal marriage and was among the small minority of young men who had not taken interest in activities associated with the Nomad Station. He played soccer and rugby only intermittently and awkwardly, would not dance to Papua New Guinea "disco music," did not sing in the community's contemporary string band, and had not been baptized and did not go to church. Instead, Wayabay honed traditional skills and spent long periods hunting in the forest and building a house in the village. He was unusually devoted to traditional customs and was proud of his ability to travel to remote feasts and initiations and dance in full costume. In all, Wayabay was a good traditionalist born a generation too late. In this context, *adameni* was a hopeful substitute for the alluring male initiation costume that Wayabay would never wear.

Gebusi men who were most successful at attracting girlfriends and brides, by contrast, were more locally modern. They could joke with some facility in *Tok Pisin*, had been to school for a few years, and gravitated toward the lifestyle of Nomad Station. They finagled a little money and managed to sport a jaunty baseball cap, sunglasses, or colorful shirt. Perhaps they even had a boom box on which they could play cassettes of rock music. They enjoyed playing rugby and soccer if not also dancing to disco music, and they were comfortable interacting casually with those from other communities. For Wayabay, however, being locally modern was difficult. He could kill a wild boar in the forest but he couldn't shoot the modern breeze.

Even for bachelors who were more self-assured, modern courtship could be stressful. On one occasion, Sayu and Didiga worked up the courage to go to a disco at the far edge of the Nomad Station. Wayabay himself was too reserved to go. I went with them to see what it was about—this alluring prospect of not just seeing marriageable women from another community but possibly dancing with them to disco music. This hoped-for attraction was constantly sung about in music cassettes and by the Gasumi guitar-and-ukulele quartet. The goal was to captivate a woman not by traditional display but with modern confidence and aplomb—talking to her directly and even gyrating with her publicly in contemporary dance.

Kamul [l] and Wayabay [r] dressed for a traditional village dance, 1998.

Disco dancing competition at the Nomad Independence Day celebrations, 1998.

The risks of this endeavor stoked hesitation as well as desire. In fact, we never got to the disco. We approached it at night, stealthily, as if stalking a wild animal. We crept slowly and noiselessly down the path, the boldest in the lead. Whispered discussion ensued every few yards as to whether we should go forward with this chance for public display and humiliation. Flashlights were turned off so no one would see us. We strained to hear if any music was in the distance. Eventually, we turned back, too nervous to proceed. During six months and several concerted attempts, I never did manage to attend a disco on the far side of Nomad Station.

The awkwardness of contemporary romance reflected not just new standards of courtship but new material demands for young men—for colorful clothes, sunglasses, shoes, and boom boxes with cassettes. Failing these, men may crave a manufactured elixir with a naked man and woman on the bottle, a potion that, with a magical splash about the eyes, could attract women. In many if not most parts of the world, teenagers covet goods and music that convey a modern aura of romance and sexual attraction. I remember a story on National Public Radio about a Brazilian woman who canoed into the upper reaches of the Amazon and made quite a profit selling Avon products like makeup and deodorant to Indians in the rainforest.

For young Gebusi men, desire for modern commodities is complicated by economic pressures to pay brideprice or bridewealth. Failing sister-exchange marriage, the brothers or fathers of young women said they would be satisfied only with a large cash payment from the would-be groom. In many areas of the world—including parts of Africa and South Asia as well as the South Pacific—inflated demands for bridewealth or dowry cause major problems for young people who want to get married. Fortunately for young Gebusi men, the amount of money they actually pay is comparatively low: for first marriages in Gasumi Corners between 1982 and 1998, the average bride payment was only 56 kina, or 28 dollars. But even this small amount was difficult for many young men to amass. And demands by a prospective father-in-law or brother-in-law easily increased a groom's sense of inadequacy.

Gebusi courtship was thus sandwiched between a rhetorical mandate for sister-exchange, inflated claims for bridewealth, desire for commodities, and the demands of modern styles of interaction. Bachelors in Gasumi Corners lamented that they would never get married. How did they find wives in fact? In large part through the idiosyncrasies of romantic attraction. In the present as in the past, attractions between a young man and woman could lead to marriage over the objections of her father or her brothers. But now, with a reduced sense of kinship obligation, and without the display of ritual attraction, romantic marriage seemed both the primary way of getting married and increasingly stressful for young men.

The special stresses that young women in Gasumi Corners were also under became dramatically evident in one attempt that was made to arrange a traditional sister-exchange marriage between two clans. . . .

Gami was 16, full-bodied, vivacious, and, if anything, readier for marriage than her slightly built older "brother," Moka. Her intended husband was Guyul, a cheerful, strapping bachelor about 21 years old. Guyul's sister was the comely and straightforward Kubwam, herself a mature 16-year-old prime for marriage. Much was made of the fact that Gami's "brother" would be marrying her groom's sister—a classic sister-exchange marriage.

Following spicy rumors that spread through the village, the courtship of the two young couples became official. Following Gebusi custom, each young woman was "seized" by the wrist and led away by a male kinsman of her husband-to-be. Kubwam appeared a bit forlorn, which is proper etiquette for a woman taken in marriage. But Gami could hardly keep from smiling despite her presumed sobriety. The four new spouses were made to sit together and were exhorted to keep their obligations to each other as husbands and wives. It was not simply a double marriage but an exchange among the four of them, and everything was going according to plan.

The two women, Gami and Kubwam, swapped residences across the four-minute walk that separated their husbands' respective households in Gasumi Corners. Each extended family simultaneously gained a daughter-in-law while losing a daughter. The two mothers-in-law made special efforts to ensure that the incoming brides felt welcome and at home. I paid visits to both households and gave small gifts. With her typical pleasant reserve, Kubwam seemed comfortable in Moka's household. And Gami was practically ebullient with Guyul's family; she smiled broadly and engaged eagerly with his kin.

The first crack in the arrangement surfaced after just a day and a half. Moka started spending time away from his new wife, going off with the remaining bachelors. Not yet 20 years old, Moka was still "young" to get married, and younger husbands sometimes took a while to settle into their new role. Though his marriage was not yet consummated, Moka's new wife, Kubwam, continued to live in his household. By itself, Moka's equivocation presented only a small wrinkle, not a major cause for alarm.

On the other side of Gasumi Corners, Gami's relationship with Guyul started off like a rocket. She had been the village belle—friendly, flirtatious, buxom, and with a thousand-watt smile. When Gami and Guyul went off together to garden and came back with moony dispositions and euphoric smiles, village gossip was ribald and irrepressible: they had consummated their marriage.

But this happiness did not last. Exactly what went wrong I never learned, least of all from Gami or Guyul themselves. But signals pointed to an abrupt U-turn in their sexual compatibility. Gami's disposition turned suddenly from sweet to sour. She wouldn't look at her husband, wouldn't work in his household, and wouldn't eat. She tried to go back to her adopted mother's home but was forced back to her husband's house. She tried again, but was again forced back. Still she refused to cooperate and returned yet again to her own family home. No entreaty made headway; no inquiry bore fruit. "Who knows what goes on in a young woman's heart or mind?!" "Gami is just stubborn and 'bigheaded.'" "She just won't be married." But why? "Just because," I was told repeatedly. "That's just the way she is."

As the hours passed, Gami's recalcitrance fueled increasing anger against her. It is a serious matter for a Gebusi woman to consummate her marriage and then repudiate it. That a woman could have sex with a husband she had publicly accepted and then reject him after a few days of romance struck against the heart of Gebusi morality. Not only was Gami's virtue on the line but also the manhood and self-esteem of her husband, Guyul. The stakes were yet higher because the marriage was a sister-exchange; Gami's rejection of Guyul also compromised the union between her "brother," Moka, and Guyul's sister, Kubwam. If her marriage dissolved, her brother's would also be forfeited.

In short order, everyone turned against Gami. Her new husband disdained her, and her mother-in-law was incensed. Her adopted mother was even more furious, as was Moka. Her "mother" slapped her, her "brother" beat her, and she endured a barrage of verbal abuse. "What is WRONG with you?!" "You are good for NOTHING!" "Guyul is a fine man!" "You think you can just 'open your skirt' and then say you won't be married?! Huh? HUH?" "Don't you care about your 'brother'?" "Don't you care about your 'mother'?" "No one in this village will protect you." "Where are you going to find a new husband? Do you think any man would want you now? Huh? HUH?" "You are alone, no one cares about you." "You can't stay here. You have no home here. You are finished."

Gami never once explained and never argued back. But she wouldn't budge, wouldn't go back to Guyul. As the hours mounted into a second day, the tension worsened. Women from other households took up the banner of village honor. Senior women badgered Gami in every way they could think of. Finally, Moka had had enough. He grabbed Gami and dragged her out the door of his house. She shrieked and screamed, refusing to leave. Heavier and at least as strong as he, she held her ground. But as Moka grabbed one of her arms, his mother and another man took hold of the other. Gami was dragged screaming and crying, feet trailing and flailing. By the time they had hauled her 15 feet from her house, she was covered in mud and bloody scrapes. Still she refused to cooperate. They pulled her by the hair, but she would not give in. Panting and screaming, they told her she could lie there and rot.

Then a senior woman came over. She was someone, here nameless, whom I otherwise liked and admired, but whom it was hard to forgive. She silently walked up to Gami, leaned down, and talked to her in low tones. Watching from my doorstep, I had a sinking feeling that I knew what she was saying, and my suspicion was later verified. It was terrible to have seen Gami hit and dragged. But it is almost unimaginable for a young woman to be threatened with a public stripping. For Gebusi, this idea is so deeply shameful as to be a kind of social death—never forgotten, never expunged. And it is triply so for a nubile young woman. It was true that Gami had badly misjudged the game and the stakes of her marriage. Her girlish flirtation and mature body had led her into the four-sided vice of sister-exchange. At first, she had complied enthusiastically, but then realized her decision was an appalling mistake that she would now risk everything to repudiate. This new threat, however, made her resistance too costly. After a minute or two, Gami got up and walked lifelessly back to Guyul's household.

I assumed that would be the end of the story, that both unhappy marriages would stay intact. But I was wrong. Though Gami stayed in Guyul's household, she would not respond or cooperate in any way. She stayed defiant, a living dead person. In exasperation, her relatives took the matter to a higher authority, the Nomad police. As chance would have it, I was at the station studying the police register when they trooped in. The village men and a Nomad police constable sat Gami down in a chair, surrounded her, and began their inquisition. "Why won't you marry this man?" "Why did you have sex with him and then refuse him?" "Do you really want to reject your own family?" "What are you going to do if you don't stay married to Guyul?" "We can bring charges to put you in jail for immoral conduct." I thought Gami would certainly crack. Alone, she faced the most powerful men not just in the village but at the Nomad Station. But she refused even to speak. Her only words were "I don't know" and "I don't want to." She hung her head and sobbed. Fortunately, the men did not touch or strike her. I don't know if my presence deterred them. But I was knotted up, frustrated at not being able to intervene. Ultimately, they gave up in desperation and returned Gami to our settlement. A public meeting was then held in Gasumi Corners. The invective again started as people debated what steps to take next. They also aired opinions about the morality of young women in the village in general—how shameless and loose they had become.

I had never made a speech at a Gebusi public meeting; I had never felt it my place to do so. And my mastery of Gebusi language was never good enough to wrap myself in their rhetoric. But this time I felt I had no choice. I knew I couldn't change Gebusi customs, alter Gami's predicament, or impose my will on theirs. Still, these were people I had lived with. They were my friends. And I thought what they were doing to Gami was wrong. As I got up to speak, I started to tremble. It was like first speech you make in junior high school when you can't remember the words and you know your voice and bearing betray your awkwardness. But I had to continue. What I said, or at least what I tried to say, was that those in the village had to respect their own custom—the custom that no one can ultimately force a woman to be married. Even in the old days, I said, some women had refused to be married. No matter what anyone had done, and no matter even what the women themselves had done, they had simply refused. I alluded to some of the failed first marriages of the people sitting around me, including some of the older women who had berated Gami. I reminded them that they, too, had ultimately refused the men they had been pressured to marry. The police, I said, respected the same custom, following the laws of Papua New Guinea. People could try to persuade a woman to marry, but they could not force her. That was all.

I don't know if my words had any effect. I was too nervous to judge people's reactions or to recall things clearly afterward. I wasn't saying anything heretical but merely putting into words the reality that I hoped they would accept—and that they were grudgingly beginning to accept anyway. Then I did something else that I had never done before. After the meeting was over, I asked to talk with Gami. Alone. Of all the things I have intentionally done with Gebusi before or since, this was the most awkward. An unrelated man simply does not talk with an unmarried woman alone—especially one like Gami, who bore the stigma of sexual impropriety. In addition, Gami had been a flirtatious and endearing young woman. Anthropology is littered with tales of well-meaning White men who scheme to help attractive women of color, only to unwittingly leave them worse than they were to begin with. So I had to be very clear about my motives.

My request related to Gami's family situation. Her father had died and her biological mother had remarried. This woman was now living near the town of Kiunga with her new husband; she was the only woman in the community to have left the Nomad area. Without money for the airfare, Gami had been left behind with her adoptive mother. Now, however, Gami's true mother was the one person who might have cared enough to help her. I knew Gami's mother from before and thought she was a good person. Because Gami could not read or write, I thought she might like me to write a letter to her mother in Kiunga—to communicate with her and solicit help. This practice is not unusual in many parts of Papua New Guinea. When I had previously visited male inmates at the national prison in Port Moresby, many of them had immediately accepted my offer to write letters on their behalf to send to their families back home. In some ways, I thought, Gami was now a prisoner in Gasumi Corners.

Apart from this, there was something else that I wanted to communicate. I wanted to tell Gami that I didn't think she was a bad or wicked person. Many young women struggle to find a man they can live with. I wanted to tell her I thought she had courage to stand up for herself. I knew

I was on cultural thin ice. I had no idea if these words would make sense or if they would backfire. But I had to try. And there was no way I could talk to her with other villagers intervening.

In the village clearing, I told Gami's adoptive mother and the others gathered there that I needed to talk to Gami, alone. They looked at me, and I looked back at them. I told them not to worry, that I was only an "old man" and that we wouldn't be long. My excuse was that Gami had never shown me the abandoned spur settlement, just 200 yards away, where her true mother had previously lived. I thought this might be a good place for her to think of her mother and to tell me anything she wanted me to write in a letter. I was touched that the villagers trusted me enough to let Gami go off with me. Gami herself had been through the wringer already, and who knows what she thought now. She had every reason to be scared of any new development, and she was, in culturally appropriate fashion, reluctant to go with me. To my distress, her relatives now gruffly ordered her to accompany me to her mother's old settlement.

As I walked slowly out of our hamlet, Gami trailed a good 15 feet behind. My first thought was to wait for her and say something innocuous. But when I slowed, so did she. It got worse when a 12-year-old boy crossed paths with us. Gami and I were the spitting image of a married couple—adult man up front and younger wife following behind. The boy was incredulous. I mumbled that Gami was going to show me her mother's house and that her adopted mother had said it was okay. As we neared the site, a second boy appeared. I repeated the story. But he was too captivated by the sight of Gami with me to be easily deterred. Even as I told him to move along, I could see him scurry away and watch from the bushes.

My conversation with Gami took place close to the main path and was very short. We stood about a dozen feet apart—as close as we ever got. Both of us looked at the ground or anywhere except at each other. I said that I was sorry for her. I said I thought she was not a bad person, but a person who had much inside that was good. I said, without repeating the obvious, I knew she had "worries." Then I said I had known her mother and I knew she was now living near Kiunga. And I asked her if she wanted me to write a letter to her mother—to see if she or other members of her family could help. Nervously, Gami said simply, "No." I continued, "Is there anything else you would like to say? Is there anything you would like to talk about or that I might do?" She replied again, "No." I responded,

"That's fine. I just wanted to ask. We'll leave it go." Then we walked directly back to the village. Gami took the lead, walking much faster than she had before.

I will never know if my awkward attempt to help Gami was an abject failure or merely a nominal one. Perhaps the idea of telling one's long-lost mother about one's moral indiscretions and predicament wasn't that appealing. Perhaps I was guilty of cultural insensitivity or of taking license against Gebusi norms of gendered interaction. I could not know and could only hope that some part of Gami sensed, amid my own indiscretion, that I was trying to help her. The best of intentions can sometimes have the worst of results. But I had to try.

What conclusions can we draw? On a personal level, my engagement with Gami and also with Wayabay led me into the uncertain territory of trying to help or intervene with Gebusi. In addition to being researchers, anthropologists are people who sometimes feel compelled to act on behalf of those they are studying. But we can't know the consequences of our actions or even if good intentions will be recognized. It seems as important as it is difficult to balance our positive intent against the specter of unanticipated outcomes. Western intervention among foreign peoples has often spawned unfortunate results, even when the intent was noble. Beyond the colonialism of the past, many large and expensive international aid projects in Africa, Asia, Latin America, and the Pacific have created little long-term benefit. Sometimes they have done greater harm than good to local people. As a caution against this potential, a sense of humility and an awareness of our own limitations—as researchers, as advocates, and as human beings—remain important.

In ethnographic terms, Gami's case and that of Wayabay illustrate the challenges Gebusi faced in trying to find marriage partners during a period of heightened modern influence, personal choice, and potential risk. In many parts of the world, personal options are expanding, including for women. Relative to unions arranged or pressured by kin and relatives, "marriage by choice" or "companionate marriage" is generally on the rise. Gami's and Wayabay's plights illustrate this larger pattern in Gasumi Corners from complementary male and female perspectives.

Modern ways of choosing a partner build on the spine of determination, physical attraction, and romance that women and men have for each other, even as the stakes of personal choice are ratcheted up. Who can say if women or men are happier as a result? But in a world of modern alternatives, the lives of young men and women are increasingly shaped by the intended or unintended consequences of their own actions, beyond those of family and kin.

Amid the clash of choice and constraint, some predicaments work out better than one might have guessed. This was finally the case for Gami and also for Wayabay. Despite their respective trials, each of them ended up finding an acceptable spouse after I left the field. In each case, their partner carried a history of difficult choices in the village that complemented their own. In December 2001, I received the following in a letter from Gasumi Corners written on behalf of Sayu: "Wayabay got married already to Gami. And ready to deliver baby." Long live their lives together. Long live their resilience.

Update: Wayabay and Gami have stayed married, and as of 2013, they had five children. Since the time of their marriage, the world of the Gebusi has surprisingly returned, at least in part, to that with which Wayabay was more comfortable; Gebusi have been reorienting more to the rainforest and away from activities associated with Nomad Station. Sister-exchange marriage also seems to have changed in valence. In 1998, men were primed to receive material compensation for sisters or daughters given in marriage. But with the later decline in the local monied economy, expectations and demands of brideprice have ebbed. Though updated information would verify the point, it seems that diverse paths of kinship connection are again being used to define marriages, at least in hindsight, as based on "exchange" between more various kin categories of "brother" and "sister."

Male–male sexuality still appears vestigial or absent among Gebusi. And yet, the idea of men having sex with men seems less anathema or taboo than it did in the late 1990s, when Gebusi avidly pursued both Christian beliefs and modern styles of courtship. Male sexual joking and camaraderie have certainly rebounded since the 1990s; these are now alive and well. With the continuing dearth of spirit séances and initiations, though, the ritual structure and cultural impetus for sexual relations between men is absent. Gebusi men have always been *hetero*sexual in overall emphasis and ultimate orientation, and this continues. But also continuing historic trends, men are now again highly homo*social* in their relations with each other, even though they are no longer homo*sexual*. Whatever male–male sexuality does take place—and this is probably infrequent or rare—occurs not as a social norm but as a private individual practice.

Finally, the tenor of courtship seems to have mellowed. Though begging more information, it seems women and men now have neither the traditional mandate of ritualized attraction, from the 1980s and before, nor the heightened expectation of money and modern allure from the 1990s. Young men and women continue to wrestle with issues of "exchange" or "compensation" as they become attracted and get married. But on the whole, the stakes and their stress seem less than they did before.

Note: As also for Chapter 5, see Gebusi video clips of and commentary on Gebusi male–male social and sexual relations ("Sexuality") and gender relations ("Gender") in 2013 on www.bruceknauft.com → Gebusi.

BROADER CONNECTIONS
Ethical Challenges, Agency, and "Companionate Marriage"

- Like cultural anthropologists generally, Bruce invariably confronted challenges of **ethics** during his fieldwork with Gebusi.
- Among Gebusi, as in many societies, young people have adopted modern customs that include greater individual **agency** in courtship and marriage.
- Bruce's response to Wayabay's request for *adameni*, and his interaction with Gami, both reveal:
  — Anthropologists may be surprised and ignorant even when they think they know a culture well.
  — Good intentions in fieldwork can still lead to awkwardness or misunderstanding.
  — Local people are often forgiving of an anthropologist's unwitting mistakes.
- As in many societies, marriage among Gebusi came to rely on personal attraction and modern courtship rather than on traditional gender roles or ritual association.

- Common with patterns in many societies, the attempted sister-exchange marriage between four Gebusi young people in 1998 revealed:
  — The modern difficulty of arranged marriages
  — Increasing **female choice**
  — Resilience of women against others' opinions
  — Increased emphasis on mutually acceptable **companionate marriage**
  — Continuing moral **stigma** against **sexual misconduct**
- Bruce's actions with Gami illustrate:
  — Anthropologists sometimes feel compelled to act as members of their field community.
  — It is important to use caution and humility when intervening.
  — It is vital to ask local people for their own opinion/s.
  — Creative solutions by local people—such as the final marriage described in this chapter—often work better than interventions by outsiders.
- Changes since 1998 suggest, regarding sex and marriage, that Gebusi at present:
  — Continue to have male social bonding and homo*social* camaraderie.
  — Rarely engage in sexual relations between men themselves.
  — Are somewhat more flexible than they were in defining marriage as an "exchange" between wider groups of kin.
  — Have somewhat less stress and anxiety than they previously did concerning modern forms of courtship and marital compensation.

Chapter 10

Sayu's Dance and After

Sayu sidled ahead of me, down the trail and into the dawn. Daybreak bathed us with its softest light as we returned from the night-long festivity. The previous evening, in a rare expression of fading custom, Sayu had been the visiting dancer at the distant village of Kotiey. In traditional costume, painted and plumed, he enacted the spirits of old in full splendor, to the beat of his crocodile drum. His jaw had been as firm as the pearl shell just beneath it, his eyes as bright as the red bird-of-paradise he had become.

As we walked back to Gasumi Corners, I remembered Sayu from 16 years before, when he had been five years old. His impish smile had lit his face like the sun rippling through cracks in the forest canopy. His play had been as full of Gebusi tradition as it could be. He would wrap his small body in leaves, smear soot on his face, and put a feather in his hair. Swelling with whimsy, he would take a length of bamboo as a make-believe drum and dance resplendently at an imaginary feast. Or lisp a fetching echo to the men's séance songs at night. Or pretend to marry a little girl in sister-exchange. Or cook sago to divine and accuse a make-believe sorcerer. More than any other child, Sayu had been in our house and in our lives at Yibihilu. Now, this dancer of childhood returned home with me at a new dawn in this rainforest of memories.

After my first years with him, Sayu's life had not been at all as I had thought it would be. About three years after we had left, his young father, Silap, died. About two years after *that*, his fun-loving mother, Boyl, also

169

died. She had since remarried and had been foraging deep in the bush
with Sayu, who was then about 11, and his younger brother, Huwa, who
was about five. Far from the settlement, and before they could return, she
fell suddenly and fatally ill. Alone, the two boys had cried and clutched
their mother as she writhed in agony and died in the night.

A search party later found them and carried Boyl's body back to the
village. Sayu's new stepfather, Doliay, was enraged by the death, and he participated in Boyl's sorcery inquest with great intensity. Shortly afterward, as
described in Chapter 7, he avenged her death by beheading Basowey.

When Doliay departed to serve his long prison term, Sayu and Huwa
were left as orphans back at Gasumi Corners. To a great extent, they raised
themselves. Six years later, following a dispute in the village, Sayu left to
embark on a young man's adventure. At age 17, he walked 80 miles to the
town of Kiunga—through lands he had never seen and enemy groups he
had never encountered. Kiunga was the district capital of 3,000 people, a
muddy gateway to the modern world, and the emerald city to those in the
forest. Quick and resourceful, Sayu finagled work as a domestic helper and
"houseboy." He lived the life of a successful teenager in town: washing
dishes, doing laundry, running errands—and learning to live in his
employer's house, ride a bike, watch satellite TV, and dance disco. Two
years later, he returned to the outskirts of Nomad, where his treasured
boom box broadcast music to everyone's delight. He had become a dandy.
But he remained thoughtful and worked hard.

When I returned to the Gebusi, two and a half years later, in 1998,
Sayu quickly became my companion, helper, and confidant, along with
Didiga, who was a good friend to both of us. I helped support them,
and we shared many good times. On one occasion, Sayu delicately with-
drew from a budding relationship with a flirtatious young woman in
Gasumi Corners. Although their relationship had not become physical,
the woman's father and brother suspected otherwise. The next day,
while Sayu and I were doing chores, her male relatives charged into our
clearing, brandishing bows and arrows. Sayu and I stood side by side
and turned to face them. I told myself to remain appropriately passive
but defiant. Livid, the young woman's brother came at us in a dead run.
As he closed to about 20 feet, he cocked his bow, drew back his arrow,
and snapped his bowstring at us. Then he veered away. I knew well
enough from my days at Yibihilu that this was merely a display of

aggression, and I bore him no anger. We all laughed about it days later. But my spine had stiffened at the time. At a public meeting, the village councilor concluded that the woman's brother and father had been wrong to intimidate us; they had to pay a fine to Sayu for falsely accusing him of impropriety.

My many memories of Sayu linked back to the present as I walked back with him from his all-night dance at Kotiey. He had danced until dawn for the first time, not to disco, as he had before, but in stately traditional costume. He had become an impressive and handsome young man in an indigenous as well as a modern sense. As his friend and part-parent, I felt a surge of pride and affection for him. I thought how deeply pleased Sayu's parents would have been to see him now. I told him what I felt: that my eyes had seen his traditional dancing with the happy heart-spirit of his dead father and his dead mother. Suddenly, I teared up. His lip quivered. I turned away so as not to cry.

The drama of the night receded slowly with the dark. Dawn approached as the trail took us back to Gasumi Corners, where traditional dancing was all but dead. On our way we walked by the Nomad Station, winding our way past its airstrip. As the light was growing brighter, I could see that Sayu's pearl shell was now crooked, his feathers skewed, and the red ocher paint smudged on his taut skin. Even on Saturday morning, he was concerned that someone from Nomad might see him in the grass skirt of a traditional dancer. Although he had been the center of ceremonial attention during the night, this had been at an old forest village. Slipping behind a shrub, Sayu exchanged his grass skirt for a pair of shorts. Now hybrid, he left the signs of his dancing on his upper body while keeping the security of Western clothes below. Around his neck, he now hung the blue beads and cross of his Catholic baptism.

As Sayu had anticipated, we met others along the way. We snapped fingers with them firmly before finally reaching Gasumi Corners, where we were greeted by those who had not made the trek. They wanted to hear the recordings I had made of the festivity. As the recorder played, we listened to the men's joking, Sayu's drumming and dance rattles, and the women's traditional singing. But there were other sounds that I had barely heard amid my focus on Sayu: the guitar and ukulele of the evening's string band, and the rock and roll of a Papua New Guinea band that one of the visitors played on a boom box. The clash of musical styles had mirrored the mix of celebrants in that old longhouse. Some had adorned themselves in leaves, body paint, and beautiful bird feathers. Others had sported a colorful shirt or hat, or even sunglasses in the night. Still others had mixed and matched cheerfully—a collage of body paint here, Western clothing there, a headdress on a hat. They had drifted through shadows thrown alternately by traditional resin torches and modern wick lanterns. All of them had paused appreciatively and even gratefully for my flashing camera, as if my modern photography would validate their hybrid tradition.

Listening to the recorded music, the men of Gasumi Corners talked of getting dressed up themselves in indigenous costumes—but not for a traditional ritual. Instead, they wondered if they could scrape together enough decorations to perform in costume for the government-sponsored contest that would be held at the Nomad Station on Independence Day. Competing communities would stage reenactments of their indigenous dances. Officials would judge the performances and award prize money to those they thought were best. The men of Gasumi Corners wanted to have at least some chance to be among the winners. They mused that maybe they would dress up Wayabay or one of their other bachelors in the full regalia of initiation—even though these men had not been initiated and never would be.

Listening to the recording and then to the men, I felt in a time warp between the past and the present. Partly this was from a lack of sleep. All-night feasts make me woozy the day after, as they do many Gebusi. By traditional design, staying up all night mixes things up and turns them back to front; the spirits of the dark meld with the humans of the day; the performance of the present enacts the cosmos of the past. But now the spirits had not just vanished with the morning mist; they seemed to be gone forever from Gasumi Corners. It was now midday on Saturday. Only a few men from our village had gone to the feast; most were now preparing to leave for the ball games at Nomad. Tomorrow, we would sing praises to God in the hot Sunday sun. Then there would be more rugby and soccer. When the men returned from the ball field on Sunday evening, their children would be going to bed so they could be up and off early Monday

Singing in
the Sunday
Catholic Church
service, 1998
[Sayu is second
from the left].

morning for a full day of school. As I drifted to sleep, I wondered if my memories of Sayu's dance were already fading. I realized I was now immersed in the changing of Gebusi culture, new meanings and connections embraced by Gebusi themselves.

The following day, my schedule returned to normal. But I didn't know what to expect during the coming weeks. Independence Day was soon, and ceremonial life would be taking another turn. Would the festivities be traditional, modern, or somewhere in between? Everything now seemed geared to this next celebration. This was true even at Yulabi, a remote Gebusi settlement where a large initiation was being held. The arrangements were timed so their ceremonies would take place just one week before the national holiday. This would allow their new initiates to get dressed up again and parade in full regalia before officials at the Nomad Station on Independence Day.

In Gasumi Corners, preparations for the national celebration also intensified. Young men talked excitedly about their local genre of so-called string band singing. A quartet of young men from Gasumi Corners had formed a singing group that featured two guitars, a ukulele, and a medley of original songs. The leader was Yamda, Nelep's son, and the other singers were Sayu, his younger brother, Huwa, and Kawuk's son, Howe. They performed one night in the village. And I was blown away. The songs were as stunning and soulful as those of the young boys I had heard earlier singing in the tree. Their tone was even crisper, soaring with rich melodies, undulating rhythms, and resonant harmonies. Hard as it was for me to admit it, their new genre was more beautiful than the séance singing of old. The songs drew important threads from traditional singing, including haunting nasal tones, falsetto harmonies, and surging refrains. But their quickened tempo, lighter lilt, and instrumental accompaniment rang clearly modern. The lyrics of the songs borrowed variously from Gebusi, English, *Tok Pisin*, the vernaculars of neighboring ethnic groups, and even phrases that had somehow been transmitted from distant New Guinean languages that very few Gebusi could translate. As in séance singing, the songs compressed poetic images that were evocative, longing, and nostalgic; they were short on content but lovingly repeated. Most of them involved contemporary contexts such as school, work, and romance. The following song was especially popular:

> *I go to school.*
> *I look at my friend from before.*
> *She looks at me and I look at her.*
> *Her eyes fill with tears.*
> *Why did you come to tease me?*

Unlike séance singing, which had been spontaneous, string band songs were carefully rehearsed. When people of Gasumi Corners gathered in the evening to hear them, they were not communing with spirits but listening to a musical performance. There was no spirit medium, no dialogue with spirit women, and no divination for sickness or sorcery. Although some senior men might call out in emotional response, the audience overall was attentive and respectful. [For music clips, see www.bruceknauft.com → Gebusi].

As the string band intensified its practice, other men tried to locate traditional costume parts. How would they use them? Judging from their winks, nods, and smiles, it almost seemed as if each man had his own plan. Sports practices also increased, and there was talk of fierce competition on the ball field. So, too, there was reference to plans for disco dancing, "dramas," and a host of humorous as well as serious games.

If initiations had previously been the biggest and grandest spectacles of Gebusi culture, the celebrations of National Independence Day at the Nomad Station had, by 1998, supplanted them. But these festivities would include more people than the Gebusi. Along with Gebusi dancing, athleticism, music, and dramatic skits were those of other ethnic groups that ringed the Nomad Station: Bedamini, Kubor, Samo, Oybae, Honibo, and even distant peoples such as the Pa and the Kabasi. Nomad was at this time the thriving administrative center for some 9,000 people scattered across 3,500 square miles of rainforest—and many of those within one- or two-days' walk came to attend. Gebusi culture was now to be presented as part of a regional interethnic festival linked, in turn, to the independence of the nation as a whole. I realized my conception of Gebusi culture was expanding to include a host of wider identifications, meanings, and institutions. Anthropologists often look to rituals of display as key expressions of a culture's values and history. As cultures interconnect, these associations increase—and the lines between them can blur. Gebusi meanings, identities, and values of culture had become at once regional, national, and even international in scale.

Ultimately, Independence Day at Nomad featured a week of festivities and celebrations. More than 1,000 people attended. Ceremonies began with two days of team sports on the Nomad ball field, escalating through several rounds and climaxing in all-star games that pitted the best players from different ethnic groups against each other. For Gebusi, their key matches were against the Bedamini—the much larger ethnic group that had raided and decimated their villages. Though pacification had stopped this, Bedamini retained a reputation for fierceness. But Gebusi had the advantage of close proximity to Nomad, where they could practice and play league sports on a regular basis. They were also playing on their home field. At the end of the competition, the headline could have read, "David beats Goliath!" In an amazing coup, Gebusi won all except one of their matches against Bedamini. Their defeated rivals were frustrated and angry enough to accuse Gebusi of sabotaging them with magic. But government officials upheld their victories. How did Gebusi respond? Though I expected a big celebration and at least a little gloating, Gebusi were subdued and circumspect. They worried that Bedamini might take revenge by breaking into the little store that we had started in Gasumi Corners or break into my own house. Their response was similar to their actions on the field: even-keeled and sportsmanlike.

As "Independence Day" unfolded, I struggled to keep up. There was excited talk of "dramas." What could these be? As dusk turned into night, a large performance area was roped off next to the government station. Hundreds of people amassed to watch the performances. And when they started, what a shock! Most of them were spoofs, farces, and parodies of local traditions acted out by villagers themselves. In one skit, a man in random black paint, and wearing an old cassowary headdress and loin-cloth, groaned buffoonishly as he tried with clumsy effort to hack down a tiny tree using a traditional stone ax. Though his efforts were futile, his slapstick antics were really quite funny, and the audience roared with laughter. The man's sardonic companion smoked a traditional pipe and refused to help cut the tree until they got into a fight. At the end of the skit, the performers explained its "meaning" in *Tok Pisin* over a battery-operated bullhorn: "In the old days, we were ignorant. We didn't know about steel axes. We tried to chop trees with stone axes, but it didn't work and we got angry and fought with each other."

In skit after skit, one or another traditional practice or belief was skewered for the audience's delight. Many customs portrayed were ones I had seen quite genuinely in 1980–82. Rites once performed with dignity and grace—magic spells, origin myths, fish poisoning rituals, spirit séances, divinations, and dances—were transformed into farce. What bittersweet comedy! As an anthropologist, it was sad to see such a mockery of rich local traditions—by the very people who used to practice them. And yet, the skits were very funny, sometimes uproariously so. I fought back tears of laughter even as I felt pangs of nostalgia for customs I had witnessed "for real" just 16 years before.

For me, the most dramatic skit was performed by friends from Gasumi Corners: a spoof of sickness, death, and sorcery divination. The opening performer was Mora—the teenager who had sought to be my romantic partner in 1981 and who was now a senior man with several children. He was caked with mud and wore a large fake phallus strapped around his waist. Smoking continually from a traditional tobacco pipe, he wheezed and coughed loudly until, in a spasm of sickness, he toppled over with a loud thud. This attracted the attention of a spirit medium, played by Yamdaw, the son of Nelep. Yamdaw's costume was absurdly traditional, including an upside-down cassowary headdress and a bark belt that was so oversized that it slid down whenever he got up. Mora then cried that he was going to die. This prompted Yamdaw to screech directly into his ear— a traditional way to forestall a friend from losing consciousness. These efforts were futile, and Mora quickly "died." After farcical wailing, a sor- cery suspect was paraded up to Mora's corpse. The suspect was Kawuk, a senior man of Gasumi Corners and staunch supporter of the Catholic Church. (During the early years of colonial influence, Kawuk had, in fact, killed a family of three—a husband and wife accused as sorcerers, plus their son.) In the skit, Kawuk was made up with black paint, white body markings, leaf strips, and feathers. Now it was his turn to be the "victim." As he was forced to wail over Mora's corpse, the body gave a dramatic "sign." A fishing line that had been tied to the tip of Mora's fake phallus was surreptitiously pulled. As Mora dramatically arched his back and moaned, this large organ raised up in a monumental erection. The audi- ence exploded with laughter. Needless to say, the corpse had indicated that Kawuk was "guilty" as the sorcerer responsible. Kawuk was then interro- gated, cried like a baby, and was summarily "killed," after which everyone ran off.

To conclude their act, the performers now distanced themselves yet more clearly from the roles they had been playing. Marching solemnly back into the performance area, they lined up in a neat row and stood at

Mora [l] and Yamdaw [r] performing the Gasumi Corners skit at the Nomad Independence Day celebrations, 1998.

attention in front of the judges. Formally and soberly, they bowed in unison to each side of the audience that encircled them—left, right, rear, and front. Finally, with military precision, they marched out, to the cheers of the crowd.

What was I to think? The richness of Gebusi spirit beliefs, the poetry and aesthetics of their spirit mediumship, and even their concern for the sick and dying were turned into farce. And yet, the skit presented a stinging critique of sorcery beliefs, inquests, and fights that had killed many Gebusi in the past. That persons such as Kawuk could play lead characters in this mocking retort—themselves having killed suspected sorcerers in years gone by—underscored this rejection. The skit was very funny, very smart, and very well performed. I was left with much to ponder.

During two nights, a total of 42 dramas were performed. Most, like those described, were spoofs of tradition. But these were thrown into relief by the remaining acts. Some of these were Christian morality plays, with large posters upon which verses from the Bible were written. Others were skits of first contact. In these, local villagers were portrayed as stupid, violent, and clumsy until they were shown the fruits of modern civilization—peace, trade goods, and store-bought food—by benevolent Australian patrol officers (played by villagers). It was hard to watch these without thinking that a core tenet of anthropology—that indigenous ways of life should be respected—was being turned upside down by local people themselves. Certainly, there were some Gebusi traditions that I was glad to see disappear. But much that was beautiful was lost in the bargain. And the new inequalities that Gebusi were experiencing—in church, school, and the market—did not always seem preferable to the practices they replaced.

The remaining skits, though few in number, suggested a more balanced view. These enacted the traumas and foibles of locally modern life. Some of these portrayed the challenges of living in Kiunga—scrounging medicine for a sick child from a pompous official, and coping with children who drift into trouble after school. In one poignant little play, an impoverished city youth stole and ran off with a suitcase full of money. The owner then returned, pulled out a gun, and shot dead the two security guards who had failed to guard his wealth. Here, the hungry boy escaped as a criminal, but worse, the powerful boss had become a murderer. Indeed, the skit echoed the life of the provincial premier, who had recently been charged with attempted murder. Despite the seriousness of such themes, the skits maintained a humorous tone. In this way, they played with alternative outcomes rather than asserting foregone conclusions.

Although local traditions were lampooned at night, they were honored for national "independence" in the full light of day. While perhaps a thousand people looked on, villagers in meticulous costumes danced in full traditional fashion, with diverse ethnic groups displaying their dances and initiations: Bedamini, Kubor, Samo, and even the Pa from across the Strickland River. Their displays were spectacular, a photographer's dream. Gasumi Corners was represented by Halowa, Yuway's married brother and an Evangelical Christian, who drum-danced with a traditionally dressed Gebusi woman from another settlement. The performance that stole the heart of the audience—and of the government judges—was by dancers from the distant Kabasi peoples, who lived three days' hard walk southeast of Nomad. With slow, dignified dancing and haunting songs, they performed both standing and sitting for over half an hour. At traditional Gebusi feasts, dancers visiting from distant settlements were typically given pride of place. Here, on a larger scale, many in the audience were visibly enthralled, appearing to have never seen this style of performance.

I couldn't help but think that Independence Day was expanding indigenous practices at the same time that it transformed them. Rather than being performed at night in a darkened longhouse for kin and friends, rituals were now reenacted at Nomad Station for a thousand strangers in the glaring heat of the day. Even a member of the national parliament was present. The performances were not geared to initiate a young man, cure a sick person, celebrate a local accomplishment, or embody the spirits. Rather, they celebrated the nation of Papua New Guinea and an interethnic brotherhood of body art and dancing. This pageantry was galvanized by government officials, who rated and judged the performances. As those from Gasumi Corners had emphasized, the small purses of prize money awarded to winning performers were a major motivation for many participants. Some villagers dressed up merely for presentation, regardless of whether the individuals were qualified to wear the costume. For most, the displays did not reflect current practices, beliefs, or rituals in their own villages. Indigenous culture was reenacted as folklore for regional and even national consumption.

If the Independence Day festivities both spoofed and celebrated traditional practices, they also played with features of contemporary life. The

A woman and man from Gasumi Corners perform traditional dancing for a crowd of hundreds by the Nomad Sub-District Office at the PNG Independence Day celebrations, 1998.

conclusion to the week's festivities included playful competitions such as drinking quantities of hot tea, pillow fighting while sitting on a beam, blindfolded women trying to split papayas with bush knives, and climbing a greased pole. The atmosphere was that of a country fair, as hundreds of people milled about. Villagers sold cooked food from stalls as music blared from boom boxes. Tables of ring toss and gambling were set up for those willing to risk 5 or 10 cents in a game of skill or chance. The final afternoon boasted a lively disco contest, at which the dance ground was thronged with bodies gyrating to the throb of Papua New Guinea rock music. Although a few brave women participated, including mothers dancing with their daughters, the dance ground was dominated by older boys. All dancing appeared to be same-sex: guys with guys, and girls with girls. The dancers' outfits presented a mélange of styles ranging from traditional costumes to spiffy modern shirts and jeans or hip-hop clothes. A couple of young men dressed up and danced buffoonishly as women in modern dress.

What was I to make of this hodgepodge? Ultimately, the Independence Day festivities were a smorgasbord of cultural diversity—traditional and modern, nearby and distant—performed for display, reflection, and playful combination. Within this mix, indigenous customs were alternately taken out of context, parodied or debunked, and reperformed with modern honor. If rituals reflect and symbolize the structure of people's social life, as Émile Durkheim suggested long ago, then the Nomad Independence Day celebrations of 1998 reflected lives that were absorbing a tapestry of different, multifaceted influences. For Gebusi, the festivities seemed to symbolize the diverse opportunities and many challenges of living so near to the government station.

In the aftermath of Independence Day, the Nomad area seemed to relax. Having worked and played so hard, people unwound in a kind of collective morning-after. Like a series of happy aftershocks following a marvelous quake, a few settlements held subsidiary feasts and celebrations. In Gasumi Corners, the period of respite lasted several weeks before gradually giving way to plans for another festivity that was especially poignant for me: the feast to commemorate my own departure.

As my time to leave inched gradually closer, my days became bittersweet. My friendships had been so deeply rekindled, and new ones had taken root. How could I go?

It ended up as an incredible finale—and I wasn't the reason for its success. Village celebrations have always served multiple purposes. And Gebusi are the first to keep anyone from getting a big head. But it was hard not to cry when I first heard the song that the Gasumi string band composed to thank me for having come back to them.

With their typical casual gusto, the village buzzed with preparations. Firewood and cooking leaves were stockpiled, sago was processed, and game hunted deep in the forest. As a contemporary twist, profits were pooled from our local store to buy a large stock of tinned fish and rice. Added to these were my own gifts to the community, both to individuals and for our collective feast. The latter included further cartons of store-bought food and a score of coveted shotgun cartridges, which Wayabay and other young men used to hunt a whole slew of wild pigs and cassowaries.

During several weeks of preparation, everyone was so busy in the forest gathering food and materials that I started to feel lonely in the village. I longed to be with them in their timbered hideaways, and I was nostalgic for the rainforest. So Sayu, Didiga, and I set off to visit those at the makeshift forest camp at Harfolobi. We canoed up the Kum River under the stately canopy of the towering trees that lined the banks. Climbing up the bluff at Yibihilu, my lip quivered to see our former village and even the site of my first house. It was all overgrown, not just with weeds but with trees turning into forest. Gone as well were so many friends from my first fieldwork, reclaimed by nature. Up at Harfolobi, I visited the grave of Sayu's wondrous mother, Boyl, and it was hard not to weep. I sat in crystal waters of the waterfall where I had bathed years before. And I enjoyed at last the easy rhythm of rainforest life—husbands, wives, and children relaxed and peaceful, and I at home among them.

After several days, obligations drew us reluctantly back to Gasumi Corners, where the festive buildup continued. Though I knew the general contours of the event to come, its specifics remained a mystery to me.

On the day of reckoning, visitors came from near and far—all of those still living whom I had known so well, others whom I had seen only occasionally, and a few who knew of me just by reputation. For several days in advance, piles of coconuts, a ton or more of sago starch, mounds of dried game, and stashes of rice and fish had spawned a veritable village industry of cutting, cleaning, wrapping, and cooking. Now it was time to pull it all from the cooking fires, divide it up, and give it away. Hundreds of visitors had come. Amid our shouts of laughter and whoops of celebration, the gift giving continued long after dusk had turned into night. By now I was no longer a bystander but a primary host. I tried to make sure that my friends and acquaintances, the government officials, and even the hangers-on, each got their appropriate share.

Then came the entertainment. Would this be a traditional dance, kindling an appreciation of historical customs? Or would it be modern? Instead of choosing a single option, my friends let all the flowers bloom. On one side of the hamlet, in the dim light of a darkened house, a visiting dancer in traditional costume performed in full dignity. Older men and women were especially drawn to this proud display of days gone by. Mothers held their smallest children, some of whom were possibly seeing a fully traditional Gebusi dance for the first time. On the other side of the settlement came strains of a visiting string band with guitar and ukulele, playing wonderful songs I had never heard. In the middle, the settlement's central clearing, was the event's pièce de résistance: a modern disco. My friends had finagled a big boom box and a set of speakers from workers at the

Nomad station and lugged them all the way to Gasumi Corners. With light from a bright lantern, the music poured forth. As older folks looked on, youngsters picked up the beat. Within minutes, they were grooving in ways that would have passed quite tolerably in most American dance clubs.

In the moonlight and gentle breeze, the joy and sadness of nostalgia blurred together. For me, it was the modern Gebusi equivalent of old *fafadagim-da*—the wistful enjoyment of strong, unfathomable longing, of being together while thinking of loneliness and loss. Swaying to different beats from one end of the settlement to the other, the village became a three-ring circus of bittersweet pleasure. I shuttled between the traditional dance, the string band, and the disco in the middle, delighting in each for their part. Together, they formed a fugue of cadences that were discordant and yet strangely harmonious. No one minded this jumble of aesthetics and experiences—and neither did I. Perhaps I had learned something new after all—not just to accept the fragmentary nature of Gebusi culture as it now was expressed, but to enjoy and revel it. I thought back to Sayu's dance and all the years of ritual splendor that preceded it. Was Gebusi ritual life now a past tradition, or a spirit of new things to come? I realized the answer could not be one or the other; it was both at the same time. Outpacing my understanding, the people of Gasumi Corners had become modern in their own special way. On the eve of my departure, I contemplated again what they had given me. Their truest gift had gone beyond their past or their present. They had shown me the discovery and surprise of continued human connection.

Update: Where does it go, the past? In the late 1990s, life at Nomad Station and in Gasumi Corners seemed so locally modern, so vibrantly diverse, so bittersweet, so hopeful. Almost as much as spirit séances or sorcery inquests in 1980, it was hard to believe that their more modern world would ever really change—yet it has. Now at Nomad, almost nothing is happening. Aside from the struggling local school and a dismal market, there is little reason for anyone to go there. I have not had the occasion to be at Nomad for Independence Day in recent years. But I can only imagine how small and restricted its celebration must be, with no government, the station shut, and little economic livelihood.

The Gebusi, however, have neither stayed still nor regretted their modern past. Sayu now has seven children. He still sings in the local string band and dances disco with the best of them. Other Gebusi have similarly thrived with their families and their local life in Gasumi Corners.

Against the hopeful opportunities of the late 1990s, Gebusi remind us that progress is not inevitable, that downturns are possible, and that change is certain, one way or the other. While I was in the field with Gebusi in 1998, the US had its own stock market plunge, followed a decade later by the crash of 2008. The Gebusi's economic downturn is lasting longer than our own. Perhaps because of this, its lesson to me seems all the greater: to adapt not just to a world of continued growth, but to one of unforeseen challenge and potential limitation.

BROADER CONNECTIONS
Nationhood, Ethnicity, and Folklore

- Features of **expressive culture** and **popular culture**—including dance, music, public display, and major celebrations and festivities—reveal much about contemporary conditions of culture and cultural change.
- The traditional dance of Sayu, a child-friend to Bruce during his first fieldwork, illustrated the discordance between declining indigenous customs and increasing modern practices.
- Many peoples feel conflicted or ambivalent about some of their indigenous beliefs and practices. At the National Independence Day celebrations, old-time customs such as sorcery divinations, spirit séances, warfare, and even indigenous material culture were spoofed and mocked, though there was also great nostalgia for indigenous costuming and dancing.
- In many societies, including the Gebusi, some indigenous practices are taken out of cultural context and enacted as performances of historic **folklore**.
- Independence Day revealed and symbolized how Gebusi, like many peoples, are increasingly now becoming part of a regional and **national culture**, including through interethnic activities and regional and national identity as citizens of a modern **nation-state**.
- Gebusi **sports** competition against Bedamini—and associated Bedamini accusations of black magic—reflect how historical enmities can inform modern **ethnic conflict**.
- Like events of **public culture** in many developing societies, Independence Day festivities reflect and symbolize the diverse alternatives and values that inform Gebusi society and culture.

- Following the theories of **Émile Durkheim,** the rituals and festivities of Independence Day at Nomad reflected the prevalent pattern of Gebusi social life during the late 1990s.

- Many peoples mix and match modern or contemporary practices and beliefs with long-standing or indigenous ones. The combination is sometimes called **syncretism.** Syncretism among Gebusi was evident in the combination of different dress styles at feasts, and more generally in the combined activity of traditional dancing, "dramas," and modern sports and games during Independence Day festivities.

- During the course of long-term or **longitudinal fieldwork,** anthropologists may form strong personal relationships and become closely associated with the people they study. At the final feast to commemorate his departure in 1998, Bruce was not just an observer but a primary participant and host.

- Decline of activities at Nomad Station in the 2000s underscores that **progress** and **development** are not inevitable and that people must also adapt to conditions of **economic downturn** or limitation.

- The Gebusi taught Bruce that older and newer patterns of culture do not need to oppose each other. This fuels our continuing surprise and discovery in making human connections across cultures.

Making do with little: A boy plays with a cardboard box hat, 2013. →

Part Three

Three Decades of Cultural Change

Chapter 11

Closer, Closer,
Further Away
Revival and Independence

2008. I had tried to send word ahead about my return. This would be a briefer visit, but no less important for that. Ten years later, what had changed? Would my Gebusi friends be yet more engaged in an outside world, their old customs further gone, their rush to be modern yet more intense?

My first inkling was the challenge of getting there. Back in Atlanta, I looked in amazement at the Mission Aviation Fellowship's (MAF) e-reply to my request for a plane ticket: the Nomad airstrip was closed. How could this be? For 45 years that airstrip had been the lifeline for Gebusi and their neighbors to the outside world. With no roads in the area, what did this new isolation mean? Had Gebusi become more remote? How had they responded, given all the change they had already experienced? These questions haunted my plans. My sinking fear was that I wouldn't see Gebusi at all. With no air transport, the overland trip to Nomad from Kiunga takes up to a week on foot, across swamps and fording the large and dangerous Strickland River. I was tempted to try this, but luckily, the MAF agent had a better idea. He suggested I land at a tiny mission airstrip at Honinabi that was open on the Gebusi's side of the Strickland River and hike from there to Nomad and on to Gasumi Corners. Maybe the Nomad strip would be fixed and reopened by the time I arrived in the country. If all else failed, I would just stay in Kiunga and make contact with whatever Gebusi happened to be residing in the corners of the town.

On leaving Atlanta, I didn't know which option would come to pass. Twenty-eight years after my first trip, I was still in suspense.

After the gruelling trip from Atlanta to Los Angeles to Australia to Papua New Guinea's capital of Port Moresby, and then to the rainforest town of Kiunga, I finally got word about Gebusi. Though none of my messages had gotten through, Father Eddy at the Kiunga Catholic mission recognized my photo of Sayu. He said Sayu was now married with several children. My appetite whetted; I was all the more eager to see my Gebusi friends. But first I had to get there.

The challenges that afflict infrastructure in outstation areas of developing countries are often socially and culturally critical. The present backstory, which I discovered later, was that the Nomad government had run out of money to pay Gebusi and others for cutting and clearing grass on the airstrip. Eventually, laborers gave up and stopped working. As grass shot up, the airstrip degraded until incoming planes could barely land. Nomad's officials, hailing from other parts of the country, flew out on the last planes and did not come back. Sadly, politics and networks allowed them to continue collecting government pay while in Kiunga or elsewhere—without living or working at Nomad at all. So government presence at Nomad shrank to almost nothing. The grass continued growing, and the airstrip was closed. When infrastructure works, it is easy to take it for granted. But when it fails, the consequences are great.

After months of cajoling and diligence, two local men who had been associated with the government had managed to raise enough money to get the airstrip partly repaired. By the time I arrived in Kiunga, the strip had been closed for nine months. Using me as a test case, MAF asked me to pay full fare for a charter flight but take little cargo, lightening the weight of the plane. The seasoned bush pilot, Nick Swaim, said we should wait for a dry day. When the weather finally cleared, I loaded my few things and we took off. Lifting up, I marvelled again at the full magnificence of the rainforest, horizon to horizon. Awe and sorrow shook me as I realized how rare such an unbroken vista of rainforest has become on our planet.

Almost before I was ready, the Strickland River passed beneath and we approached Nomad Station. Nick circled and careened us down to just six or eight feet above the ground—so he could carefully inspect the strip. I looked across anxiously as he pulled up suddenly to get us back over the treetops. He gave me the thumbs up; we would try to land. My pulse raced with the plane as it circled in for a final descent. On touching down, we caught a rut and skidded right and then left. But Nick got us calmly straightened out and brought the plane to a gentle stop. It was only later that I discovered the greater risk—that if we had hit a deeper rut, the plane would have catapulted forward. If the lone front propeller hits the ground, its powerful torque can flip the rest of the plane to disaster.

But, oh, to be safely back! I gazed out eagerly as we taxied, remembering the same experience in 1980 and in 1998. Who and what would I find? Each time was so new.

Word about my arrival had finally gotten to Nomad that very morning, and Sayu and Didiga had rushed to the airstrip—arriving in time to meet me! I could hardly believe it. We hugged and hugged and snapped fingers. At first we could barely say anything, overcome by the joy of simply being together again. Their faces were now middle-aged, but their smiles were bright and deep as ever.

As I got my bearings, I realized that the clothes on those around me were plainly ragged, unlike before. Looking up across the Nomad Station, I saw that it, too, was ragged. Houses had deteriorated and most were boarded up. The Nomad school, so full of boisterous children the decade before, was empty, closed to students. Even the schoolyard grass was burned and charred black. The Nomad ball field, having seen so many rivalries and triumphs in years past, was now overgrown with two feet of grass. Gebusi themselves were smiles all over. But in what circumstances were they living?

Not wanting to linger at Nomad, we gathered up my few supplies. I shook hands and exchanged warm greetings with Father Aloi. An Indonesian who was now the Gebusi's Catholic priest, he had waited months to leave Nomad for a much-needed break and so was eager to board the plane that had just brought me. News about Father Aloi had been encouraging—that he loved the Gebusi, was actively learning their language, supported their customs, and was shaping the church to fit local needs. Also boarding the plane was "Bruce," named after me, who was venturing to school in Kiunga. As the Cessna quickly taxied and took off, the rest of us trotted off in high gear to Gasumi Corners. I apologized to everyone that I had not been able to bring many supplies or gifts, since a heavier plane couldn't have landed. Reassuring me, my friends understood but hardly seemed to care. My questions deepened, though, when I arrived in the village and saw that people's possessions were few, their clothes torn, their pots battered, and their knives and axes more worn than before.

My first priority was simply to see who was still alive. To my huge relief, most of my closest friends had survived; a surge of welcomes came from Kilasui, Mosomiay, Hogaya, Wayabay, Agiwa, Yokwa, and my great old friends Yuway, Keda, Kawuk, and Hawi. Among the women, Mus, Dohayn, Dasom, Tabway, Kuni, To'ofun, Towe, Hahap, Oip, and Nelep were still living. Complementing the adults was a bounding gaggle of children born since my last visit; I struggled to record and remember their many names. As my tabulations showed, time had been kind to the people of Gasumi Corners: through natural increase, they who had grown 38% between 1998 and 2008—from 122 to 168. Among the additions was one new "Knauft": Didiga's first son, to whom he gave my last name.

Children in Gasumi Corners, 2008.

Among some peoples of the developing world, a swelling tide of children is a major problem: too many mouths, poverty, poor health, and lack of education. But given Gebusi's extensive tracts of land, their surge in numbers was more a vibrant replenishment than a crisis.

How else had the community changed? Back at Nomad, with the airstrip virtually closed, the government was gone, the offices vacant. There was no Nomad school, no effective medical clinic, no sports leagues, no development projects, and—in the absence of a cash economy—a Nomad market that was poorly attended, with just a few sellers offering paltry goods to nonexistent buyers. Against this, Gasumi Corners itself was a different story. Its biggest change was also the most obvious—a great new longhouse in the center of the community! I knew immediately what this meant: a whole new generation of Gebusi had been initiated since I had last been there. Their transmission of indigenous culture across generations had been rekindled and maintained. What a joy! Given this, I suspected I would soon learn of other traditions that were also reemerging.

When I first entered the house, as if there were any doubt, I was besieged by a flurry of traditional welcoming. My fingers were snapped again and again, my gift exchange names called out, and the floor swept clean. After being begged to sit down, I was offered water, bananas, and, most significantly, round upon round of strong sweet tobacco from traditional bamboo pipes. In short order, festivities were punctuated by waves of good-natured sexual joking, as I had remembered from 1980. In marked contrast to a decade earlier, men were delighted almost to tears that I could joke back with them in traditional style.

As our conversations started in earnest, I found that my long-standing interest in Gebusi customs was not as marginal to my friends as it had been before. Alongside the resurgence of traditions was new curiosity about the Gebusi's past, including the life stories and genealogies that I had brought with me. I gave a full copy of these to Didiga, who could read and recite the information as a kind of community history. That night, I stumbled to bed astounded: Gebusi were reclaiming their past in ways I could not have imagined.

On awakening, I found my friend Keda, now more usually called Joseph, reading one of my books about the Gebusi that I had brought. My first surprise was that Keda could read. In fact, he had just finished reading my story of Doliay—how he had beheaded Basowey as a sorcerer and later became a staunch Christian. Unfortunately, Doliay had died since my last visit. With his passing, only two of the six young men we helped initiate in 1981, Hawi and Yuway, were still alive.

The decade before, I had tried hard to respect and document Gebusi desires for change and the forces that had underlain them. But I had also wondered how Gebusi could benefit from outside influence without losing the richness of what was already theirs. Now they seemed more self-determined and more able to balance modern desires with appreciation of their cultural past.

To my delight, this balance now included traditional dancing. Within three days of my arrival, a dance with full regalia was held in a large house just five-minutes' walk from Gasumi Corners. In good classic style, the dancer was from a distant village; in this case, his dance helped cure a man who was regaining strength following illness. In style, form, and costume, the dance was similar to those I had seen so many years earlier. Indeed, men's chewing and drinking of kava, the local root intoxicant, were more pronounced than they had been before—and the upcoming younger men were the most active drinkers.

Thankfully, I also determined that Gebusi violence concerning sorcery had remained minimal or negligible. During the intervening years, the greatest potential exception to this trend was itself revealing.

When Sayu had married Dankop, her brother, Harfay, did not himself have a wife—and Sayu had no sister for a marital exchange. The two men had fought, and Harfay had then gone off in a huff to work at a distant logging camp. When he did not return, his family and others in the community suspected he was dead. Indeed, they took the rare initiative to seek out advice in a distant village from one of the few remaining Gebusi spirit mediums. The medium confirmed that Harfay was dead—and implied that Sayu was the assault sorcerer responsible. The dispute against Sayu rose to such a pitch that Father Aloi, the priest in Gasumi Corners, got wind of it. Through his radio contacts, he determined that Harfay was in fact still alive and had simply signed on for another term of logging work. But Harfay's family didn't believe this, insisting he was dead and that Sayu was responsible.

Father Aloi then convinced Sayu to himself trek to the distant logging camp, find Harfay, and bring him back. When the two young men returned together in good health, the community was amazed. Harfay's mother even thought that her son had been brought back from the dead. In the bargain, suspicions of sorcery—including the spirit medium's pronouncement—were shown to be manifestly false. Enmity turned to friendship. Though this "good news story" certainly does not apply to all Gebusi disputes, it does reveal how lack of ability to validate sorcery accusations dovetails with community uncertainty and Christian beliefs to undercut violence. As before, it continued to be said that without connection with traditional spirits, it was impossible to know who the sorcerer was or even if sickness or death was caused by sorcery at all.

Instead of spirit séances, the lovely string band singing that had come to the fore during the 1990s had persisted and expanded. As such, Gebusi continued to enjoy plaintive songs of longing, sexual attraction, and allure accompanied by guitar and ukulele—now accompanied as well by active bouts of sexual humor and joking.

Figures bear out the link between Gebusi's changed forms of cultural expression, spiritual belief, and reduction of violence. Of the deaths that occurred in Gasumi Corners since 1989, none appear to have been homicides; the killing rate seems to have been zero. Since in earlier years almost one of every three adult Gebusi had been killed, this is a major positive change—and one that testifies to the human ability to quell violence through cultural self-management.

Influencing this trend in Gasumi Corners is the St. Paul's Catholic Church. During the 2000s, the Catholic Church was the one nontraditional institution that grew and intensified, even as the Evangelical and Seventh Day Adventist churches declined. Part of this was due to the skill of Father Aloi, including his initiating development projects with the Gebusi. Often traveling to settlements in the bush, Father Aloi went by foot and canoe or motorboat, accepted local food, and tried to appreciate local customs wherever he went. He recounted with a laugh having unwittingly smoked a large amount of marijuana that was "innocently" put in a traditional tobacco pipe by a mischievous welcoming villager in a distant Bedamini settlement. As it turned out, the raising and selling of marijuana has become a major problem in the general Nomad area, especially east of the Gebusi. This problem has intensified as the local cash economy based on garden produce and other forest products has collapsed.

In the mix, the pervious separation and asymmetry between Catholic leadership and Gebusi's received culture seemed less than before. More generally, Gebusi had confronted the new reality of their postmodern isolation by extending and developing their own culture. In the process, they found newly traditional as well as modern ways to express themselves and to create renewed avenues of meaning, value, and livelihood. I admired them for adapting so effectively to conditions of staggering economic decline. Rather than lamenting for the past, they drew upon their cultural history as their deepest resource.

Six months after I returned to the US, we ourselves experienced the stock market crash of 2008. The Dow Jones average plummeted 54%. A number of my friends lost their jobs or their savings. I remembered the Gebusi for all they still have to teach us, including how, amid the convulsions of an ever-modern world, we can rediscover vitality and renew our lives when times get tough.

2013. Once again, my outbound voyage was chocked with uncertainty. Once again, it was hard to find a plane that would land at Nomad. But this time it proved impossible. Instead we flew to Honinabi, landing not on the edge of Gebusi territory, but among a group further north, the Samo. One-third of a century after I first met the Gebusi, it was a longer trek to reach them than ever before. To me personally, Gebusi were closer than they had ever been. But geographically and logistically, they were, if anything, yet further away.

Flying to Honinabi was a new experience for me, and also for my colleague, anthropology graduate student Latham Wood, from the University of Oregon. Himself of mixed Pacific Island descent, Latham was not just a wonderful guy but an experienced hand in Melanesia, including several years of field experience as a Peace Corps worker in another part of the region. Though new to Gebusi, Latham spoke *Tok Pisin* fluently and also had experience as a videographer.

Word having arrived ahead, I was moved to find a large throng of Gebusi welcoming our plane even at Honinabi; they had made the long hike up to welcome us and carry our goods. Sayu and Didiga are family to me now, and I hugged them with the joy of long-lost brothers. Within minutes, our cargo was shouldered and we were all off down the track.

Fortunately, it had not been raining so the Nomad River was not in flood. As such, we negotiated the track and forded the river to Nomad and on to Gasumi Corners without major incident—except that a makeshift handrail gave way on a single log bridge over a steep drop. Luckily I managed to grab a support beam while falling. I scraped myself badly but thankfully avoided broken bones or other injuries. No one else was hurt.

Against this ominous preamble, our entrée into Gasumi Corners seemed all the more grand. Sayu had rushed ahead with news of our arrival, and by the time we got there, a whole new ritual of welcome was enacted before us. Just when I thought I knew what to expect, I was surprised yet again. To the left, just in front of the St. Paul's Catholic Church, stood my old friend Gwabi, caked with brown mud and threateningly wielding an ax in the old traditional style, as if to strike us. Beside him was an entry portal configured from poles rimmed with leaf strips, behind which we could dimly see Gebusi in costume holding instruments. Ignorant but beckoned, I was coached along with Latham to approach and walk unflinchingly past Gwabi's threatening ax and duck through the portal. As we did so, the cultural heavens seemed to open. Music and song poured forth from performers who were festooned in a newly exquisite style of bird-of-paradise costumes. Wreaths of flowers were draped over our heads by pretty young women. I had never seen anything like it. People cheered and clapped as we went down the line, snapping fingers with everyone in turn. Each of my friends who I found to be still alive jolted my feelings more deeply. Laughing, smiling, practically crying, I finished the welcoming line and we proceeded to the village.

Latham's presence helped put my own in perspective. Now an older man, and accorded deference, I was typically placed at the center of gatherings in the village's central house—a large-roofed but otherwise open structure that was similar to but not exactly like a traditional "longhouse." In contrast to my early days among Gebusi, when I had been a curiosity but otherwise a fly-on-the-wall at public meetings, now I was often the center of attention—if not the main attraction! Amid the happiness of not just catching up but being communicated with earnestly and at length, I admit some envy at Latham's ability to talk more casually and privately on the periphery with the younger men. He also shared with

Traditional ritual antagonism: Gwabi   Welcoming finger-snap with Halowa,
in a ritual display with an ax by the   2013.
Catholic Church, 2013.

them the modern benefit of conversing in *Tok Pisin*, which I myself had
never properly learned. Among other things, Latham found out—as I had
not—that some Gebusi men had been desperate enough for money to
walk long distances trafficking parcels of marijuana from their tropical
lowlands to the New Guinea highlands.

By and large, however, and as Latham agreed, Gebusi have continued
to accommodate with remarkably good spirit—and with good result—to
their continuing isolation and lack of money or goods. Added to the
ongoing closure of the Nomad airstrip and government office has been
the decline of other modern institutions, including even the local Catholic Church. With the departure of Father Aloi the Church has ebbed in
influence, attendance, and local significance, though it still labors on. Left
on their own, the people of Gasumi Corners have reoriented increasingly
to the abundance of the deeper rainforest. Indeed, their nutrition and
health seem better than ever! Rather than amassing prized foods to sell to

government workers, Gebusi now grow and harvest these fully for themselves. They have retained and expanded their use of peanuts, pineapple, corn, pumpkins, manioc, and several root crops—adapting their cultivation to local conditions. Of particular importance is sweet potato, which was indigenously raised as a rare and scrawny tuber. Now, by contrast, sweet potatoes are grown abundantly by using mounding techniques and ingenious means of keeping away pigs. As such, they have become a major food staple alongside plantains and sago—and are much more nutritious than either of these.

This time I had the luxury of making deeper travels into the forest with Gebusi than I had in some years. And I quickly realized how adept and effective they had become at using canoes. Historically, living near a riverbank left a settlement vulnerable to attack; for defensive purposes, Gebusi preferred their houses perched on ridgetops. Even then, settlements were easily uprooted by raiding, killing, and accusations of sorcery. Under such conditions, it hardly made sense to invest heavy work in carving hand-hewn canoes from tree trunks—not to mention with stone adzes. And canoes once made could be stolen by enemies. In 1982, the community of Yibihilu was at the downstream juncture where the Kum River became fully navigable; Gebusi had two or three canoes but mostly travelled overland. The neighboring community lived a good distance from any major river and had no canoes at all.

Canoeing on the Kum River, 2013.

Now, however, rivers are routes of connection rather than barriers of separation. With increasing years and then decades of peace and residential stability, many Gebusi have gravitated increasingly downstream along their large and most easily travelled rivers. This includes those further downstream at Gasumi Corners, whose waterway to the Kum River is just five minutes' walk from the main settlement. Their neighboring community, Yehebi, has relocated entirely from its ridgetop to a bluff along the large Sio River. Every family has a canoe or two, and these are easily shared. Gebusi are now skillful oarsmen (and women!) and are quite comfortable spending from dawn to dusk on the river. Fishing is at once relaxing, productive, and a great supplement to nutrition. Further, Gebusi now cut large gardens along the banks of their rivers. Some stretches of riverbank boast one large food-producing plot after another. Rather than trudging through the forest and hauling produce back laboriously, Gebusi now rely increasingly on canoes to easily ferry themselves, supplies, and food directly to and from their garden settlements. In reorienting back to the rainforest, they have now, to a significant extent, become "canoe people."

In all, Gebusi seem to benefit greatly from increased nutrition, diet, and health. And this is despite the collapse of medical services (apart from infant inoculations, which thankfully continue at Nomad due to the heroic efforts of two Catholic nuns). In concert with the low rate of violence and continued absence of killing, Gebusi enjoy increased fertility and a burgeoning rise in population. In 2013 the population of Gasumi Corners had grown to almost 200 persons, marking an annual increase of about 3.5% since 2008, and, similarly before that, since 1998. Along with

Tabway with five of her grandchildren, 2013.

this has come greater longevity. In the deeper past, most people died by what we would consider middle age, and it was unusual or rare for a man to live long enough to see the birth of a single grandchild. Now, however, enjoying grandchildren is not just cherished but commonplace. Kawuk, who has lived well into his 60s, and his wife, Tabway, have 12 grandchildren while remaining active and vibrant.

Amid their other changes, land for Gebusi still remains a plentiful rather than a limited or contested resource. Their biggest threat, however, is both one that Gebusi crave and one that could profoundly impact their land and livelihood: the construction of an LNG (liquified natural gas) pipeline.

As part of its Hides project, ExxonMobil has constructed an 11+ billion-dollar gas pipeline from the southern highlands of Papua New Guinea, well east of the Gebusi, all the way down to the New Guinea south coast. The next huge phase of this project looks to build a second LNG pipeline from the Faiwol area, far northwest of the Gebusi, and link it across hundreds of kilometers of pristine rainforest with the existing Hides pipeline. As of 2016, the plan for this pipeline is to cross at least part of Gebusi territory.

Even in the 1960s, oil companies were exploring hopefully in the Gebusi's general area south of Nomad. Since this time, Gebusi have been aware of—and enthusiastically hopeful for—benefits from resource development by outside companies. But to the present, at least, none of these developments have panned out in the Nomad area. Whether and when the current opportunity—and threat—will become reality is hard to gauge.

This fact—the uncertainty and unpredictability of development—is itself important. As might be expected, ExxonMobil's project planning and pipeline construction schedules are deeply held secrets. And these can change, sometimes radically, over time. Between 2010 and 2015, the global price of LNG declined by about 30%, making the building of a multibillion-dollar new pipeline correspondingly costly against expected profits. The price of LNG, however, is generally projected to rise consistently, if slowly, in future years. Who knows what ExxonMobil's calculus is concerning the profitability—and risk—of building this new pipeline? Given the surprising drop in global oil prices in recent years, many energy multinationals are hedging their bets. From a local perspective, however, the company is in the driver's seat. Having secured initial rights to the pipeline's route, ExxonMobil appears free to build when they want, wait for as many years as they want, or defer or abandon the project altogether in the future.

The helicopter buzzed and circled overhead, and we all went running: the pilot was scouting a place to land—right in Gasumi Corners! Trying to enlarge the village clearing, young men starting chopping with frenzied abandon at the valuable coconut trees that ringed the area. As the copter floated away to the field by the Catholic Church, we rushed in its wake, arriving in time to see it land and a man emerge. Dr. "Hitchcock," I presume?!

I had tried to tell Gebusi about the potentials, the risks, and the frank unpredictability of ExxonMobil's LNG pipeline project that *might* cross part of their land. To help ensure they'd get fair compensation if the project indeed went ahead, I trekked to distant tribal borders with Gebusi landowners to mark the GPS coordinates of clan and tribal boundaries. I also wrote up, submitted, and posted on my website a report on the land tenure principles of Gebusi and neighboring groups—hoping their customary strictures concerning land wouldn't be trampled to oblivion if and when they could receive compensation.

Trying to explain all this to Gebusi was not easy. What was liquified natural gas? How would a three-meter pipe be sunk for hundreds of miles beneath the rainforest ground and even tunneled under major rivers?

Company helicopter hovering in Gasumi Corners, 2013.

Who would get money and when and how much? What, anyway, *was* a GPS? The young Gebusi man with the greatest education, a year or two of secondary school, had been away at Kiunga during my more recent visits and didn't really know me. He asked for my business card and saw that I was part of the Emory School of Arts and *Sciences*. When he heard I was taking a GPS to map land in some relation to "minerals" (the generic term for exportable resources on or under the land), he thought I might be a scientist who could somehow extract or beam the minerals *into* my GPS and then take them away with me—potentially stealing them altogether! It was as important as it was difficult for me to explain in Gebusi, and with Latham's thankful help in *Tok Pisin*, how a GPS worked and that the liquified natural gas was not on Gebusi land but only potentially passing *through* it—along with a host of other details.

Even harder, though, was that as a senior and respected honorary member of the community, with presumed outside knowledge, I didn't know and couldn't say anything meaningful about the most important questions: When would the pipeline project come? How much money would it generate? Who would get it? Would anything come to pass at all? I felt slammed in a way I had never experienced by the blatant uncertainty of capital development—and, moreover, its potential or probability for *lack* of development or *under*development. Amid the inflated hopes and expectations of Gebusi—like the earlier drawings of schoolchildren at Nomad, picturing their future selves so hopefully as machine operators, nurses, pilots, policemen, and rock singers—it was easy to see that my raising the prospect of a major development project on the Gebusi's doorstep could easily fuel inflated expectations. And also that these might only be crushed in reality afterward. Yet, it didn't seem right to keep Gebusi in the dark concerning everything I knew and had found out.

Though applied anthropology may generally be considered to be any application of anthropology to address social problems, anthropologists often distinguish more finely between "applied" anthropology and "engaged" anthropology, as elaborated further below. Applied anthropology specifically can be seen as practical work for which outside entities contract and pay anthropologists to conduct tasks in relation to or on behalf of local people. The information or reports that result are often owned by the entity that has paid for it, and the work is generally geared to satisfy the objectives and ultimately the demands of the organization that provides the funding. Applied anthropology as such can be wonderfully helpful and of great benefit, fostering anthropologists to gather information and help design or implement projects that are good for and desired by local people. Humanitarian aid organizations around the world hire anthropologists and others in this hopeful regard.

But things don't always work out as hoped. Depending on the ideologies, finances, and politics of the sponsoring organization—not to mention the expectations, politics, and demands of government officials or of local people themselves—even when well-intentioned, aid projects, and applied anthropology as well, can run the gamut from inspiring to insipid, from excellent and glorious to awful and disastrous. Things are seldom as simple or as effective in practice as envisaged or described at the outset. This is not to debunk applied anthropology, far from it! The range of those doing good applied anthropology grows by leaps and bounds each year. It is rather to acknowledge that applied anthropology, like any human endeavor, has its politics, its ideologies, and its blind sides. If our goal is to help facilitate the progressive desires of local people, it's important to be aware of these challenges, to negotiate them as effectively as possible, and to honestly assess—often in the absence of simple or easy answers—how and how much to participate in others' projects.

Before I had left the US, I had been contacted by a colleague and brought roughly up to date about current work subcontracted by Exxon-Mobil to map the distribution of peoples along potential pipeline routes. One of these subcontractees, Garrick Hitchcock, has a PhD in anthropology and had done fieldwork in New Guinea further to the south. Nonetheless, I had had little idea that Garrick might visit me personally right in Gasumi Corners, much less by helicopter. As he landed, however, I put the pieces together and tried to welcome him as best I could. He seemed like quite a nice fellow. We triangulated, with me translating into Gebusi for the benefit of those around, as Garrick described the general process of "social mapping," which involved finding out who lived where and their relationship to their land. As an applied anthropologist, he among others would be return-ing to the Gebusi (as well as to many other peoples) to conduct this "map-ping" in coming weeks and months on behalf of ExxonMobil. The exact process was only partly clear to me and certainly less so to Gebusi them-selves. This included the fact that these pending visits were not designed to give compensation for land or resources and that there was no way of know-ing if a pipeline would be laid, if it would actually cross Gebusi land, and, if it did, if any compensation from ExxonMobil to any Gebusi would result.

The specter of wealth and benefits flowing to Gebusi seemed so fantas-tically possible, so close, and yet so far away—in a word, so magical. So, too, it seemed magical if not downright divine to those around me that of all the miles of rainforest, and even as planes couldn't land at Nomad, the extravagant company helicopter had landed right down in Gasumi Corners so the company "boss" could meet me. Even as I shuddered at the prospect of power or influence being projected onto me by Gebusi, I felt I was in my own warp of surreality next to Garrick. He told me pleasantly that he would *like* to do what *I* was doing—get close with local people and trek in the rainforest. But liability strictures in his social mapping subcontract from ExxonMobil required him (due to risk of malaria, among other things) to sleep each night at his base by Kiunga in a secure and air condi-tioned room. In practical terms, this meant that he buzzed daily over tens and even hundreds of miles of rainforest—in a helicopter that cost thou-sands of dollars each *hour*—but he couldn't camp a single night or connect with local people except for precious brief minutes while his chopper stayed waiting. How bizarre: an applied bush anthropologist copters the skies, spending hundreds of thousands of dollars and more, removed from effective local contact, while the impoverished Gebusi and I on a shoestring remain both so richly connected and so remote from the money that flows so easily. And yet, *without* a Garrick Hitchcock, who would undertake the key task of actually finding out who is located where along the entire pipe-line route, and what their customs are concerning the allocation of land?

I myself was complicit. Not only was I friendly to Hitchcock, but he had generously given me e-mail suggestions and directions ahead of time about getting and using a GPS. More than that, his boss, also an anthro-pologist, who I had known for many years, had contacted me before my fieldwork to ask if I wanted to get paid as a subcontractee from ExxonMo-bil—that is, to do social mapping work among Gebusi and neighboring peoples for the pipeline project. If I had agreed, I would have be paid a ton of money. I had declined—but not completely.

On the one hand, I didn't want to be in a conflict of interest between working for and on behalf of ExxonMobil and the Gebusi. So I declined to sign any contract. But I *did* want to increase the chance—in whatever way I realistically could—that Gebusi would get their fair share of any land compensation package if and when the pipeline crossed their land. So I agreed to take a GPS and map Gebusi tribal boundaries, with Gebusi's own encouragement and support, to document the extent of their territory. And I decided on my own to write a formal report on the principles of Gebusi land tenure. This because local customary land law is *supposed* to be respected by the government and by corporations under conditions of resource extraction and development. But in fact, when payments for compensation stand to be made to local people, a feeding frenzy of competition, including influx and bribery by outsiders, is often a huge if not paramount result. To increase the accuracy and credence of my report, I researched and wrote it up while still in the field, so I could directly clarify its details with Gebusi themselves—and so they would know just what it said. When I left the field, I sent the report to Garrick and his boss and also posted it on my website, where it is publicly available.

As such, I was not technically an applied anthropologist. But I *was* actively engaged in working on practical issues that were of concern and interest both to Gebusi and to outside identities. Anthropologists often call such work "engaged anthropology." In essence, this is practical work by anthropologists that may not be formally contracted but that nonetheless engages and actively facilitates concrete plans or desires of local people, including in areas of economic development, health, education, safety, or politics. Long an informal or personal aspect of fieldwork, engaged anthropology has in recent years become one of cultural anthropology's greatest new areas of explicit practice, research, publication, and professional recognition.

At the bottom end of a very long food chain, Gebusi have no effective bargaining power against a corporation like ExxonMobil. And my own efforts, despite their good intention, may also have little effect. By all indications, Gebusi will gladly take whatever compensation they are offered for the small fraction of their land that the pipeline might cross. Sadly, the wider pattern in such cases is for windfall compensation to be given only to the specific landowner/s whose land is directly affected. The multinational corporation hopes to make billions of dollars, the various levels of Papua New Guinea government take their large financial cut, but the local landowners get far less than a penny on the dollar. This nonetheless provides them a huge fortune, at least in local terms. But the great bulk of inhabitants across whose land the pipeline does not *directly* go, are given very little money or, more typically, nothing at all. In parts of Papua New Guinea previously affected by such projects, the huge inequalities thus created—a few people on selected parcels of land get huge payouts while their neighbors get few or none—have fueled major conflicts and civil strife. But among Gebusi, for better as well as for worse, the bittersweet fruits of resource development are not as yet at hand.

In many world areas, social or religious movements have developed to address frustrated desires to be or become modern. For many years in some parts of Melanesia, so-called "cargo cults" sprang up, whereby magical or ritual means were developed as hopeful ways of attracting or directly creating Western wealth and commodities. Outsiders tended to see these cults as superstitious and irrational ways of mimicking or aping Western productivity—without producing anything of value. From the perspective of those living in remote areas, however, these terms can seem somewhat reversed. Who can explain why so much money from the outside world comes to some places and people, and not at all to others? Who can explain the vast riches and resources of multinational corporations, how they bet billions of dollars on the global price of gas, how stock market algorithms make and break great fortunes in the flash of an eye? And how should all of this be impacting some group in rural Papua New Guinea whose future will be radically influenced by either the presence of a pipeline or its absence?

Not just in the rainforest but from a larger perspective of human experience, the ideologies, beliefs, and practices of modern global capitalism—including the multinational mining, logging, and petroleum projects that mightily impact Melanesia and so many other world areas—can seem as idiosyncratic, counterintuitive, and irrational as the traditional New Guinea religions that seemed, on first blush, to be their antithesis. Imagine the reaction of New Guinea highlanders when explorers first ventured in so laboriously and looked so insistently for little pellets of this useless yellow substance—gold—that they sometimes had put in their teeth. How seemingly irrational! In both directions, the notion that "they just don't understand" can seem equally valid.

Among Gebusi, attempts to engage the modern world—and also to accept their ultimate inability to do just that—seem not just understandable but creative and effective. Gebusi provide an insightful example of how to manage a local modernity under conditions that, as Karl Marx otherwise put it, are not of their own choosing. Against this backdrop, our common tendency to polarize the advanced against the backward, the civilized against the undeveloped, can all too easily obscure—and reinforce—the huge difference that continues to separate the earnest activities and meaningful engagements of economically poor and disempowered people from those with enormous wealth.

As they wrestle with their continuing hopes and their long-standing frustrations of attaining modern development, Gebusi may in some ways be ahead of our own 21st-century curve, rather than behind it. Amid our own hopes for continuous economic growth, uncertainty and significant downturns—economic, political, and ecological—are themselves almost certain over the course of time. In relation to these, the adaptive responses and even the seemingly quaint enchantments that we find so rich among people in developing countries may be useful to learn from as we confront our own futures. Gebusi illustrate the ability of people to create dignity and meaning amid conditions of major challenge as well as change.

Back in Gasumi Corners, life goes on. The government may have "died," but Gebusi do not blame themselves for lack of outside support. Rather, they develop and assert their own customs and beliefs as indigenous people. In the process, they have taken responsibility and initiative, drawing on cultural resources and their own environment to shape their destiny.

As our days and weeks rolled on, Latham and I enjoyed the casual flow of evening conversation, serene treks to distant lands, establishing gift exchange names with new companions, updating histories, and, most of all, catching up with my previous friends and acquaintances. Men were warm with each other, and relations with women were noticeably more relaxed and friendly

Men joking about
recent events in
Gasumi Corners,
2013.

than they had been before. Gender taboos have crumbled, and Gebusi men and women now live in houses with no walls between them. Sexual joking and repartee remain strong among men, with women often smiling from the sidelines. When I asked them earnestly if there would be a new longhouse and another initiation, they answered, as before, "Who knows?" And when they asked me earnestly if and when I would again return, I, too, had to answer honestly, amid my hopes, that I also didn't know.

As had become my custom in 1998 and in 2008, we went up by canoe and paid homage to the old village site at Yibihilu, now verdant in its own new way, fully grown over with grass and trees. It is now almost unrecognizable, just another part of the immense forest. We talked and laughed and sighed about days and people gone by, the passage of time. Despite and even because of this passage, their memory remains bright for me, a beacon of pleasure from the past.

No matter how often I return to the Gebusi, their story is always fresh. Each time, my expectations of who they have become are wonderfully recast. In the process, my life as well as my understanding becomes richer. Gebusi have taught me that our understanding of peoples and cultures—across the world and around the corner—is never finished. Today's new finding may be changed tomorrow. This does not mean our efforts to understand are either inadequate or doomed to be history. It simply means our work, like our lives, engages new realms of experience that continue to inspire both our minds and our hearts.

So, too, my Gebusi friends, their families, and their future will always be meaningfully growing and changing. As long as I live, I hope to keep contact with Sayu, Didiga, and my other Gebusi friends. Since 1980, their culture has been transformed for me from an alien world to one of powerful value and then to one of friendship and family-like connection. Across the miles and the years, what more can one ask?

Note: See Gebusi video clips of and commentary on "Gebusi Underdevelopment" on www.bruceknauft.com → Gebusi.

BROADER CONNECTIONS
Cultural Survival, Development, and Applied Anthropology

- Problems of **infrastructure** and **government** are common in rural areas of developing countries.

- Like people in many world areas, Gebusi facilitate their **cultural survival** by rejuvenating selected older practices and, in the process, **reinventing culture**.

- In formal economic terms, Gebusi live in extreme **poverty**—they earn less than a dollar a day. But they are arguably richer now in cultural meaning and social quality of life than when they were more "developed."

- With passage of time, Gebusi, like many peoples, take increasing interest in their own cultural past, including ethnographic documentation, books, and other information given to them by the anthropologists who have worked among them. This process of giving back to local people is sometimes called **cultural repatriation.**

- Peoples undergoing **cultural loss** do not recoup the full range of their previous beliefs and practices, including during periods of cultural rejuvenation. Gebusi have not reestablished spirit mediumship or shamanism, séances, sorcery divinations, or other traditional practices that escalated violence.

- The homicide rate among the people of Gasumi Corners appears to have continued to be zero since the late 1980s. This illustrates that (1) violence is not innate or inevitable but is strongly shaped by social and cultural influences over time, and (2) culture change on its own terms can have positive results in managing and quelling conflict.

- Gebusi illustrate the importance of complementing our understanding of large-scale changes, including **globalization,** chronic **poverty,** and challenges of **development,** with a human appreciation of how people **adapt** and find **meaning** and **value** in their own culture.

- Though largely devoid of **economic development,** Gebusi have intensified their use of traditional resources of the primary **rainforest** while also cultivating newly introduced **root crops** and other foods to enrich their subsistence livelihood.

- Based on self-reliance, Gebusi now appear to have better **nutrition,** better **health,** higher **fertility,** and greater **longevity** than they did previously.

- Like many rural peoples in developing countries, Gebusi face the specter of major **resource development** by extractive **multinational corporations.** In this case, a potential major liquified natural gas pipeline built by ExxonMobil.

- Like many peoples, the economic future of the Gebusi is difficult to predict, highly uncertain, and could result in long-term **underdevelopment.**

- **Applied anthropology** in general is any application of anthropology that addresses or attempts to improve social problems. In narrower and more specific terms, applied anthropology pertains to the employment of anthropologists to investigate or address social problems when this work is funded and contracted by entities that have specific practical objectives of their own. By contrast, **engaged anthropology** engages the anthropologist with the practical desires and plans of local people in ways that are largely or effectively beyond the purview of financial support and management by outside agencies or institutions. Though this contrast sometimes blurs in practice, it highlights the importance of considering the specific social and economic conditions under which efforts to help local people are configured and potentially controlled.

- Poor peoples like the Gebusi typically have very little influence over larger political and economic conditions—the broader **political economy**—that may radically change their lives.

- Gebusi reveal that **culture change** can be surprisingly productive over time and that human cultural connections have the potential to facilitate these changes, both within societies and, in their own limited way, through the efforts of anthropologists.

Chapter 12

The Larger Future

Around the world, traditions fade. But important parts of them are rediscovered, reinvented, and expressed in new ways. This pattern continues for Gebusi and their neighbors. On one hand, they face deepening challenges of marginality, isolation, and poverty—at least as measured in money. At present, the Nomad airstrip remains closed, the government departed, the cash economy moribund, and the area more remote than ever even as ExxonMobil, the world's largest energy company, could be knocking at their door. No Gebusi have yet graduated from high school, and though the Nomad elementary school has reopened, it is poorly and inconsistently staffed. Gebusi still have no roads to anywhere. Yet, they are buoyed up by the vibrant resources of their own traditions, the good fortune of access to their indigenous lands, a keen sense of humor and vitality, and the benefit of having shed violent parts of their deeper past.

As our twenty-first century connects the world more tightly than ever, Gebusi are no more accessible, and in some ways more remote, than they were when first I met them in 1980. The breathlessness of our digital world easily covers up the spotty and uneven nature of global development. Some get richly "developed," at least temporarily, while others do not, or get poorer. Amid the rush to the future, our integral connection to those less advantaged remains as important as it is underemphasized.

Even apart from ExxonMobil, Gebusi's regional context has already been greatly and unevenly impacted by outside influence. This includes colonial pacification and the introduction of steel tools in the 1960s and 1970s, and the advent of Christianity, schooling, and the Nomad market for Gebusi during the late 1980s and the 1990s. These latter changes have ultimately hinged on government royalties from the huge Ok Tedi gold and copper mine, some 100 miles to their northwest. In operation since the 1980s, in 2010 the mine supplied a whopping 32% of the export earnings of the entire country of Papua New Guinea as well as almost one-fifth of the nation's overall domestic production.

The bulk of the enormous revenue from this megamine supports the Papua New Guinea national government and its budget. A small portion of the mine's income goes to towns and areas where resources are being developed. But only a tiny trickle winds its way through the siphoning maze of government bureaucracy to outstations like Nomad. In past years, this dribble of money supported a skeleton of infrastructure across the expansive rainforest of the country's large Western Province where the mine is located—a huge area that constitutes 20% of the nation's landmass but harbors just 3% of its population, including the Gebusi. Now, sadly, even the meager funds Nomad has been allocated are spent on the salaries of government workers who live in places like Kiunga—though they are still paid to work at Nomad, where the airstrip is closed.

Increasingly in developing countries—and especially those dependent on the export of raw materials—government services are deferred to or replaced by relief organizations, NGOs, or the social service wing of extractive multinational corporations. Paralleling the state, these agencies and organizations may—on their own terms—support local education, health care, infrastructure, and even security. For many like Gebusi who do not live in or near areas of resource development, however, social services can decline to near zero. This pattern of rural and also urban neglect, even amid global or national economic growth as a whole, is common in the developing world.

At the upper end of the funding chain, larger challenges of national income commonly intensify the problem. For Gebusi and those in the Nomad area, the best hope for repairing the local airstrip is hence an agreement for ExxonMobil to do this—if and when their new pipeline is built. As for Ok Tedi, its assistance to local people and the general economy is diminished not only by government action and inaction but by environmental problems. Indeed, the Ok Tedi mine has produced one of the biggest ecological disasters in the world. Rock-born toxic waste from the mine, including heavy metals, has hugely and lastingly polluted what was one of the world's final remaining large, pristine rainforest river systems.

As plans emerge to extend the life of the aging mine until 2025, it remains to be seen if future royalties from Ok Tedi will be redirected to improve conditions at Nomad for Gebusi and their neighbors. The prognosis seems doubtful. From mid-2015 through the beginning of 2016, the mine has been closed altogether because low river levels and sediment from the mine itself prevent barges from exporting its ore. Tabubil, a planned township established to serve the mine, and its workforce, is being mothballed, its schools shut, and workers sent home. How fully the mine will reopen and under what conditions is presently unclear, but yet more questionable is whether the Nomad area and Gebusi will derive any benefit.

The Ok Tedi mine does not *directly* affect the Gebusi's own river system and ecology. But as is generally the case, larger forces and factors exert strong influence. In the present instance, the desire to keep Ok Tedi open for the sake of national income has led the government of Papua New Guinea to itself take over the mine and to try to keep it operating, despite its mounting toxic effects. Against this, the huge cost of addressing Ok Tedi's ecological quagmire reduces money available for infrastructure support for Western Province as well as for the central government itself. There is hence a direct conflict between the government's desperate need for its own revenue and its mandate to protect the country's environment, in addition to providing services for people in outstation areas.

These circumstances illustrate how local conditions are invariably part of a larger political economy—a deeply interconnected web of broader economic and political forces, interests, and institutions. These are regional, national, and ultimately international in scale and influence. Entangled within them, developments among Gebusi can hardly be seen in isolation, even as the Gebusi's own ability to control or influence these larger forces is minimal.

In significant parts of the world, the challenges posed by globalization dwarf what Gebusi have experienced. For the last several years, my interest in the Gebusi and in Melanesia has been complemented by designing and

directing projects of engaged anthropology that have exposed me to struggling parts of the developing world in areas such as West Africa (including
Liberia and Guinea), East Africa (including Burundi, Rwanda, and Congo
[DRC]), the Andes (Ecuador), Southeast Asia (Burma/Myanmar), and the
Altai-Himalayan areas of Tibet [China], Mongolia, Nepal, Bhutan, and
northern India. In each case, my goal has been to identify and put together
networks of influence that combine anthropologists, leaders of civil society
organizations, and policy makers—sometimes including high-ranking government officials and administrators from the UN. All too often, these
groups communicate and operate separately, in self-contained worlds.
Against this, our projects have developed ways to bring together members
of such diverse constituencies for engaged dialogue within and between
developing world regions themselves. The larger goal is to produce con-
structive dialogue and engaged learning that can influence practical policy.
In the process, the projects encourage best practices among networks of
scholars, policy makers, and civil society activists within these world regions
themselves. (See www.bruceknauft.com → Engaged Anthropology.)

     In the course of these projects, I have realized how important it is for
regions of the developing world to manage natural wealth for the public
good—lest it become a curse of social, political, or military conflict.
Whether it be diamonds in West Africa, precious minerals in East Congo,
hydropower in Tibet, cocoa in the Andes, copper and gold in Mongolia,
oil in Nigeria, or liquified natural gas in the Western Province of Papua
New Guinea, the material resources of developing countries—which
industrialized countries crave—can be a source not just of prosperity for
some but also of inequality, oppression, and even violence for others. The
conflict in East Congo, fueled by greed for enormous mineral wealth, has
claimed more than five million lives—the greatest human-caused loss of
life since World War II and the Holocaust. At the other end of the spectrum, rapidly developing countries in significant parts of East Asia, South
and Southeast Asia, and South America experience a significant increase
in living standards, even though this wealth is spread unevenly and may
not confer personal agency or political freedom.

     The uneven nature of capitalist development makes it difficult to gen-
eralize about the impact of globalization on society and culture; we are
provoked to probe more deeply into specific patterns that both connect
and divide people in different world areas. This cautions us to avoid either

rosy assumptions of global development or pessimistic ones of catastrophe or degradation. Challenges are great, but so, too, are local abilities to respond with insight and dedication. From my own perspective, a combination of scholarly and engaged anthropology is needed to determine both how patterns of development and exploitation occur and how these can be managed or changed. Within this process, culture is not simply a passive bystander to economic development, political control, or manipulation. Rather, cultural identity—including ethnic identity, national history, class identification, and religious affiliation—is often at the heart of the matter, including how and why benefits are apportioned or unequally distributed.

Given this, it seems increasingly important for cultural anthropologists to communicate with those beyond a scholarly world, not just to study but to practically address and mitigate human problems at home and abroad. In their own small part of the world, Gebusi developments don't and can't provide full answers to these larger issues. But they do illustrate how culture, political economy, and the human and physical environment are interwoven and creatively responded to, including in the world's most seemingly remote regions.

In some respects, social and economic developments converge globally to make people more similar across the world. Modern institutions of schooling, health care, government, development projects, local markets, and churches or their equivalent are influential in most areas of today's world, as they have also been for Gebusi. But against such international influences, the resurgence of local cultures cannot be discounted. Arguably, in fact, the reemergence of cultural diversity across the world is now as great, if not greater, than it has ever been.

Through culture, the paths of the past fertilize those of the present, even if the latter seem increasingly well trodden. People like the Gebusi experiment continually with this mix. As an ethnographer and as a person, engaging this process has been an intellectual challenge and also an emotional one. Addressing the dynamics of cultural change requires a balance and sometimes a healthy tension between the analysis of our minds and the humanist ethics of our hearts. Where would we be without both of these in our lives and in our work?

Over the years, as I have felt and pondered changes in Gebusi culture, I have moved increasingly beyond a view of Gebusi as either fundamentally indigenous or orphaned from their rich past. Instead, I view Gebusi as emergent, vibrant in their present. Gebusi themselves have negotiated their challenges better than I could have imagined. The same is true of peoples in many parts of the world today. For Gebusi, I think they have managed well in part because of their abiding flexibility, on one hand, and their sense of playfulness, on the other. My Gebusi friends might embrace new events and activities as if they were separate from their past, or they might rediscover older customs in a new light. But in either case, they convey strong awareness—through humor and irony, play and performance—that developments are neither as fixed nor as serious as they might otherwise appear. Even as some of their beliefs or practices are left aside and in some cases actively abandoned, others are reinvented.

Gebusi still desire money, modern goods, and more contemporary styles of life. But they are no longer as subordinate to outside authority figures—pastors, teachers, government officials, and buyers at market—as they were during the 1990s, when they identified closely with developments that were taking place at Nomad Station. Since that time, the people of Gasumi Corners have reasserted their own social world and have reinforced the integrity of their own community, including in relation to the rainforest. How and how much this pattern will continue—including in relation to the potential but uncertain intrusion of ExxonMobil's LNG pipeline—remains an intriguing question.

Like other peoples in the world, Gebusi are becoming more contemporary or modern in their own distinct way. Gebusi still value quiet moments in the rainforest, the bonds between kin and friends, and the aesthetic splendor of their traditional costuming and performance. They also engage and aspire to features of so-called modern life, including modern manufactured implements and commodities, clothes, a desire for money, and interest in new forms of aesthetic expression and music. The resulting combinations are distinctive to Gebusi and not the same as in other countries or even other parts of Papua New Guinea. Like the mixed vocabularies that pervade their string band songs, contemporary life for Gebusi cannot be framed solely in terms of external influences or indigenous dispositions; rather, they are a product of both. This rich tapestry is their culture.

Good company in the
rainforest, 2013.

In their own context, Gebusi are especially fortunate to have the continuing bounty of their land. They retain the land of their villages as well
as the gardens and pristine forests that provide them abundant food.
Many peoples who experience so-called modernization are not so lucky.
By contrast, Gebusi have not had to endure violent subjugation, land
alienation, punitive taxation, exploitative wage labor, slavery, depletion of
natural resources, or degradation of their immediate natural environment. This history has provided them the flexibility to either orient
toward outside activities or thrive on their own, including their livelihood
in the primary rainforest.

I have been fortunate as well. I have had the rare opportunity to know
the Gebusi, to be part of their lives, and to share in their customs across a
rich spectrum of traditional, modern, rediscovered, and hybrid orientations. These have spanned a remarkable diversity during just three-and-a-
half decades, making my good fortune all the greater. The Gebusi in 1980
were neither pristine nor fully "traditional," but their history gave them a
special opportunity to develop their culture, in significant part, on their
own terms. By 1998, the Gebusi's path of cultural development had not
just taken off but run circles around its previous scope and scale, including
changes in subsistence, economy, religion, marriage, politics, aesthetic life,
and even their sense of time. Due to these changes, Gebusi will never be as
independent or remote from outside influence as they once were. During
the last decade, a negative turn of the economic wheel has slammed
Gebusi, and their lack of money and services has since become chronic. In

the mix, Gebusi traditions are more fully reasserted and more fully combined with newer developments. These are resurgent not as simple replicas of older history but as cultural resources that deeply enrich the present from the past.

As part of their openness, the Gebusi warmly welcomed me from the start. They have given me the greatest gift that people can give and that we can all appreciate: the sharing of life across differences of culture.

Farewell: On the day of departure, I had no shame. The morning started rainy, and I hoped it would continue so the plane wouldn't come. I didn't care that my few boxes were already sealed and that everything else had been given away. Eventually, though, the rain let up, and I trekked in sorrow with everyone else to the airstrip.

I started choking up well before the plane emerged on the horizon. I knew it would happen, just as it always does. I fought back tears, but they kept coming. I have known the people of Yibihilu and now of Gasumi Corners for so many years, first when they were young, now with their own children as well. There is always the question of when and if I will see them again. Their place is remote, the logistics are hard, and the tropics grind hard on my body. My Gebusi friends know this. Those who are older know I may never see them again; each time, more of them have departed before I can return.

Instead of taking pictures at the end, I take mental pictures that are more indelible. I move down the sorrowful line of those gathered to say good-byes and I force myself to peer in the face and gaze in the eyes of each man and woman, each boy and girl from Gasumi Corners. Snapping their fingers in the best and most forthright manner, I burn into my mind the living image of each of these unique persons so as never to forget their exquisite humanity. Their tear-streaked faces mirror my own as we fight the impulse to turn away. I cry, oblivious to onlookers, a six-foot white guy bawling with a crowd of villagers.

I lose it when I come to Sayu and Didiga. I have become so close to them over the years, since they were very small. They have shared their lives with me, and I with them. It is hard to not know when I will see them again, and that until then I will have so little contact.

I remember Yuway. He led me on my very first patrol to the Gebusi. He was my most sensitive and caring helper when I was first learning the language, and was my best friend. I saw him fall in love and get married, and I know his five children, who are now grown. Throughout, Yuway was one of the nicest and most decent people I have ever met. When I last left him, I looked into his eyes and blurted out, "Friend. Oh friend. When will I ever see you again?!" His wisdom was greater than mine. With a weepy and yet dignified smile, he told me, "I'll see you later, in heaven."

My last sight of Yuway then was at the edge of the airstrip; he had walked down the path to its end. He waved me a final goodbye as my plane soared off. As I sailed toward the heavens, Yuway awaited his own.

Yuway died on June 16, 2009. This book is dedicated to the spirit he embodied, to Sayu and Didiga, and to the past, present, and future of the Gebusi.

Who can deny the world of change in cultures? Or the richness of humanity despite all that would suppress it?

Yuway with his wife, Warbwi, and two of their children, 2008.

BROADER CONNECTIONS
Globalization, Political Economy, and the Future of Culture

- As Gebusi illustrate, **globalization** affects all societies and cultures but is also highly uneven in its impact and affects. Globalization can intensify **poverty** and **inequality** at the same time that it informs **economic growth.**

- For Gebusi and virtually all peoples today, **political economy** includes interconnected economic and political forces, interests, and institutions that are regional, national, and ultimately international in scale and influence. The ability of local people to influence or change these larger forces is often minimal.

- Amid globalization, some traditions fade while others are rediscovered and expressed in new ways. This reflects the **reinvention of culture.**

- Trends of **economic development** do not always move "forward." In significant ways, Gebusi are more remote now than they were in 1980: the local airstrip is closed, schooling and health care are minimal, and police and government presence is absent.

- For Gebusi, like people in many developing countries, the larger political economy is strongly impacted by hard-to-predict patterns of **resource extraction,** including by **multinational corporations.** For Gebusi, this is illustrated both by the Ok Tedi gold and copper mine and the potential building of a large liquified natural gas pipeline through their territory by ExxonMobil.

- The Ok Tedi mine illustrates how exploitation of natural resources can at once be an economic benefit and also a **resource curse** that causes conflict, corruption, and environmental degradation.

- Culture includes key features of personal and **group identity**—such as ethnic, racial, national, and religious affiliation—that inform exactly how regional and global forces affect local conditions.

- Basic services of the **modern state** and its **government**—activities and functions that the state is expected to carry out—typically include **education, health care, infrastructure,** and **security.**

- In poor developing countries, **government services** are often taken over in part or more generally by **NGOs (nongovernmental organizations), aid agencies,** or even **multinational corporations.**

- Bruce's project work in Africa, South America, and Asia addresses practical issues of social and cultural recovery under conditions of stress and challenge. This provides a significant example of **engaged anthropology.**

- It is increasingly important and useful for cultural anthropologists, as **practicing anthropologists,** to develop meaningful dialogues with policy makers and members of civil society to facilitate positive social change. It is vital that local constituencies be strongly involved and influence outcomes.

- As Gebusi illustrate, including with respect to historic patterns of violence, local initiatives are often better at instituting positive change than those envisaged or directed primarily by outsiders.

- Many peripheral peoples in the world today have a history of having been subject to **colonialism** and/or to coerced labor or slavery, tribute or taxation, land alienation, out-migration, or indebtedness due to reliance on cash crops or commodities. Gebusi are fortunate to have not suffered greatly so far from such negative impacts.

- Like other peoples, Gebusi are becoming contemporary or **locally modern** in their own distinct way. Gebusi flexibility and playful creativity are especially useful and effective in this regard.

- Both personally and professionally, cultural anthropologists such as Bruce are fortunate that the people they live among during fieldwork share their lives across differences of culture.

- Over time, cultural anthropologists and the people they study may become closely connected personally as well as professionally.

- The vibrancy and creativity of cultural change are irrepressible and cannot easily be suppressed or denied.

List of Persons

Harfay	1982	infant	*194–195*
	1998	bachelor	
	2008	had had affair with Kubwam but unmarried	
	2013	unmarried/widower, no children	
Hawi	1980–82	carrier for Bruce and Eileen on first expedition, initiate, friend of Doliay	*18–19, 26, 31,*
			38–39, 81,
	1998	married with four children, lived at Nomad Station, devoted member of the Evangelical Church, helped keep track of aircraft cargo	*82–83, 93, 99,*
			100, 101, 116,
			117, 192, 194
	2013	still alive, two surviving children and four grandchildren	
Haymp	1982	initiate	*93*
	c. 1983	father of Kubwam	
	1998	deceased	
Hiali	1981	younger brother of Silap, died of sickness 11 days after being initiated, unmarried and childless	*93*
Howe	1982	young boy, son of Kawuk	*115, 174*
	1998	young man, member of Catholic Church, singer in the Gasumi Corners string band, bachelor	
	2008	married with three children	
	2013	married with four children (plus one deceased)	
Huwa	1998	orphaned teenage younger brother of Sayu, Gasumi string band singer	*170, 174*
	2013	married with two children	
Imba	1982	senior respected man of Yibihilu, father of Didiga and Bene	*31–32, 117*
	1998	deceased	
Kawuk	1982	cofounder of Yibihilu longhouse, married with two small children	*174, 177, 178,*
			192, 201
	1998	senior man of Gasumi Corners, devoted member of the Catholic Church, married with five children	
	2008	security guard for the Catholic Church, five children and six grandchildren	
	2013	still married with five surviving adult children and thirteen grandchildren	
Keda	1982	teenage younger brother of Yuway	*124, 192, 193*
	1998	married with children, active Catholic Church member	
	2008	Catholic Church lay leader, father of three children	
	2013	still alive and married with three children	
Kubwam	1982	born in Yibihilu shortly after Bruce and Eileen's departure	*159–160*
	1998	temporary wife of Moka	
	2008	divorced Gebusi husband, married Bedamini man, moved to Bedamini territory	
	2013	living in Bedamini territory	
Kuma	1982	young boy, son of Bosap	*137–138*
	1998	marriageable bachelor	
	2013	married to daughter of Doliay, father of five children	

Uwano	1982	young adult man, "breadfruit" name exchange partner of Bruce	*129, 130*
	1998	deceased October 9, with five surviving children	
	2013	four surviving grandchildren	
Warbwi	1982	new wife of Yuway	*120, 121*
	1998	wife of Yuway and mother of five children	
	2008	still alive, mother of five children	
	2013	still alive, widowed, five children and two grandchildren	
Wayabay	1982	young boy, son of Swamin	*153–157, 165–166,*
	1998	bachelor, hunter, and house builder	*167, 172, 181,*
	2001	husband of Gami	*192*
	2008	married to Gami, father of their three children	
	2013	married to Gami, father of their five children	
Willy	1998	boy, son of Doliay	*128, 129*
Wasep	1982	husband of Nelep, father of Yamdaw and Korlis	*83, 117, 142*
	1998	deceased	
Yaba	1982	widower, jokester in Yibihilu	*79–81*
	1998	deceased, widowed and childless	
Yamdaw	1982	young boy, son of Nelep and Wasep	*177*
	1998	married with children, lead Gasumi string band singer, devoted member of the Catholic Church	
	2008	Catholic prayer and service leader, father of three children	
	2013	first wife deceased, newly remarried with three surviving children from first marriage	
Yuway	1980–82	initiate, carrier for Bruce and Eileen on first expedition, language helper and friend of Bruce	*14, 18, 29, 33, 34,*
	1998	husband of Warbwi, father of four children, member of the Seventh Day Adventist Church	*42, 48, 49, 93,*
	2008	member of the Catholic Church, father of five children	*99, 101, 113,* *117, 120–125,* *127, 134, 179,*
	2009	deceased	*192, 194, 221*
	2013	two surviving grandchildren	

Index